Pro Kotlin Web Apps from Scratch

Building Production-Ready Web Apps Without a Framework

August Lilleaas

Apress®

Pro Kotlin Web Apps from Scratch: Building Production-Ready Web Apps Without a Framework

August Lilleaas
Oslo, Norway

ISBN-13 (pbk): 978-1-4842-9056-9   ISBN-13 (electronic): 978-1-4842-9057-6
https://doi.org/10.1007/978-1-4842-9057-6

Managing Director, Apress Media LLC: Welmoed Spahr
Acquisitions Editor: Jonathan Gennick
Development Editor: Laura Berendson
Coordinating Editor: Jill Balzano

Cover Photo by George Tasios on Unsplash

Distributed to the book trade worldwide by Springer Science+Business Media LLC, 1 New York Plaza, Suite 4600, New York, NY 10004. Phone 1-800-SPRINGER, fax (201) 348-4505, e-mail orders-ny@springer-sbm.com, or visit www.springeronline.com. Apress Media, LLC is a California LLC and the sole member (owner) is Springer Science + Business Media Finance Inc (SSBM Finance Inc). SSBM Finance Inc is a **Delaware** corporation.

For information on translations, please e-mail booktranslations@springernature.com; for reprint, paperback, or audio rights, please e-mail bookpermissions@springernature.com.

Apress titles may be purchased in bulk for academic, corporate, or promotional use. eBook versions and licenses are also available for most titles. For more information, reference our Print and eBook Bulk Sales web page at http://www.apress.com/bulk-sales.

Any source code or other supplementary material referenced by the author in this book is available to readers on GitHub (https://github.com/Apress). For more detailed information, please visit http://www.apress.com/source-code.

Printed on acid-free paper

Dedicated to my mother and father, who made it all happen,
and
in loving memory of Ann-Cecilie Saltnes (11.03.1980–04.07.2022)

Table of Contents

About the Author

 **August Lilleaas** has been building web apps, user interfaces, and real-time systems since 2004 and mobile apps since the app stores opened in the late 2000s. After picking up Clojure in 2012, he left the frameworks and ORMs behind and started to build web apps from scratch and has shipped to production using Clojure, Groovy, Node.js, Elixir, and Kotlin. He has worked as a consultant for a decade and is now an independent contractor and startup founder.

About the Technical Reviewer

 **Andres Sacco** has been a professional developer since 2007, working with a variety of languages, including Java, Scala, PHP, Node.js, and Kotlin. Most of his background is in Java and the libraries or frameworks associated with it, like Spring, JSF, iBATIS, Hibernate, and Spring Data. He is focused on researching new technologies to improve the performance, stability, and quality of the applications he develops.

In 2017 he started to find new ways to optimize the transference of data between applications to reduce the cost of infrastructure. He suggested some actions, some of them applicable in all the microservices and others in just a few of them. As a result of these actions, the cost was reduced by 55%. Some of these actions are connected directly with the bad use of the databases.

Acknowledgments

Thanks to my fiancée, Tina, who believes in me and lets me know. Thanks to Jonathan Gennick for giving me the opportunity to become a technical writer. Thanks to everyone else at Apress for being a pleasure to work with. Thanks to Marius Mårnes Mathisen for catapulting my career way back when, despite my complete lack of programming education and professional experience. Thanks to Kolbjørn Jetne for further catapulting my career, despite my complete lack of consulting experience. Thanks to Magnar Sveen, Christian Johansen, and Alf Kristian Støyle for all the discussions, input, and inspiration through the years. A special thanks to Finn Johnsen, who helped form most of the patterns in this book and was a vital fellow traveler in my initial quest for escaping the framework and bridging the gap between the old and the new.

Finally, thanks to my son, Tobias, and my daughter, Lone, who are awesome. And, at my daughter's request/demand, "Pappa er en bok."

Introduction

Welcome to *Pro Kotlin Web Apps from Scratch*! In this book, you'll learn how to build professional and production-grade web apps, completely from scratch, without the use of big and unwieldy frameworks.

My personal web app journey started with frameworks, but when I learned more about what goes on under the hood and grew weary of fighting framework bugs and limitations, I started teaching myself how to build web apps from scratch instead. As it turns out, frameworks aren't a requirement!

You're in good hands when you're building from scratch, thanks to modern programming languages like Kotlin and amazing third-party open source libraries. Back in the day, you needed thousands of lines of boilerplate and XML configuration to wire up a framework-less web app. No wonder people preferred frameworks! Nowadays, though, all you need is a couple of handfuls of explicit code, completely free of bloat and magic, that only does what you tell it to.

In Part I, you'll set up a web app skeleton, completely from scratch. This code base forms the basis for Part II, where you'll learn a handful of patterns and practical solutions that build on the skeleton from Part I. Part III covers how to choose the right library and Kotlin tips and tricks that I didn't get to cover in the preceding parts. Finally, three appendixes explain how to replace some of the libraries chosen in Parts I and II, to demonstrate that you have free rein to choose different libraries than me and still write pro Kotlin web apps from scratch.

I've deliberately kept the chapter about Kotlin tips and tricks in Part III as short as I've been able to manage. Instead, you'll learn Kotlin tips and tricks in Parts I and II, and you'll learn how to build web apps from scratch alongside explanations of the various Kotlin language constructs you're using.

PART I

Up and Running with a Web App

CHAPTER 1

Setting Up a Development Environment

In this chapter you'll set up a development environment for Kotlin. You'll install IntelliJ IDEA, a Java Development Kit (JDK), you'll write a small Kotlin program, and you'll compile and run it using the Gradle build system.

This chapter explains how to do everything using IntelliJ IDEA. For the other chapters in this book, though, using IntelliJ IDEA is not a requirement. For example, both the Eclipse IDE (integrated development environment) and Visual Studio Code have Kotlin plugins available, made by the Kotlin community. If you choose to use another editor, make sure that it supports *auto-completion* and *automatic imports.* Extension functions are prevalent in Kotlin, and you must import them before you can use them. You'll avoid lots of tedious manual work if your editor can search and match all available extension functions (auto-completion) and automatically add an import statement when you select one of the auto-completed options (automatic imports).

Get Started with IntelliJ IDEA Community Edition

You'll need an editor to write your code and a way to compile and run your code. IntelliJ IDEA gives you both.

IntelliJ IDEA is the canonical integrated development environment (IDE) for static languages on the Java platform. The free community edition of IntelliJ IDEA has everything you need, both for this book and for production-grade Kotlin development. Additionally, JetBrains makes both Kotlin and IntelliJ IDEA, making IntelliJ IDEA uniquely well suited for Kotlin work.

© August Lilleaas 2023
A. Lilleaas, *Pro Kotlin Web Apps from Scratch*, https://doi.org/10.1007/978-1-4842-9057-6_1

Download and Run IntelliJ IDEA

You can download and use IntelliJ IDEA Community for free from JetBrains. Go to the IntelliJ IDEA download page, shown in Figure 1-1, at the address `www.jetbrains.com/idea/download/` and download the community edition from there. JetBrains provides a .dmg file for macOS, an .exe file for Windows, and a tarball with a shell script in *bin/idea.sh* for Linux.

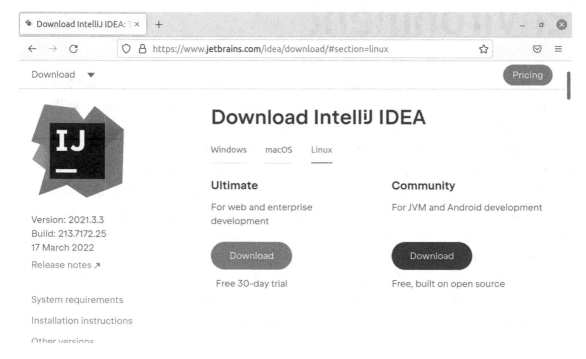

Figure 1-1. *Download IntelliJ IDEA Community Edition for your platform*

For more details on how to install and run IntelliJ IDEA, refer to the JetBrains website. For example, the download page has a link with installation instructions in the left sidebar, as seen in Figure 1-1.

Create a New Kotlin Project with IntelliJ IDEA

There are many ways to create a new Kotlin project. For this book, you'll be using IntelliJ IDEA to do it. It's nice to have a GUI to hold your hand through the process if you're not familiar with Kotlin and/or the JVM.

When you launch IntelliJ IDEA, you should see the splash screen shown in Figure 1-2.

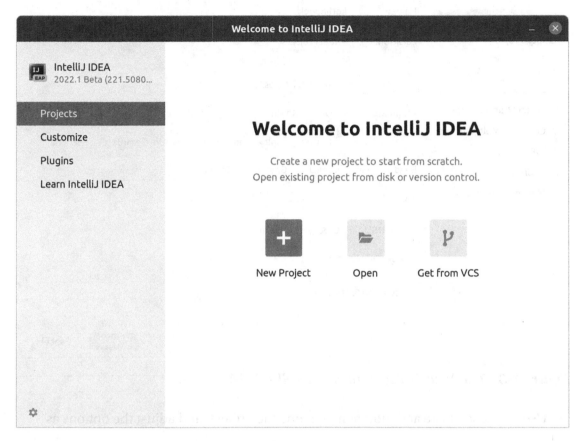

Figure 1-2. *Your first taste of IntelliJ IDEA*

Click "New Project" to create a new Kotlin project using the built-in wizard in IntelliJ IDEA, shown in Figure 1-3.

5

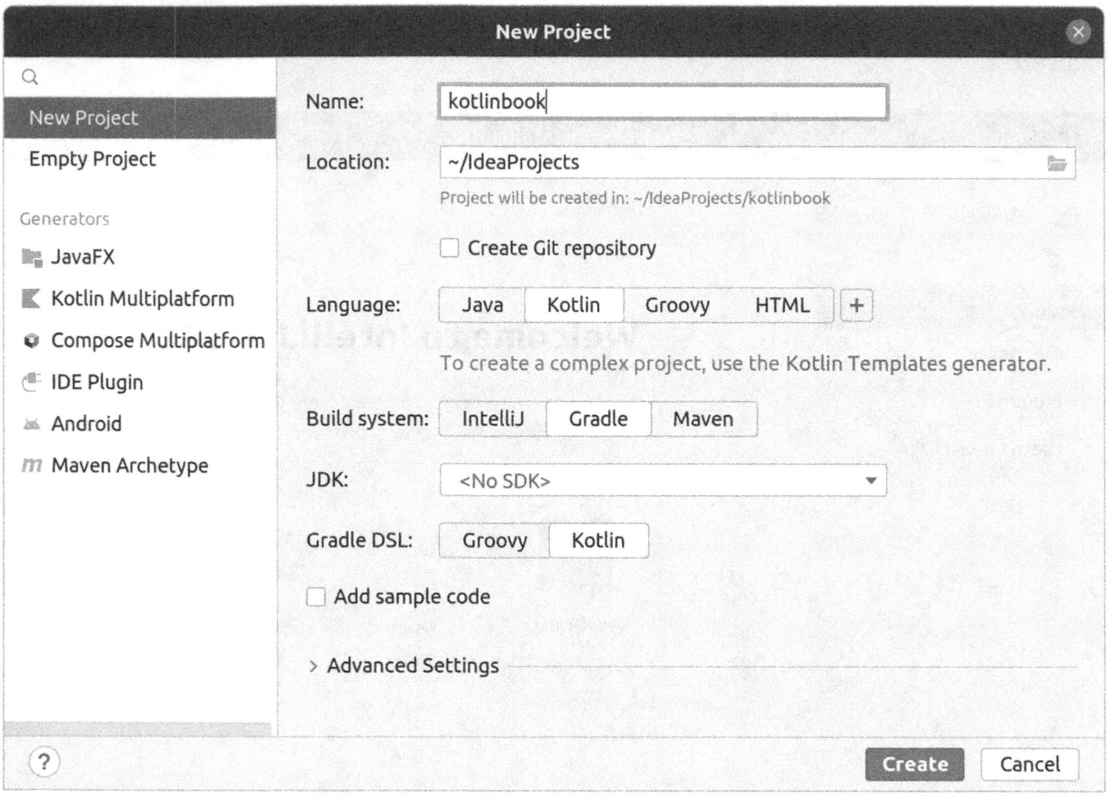

Figure 1-3. *The New Project screen in IntelliJ IDEA*

Use your good taste and judgment to name the project, and adjust the options as follows:

- Make sure you select "New Project" in the left sidebar.

- Set *Language* to *Kotlin*.

- Set *Build system* to *Gradle*.

- Set *Gradle DSL* to *Kotlin*.

- Uncheck *Add sample code*.

You need a JDK, and the easiest way to get one is to have IntelliJ IDEA download one for you. Click the red "<No SDK>" dropdown in the New Project dialog shown in Figure 1-3 and choose an appropriate JDK from the popup that appears, shown in Figure 1-4. JDK 17 or JDK 11 is a good choice, as those are stable Long-Term Support (LTS) releases.

Figure 1-4. *Use IntelliJ IDEA to download a JDK*

There are multiple vendors available. They are all full-fledged JDKs that adhere to the JDK specifications. For the most part, it doesn't matter which one you choose. The differences lie in a handful of edge cases and different defaults. For most web apps, you'll be able to switch between vendors and not notice any differences. I personally prefer Amazon Corretto, mostly out of habit. But I've used other vendors in real-world web apps, such as Azul Zulu. I tend to choose whichever vendor is most convenient on the platform I use, such as Azul Zulu on Azure, Amazon Corretto on AWS, and so on.

Make sure you choose a JDK of version 11 or newer. Versions 11 and 17 are both Long-Time Support (LTS) releases, which means they'll receive security updates longer than other versions. And later in this book, you'll use libraries that require at least version 11 to work.

You can also choose an existing JDK if you have one installed. Alternatively, you can manage JDK installations yourself, by using something like sdkman (`https://sdkman.io/`) on macOS and Linux and Jabba (`https://github.com/shyiko/jabba`) on Windows.

Tip   You can have bad luck and choose a JDK version that's incompatible with the Gradle version used by IntelliJ IDEA. For example, the 2021 version of IntelliJ uses Gradle 7.1, which only works with JDK versions lower than 16. If this happens, delete your project and start over, using a different JDK or Gradle version.

After IntelliJ IDEA finishes downloading the JDK, click the "Create" button at the bottom of the New Project dialog shown in Figure 1-3, and your brand-new project appears, as shown in Figure 1-5.

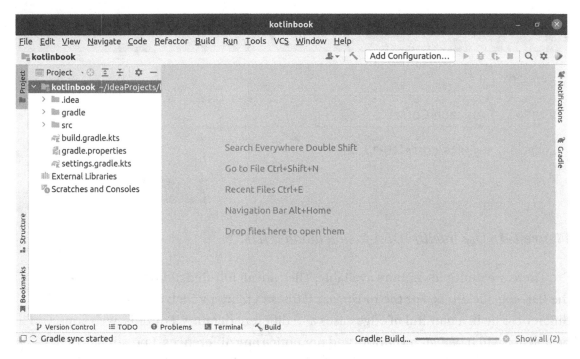

Figure 1-5. *IntelliJ IDEA after it has finished with project initialization*

With this setup, IntelliJ IDEA won't create sample code or pre-generated files, other than a Gradle build system skeleton. All you have now is a way to compile and run Kotlin code. And that's all you need in this book. There's no framework with tens of thousands of lines of code that needs to run first to get anything done.

Tip   Gradle is a build system for the Java platform. This is where you add third-party code as dependencies, configure production builds, set up automated testing, and more. Maven is also an excellent choice for building production-grade Kotlin web apps. Most examples you'll see in books and online documentation use Gradle, though, and I've only used Gradle in real-world Kotlin apps, so that's why I use it in this book.

Kotlin Hello, World!

It's common when learning a new language to make one's first program to be one that outputs "Hello, World!" This ensures that everything is up and running, that you can compile Kotlin code, and that you can run it and see that it outputs something.

Kotlin Naming Conventions

Before you create your first file, you need to know where to put it and what to name it.

Kotlin is very flexible about the naming of files and folders and doesn't enforce a specific structure. However, it's common to follow the Java conventions, and this is what the official Kotlin style guide recommends. This is especially helpful in team situations, so that everyone knows where to find and place things.

The conventions go as follows:

- Place Kotlin code in *src/main/kotlin*.

- Create a *package* named after the project itself and put all your files in it. A package is a namespace that tells code apart. This helps avoid name conflicts with third-party code.

- The directory structure matches the package names. The package myapp.foo exists in *src/main/kotlin/myapp/foo*.

- File names are in upper camel case, also known as PascalCase, the same as Java. Note that in the wild, it's relatively common to see underscores too, underscore_case. This book uses PascalCase throughout.

In this book, you'll place all your code in the package kotlinbook.

Write Some Code

You are now ready to create your first Kotlin file. Taking the preceding conventions into account, the file name to use is *src/main/kotlin/kotlinbook/Main.kt*.

To create the file in IntelliJ IDEA, follow these steps:

- Expand *src/main/kotlin* in the left sidebar in IntelliJ.

- Right-click *src/main/kotlin* and choose *New* ➤ *Package*.

- Name it `kotlinbook` and hit Enter on your keyboard.

- Right-click the newly created package/folder *kotlinbook*, and choose *New* ➤ *Kotlin Class/File.*

- Choose File, choose the file template named simply "File," name it *Main* (IDEA will automatically add the *.kt* extension), and hit Enter on your keyboard.

IntelliJ IDEA should now look like what's shown in Figure 1-6.

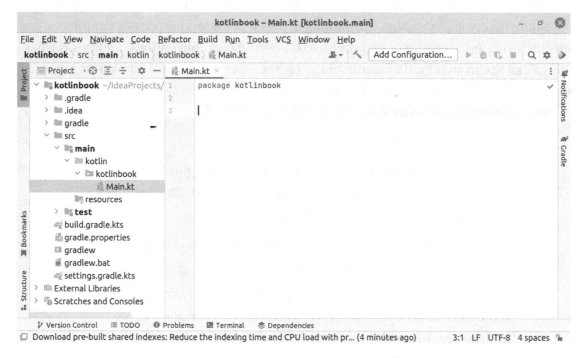

Figure 1-6. *A Kotlin file inside a package in IntelliJ IDEA*

Kotlin is a multi-paradigm language and has support for object-oriented, functional, and data-oriented programming (Sharvit, 2022, Manning). This book will use functional and data-oriented styles as much as possible and only use the object-oriented style when third-party libraries require it.

In your first file, write a top-level function with the name `main`, as seen in Listing 1-1. This is a special function name, which tells the Kotlin compiler and the Java runtime to call that function as the entry point to your program.

Listing 1-1. Print "Hello, World!" in **src/main/kotlinbook/Main.kt**

```
package kotlinbook

fun main() {
    println("Hello, World!")
}
```

Tip   You can also declare your function as `fun main(args: Array<String>)` `{ ... }` if you want to read the command-line arguments passed to your application. Java requires that your main function takes an array of strings, but Kotlin does not have this requirement.

Run Your Code with IntelliJ IDEA

IntelliJ IDEA can run your code directly. This is the fastest way to run your code and takes maximum advantage of the fact that you're using an IDE.

The little green arrow next to a function, as shown in Figure 1-7, indicates that IntelliJ IDEA can run that function directly. Click it, and IntelliJ IDEA will do as you command and run the function.

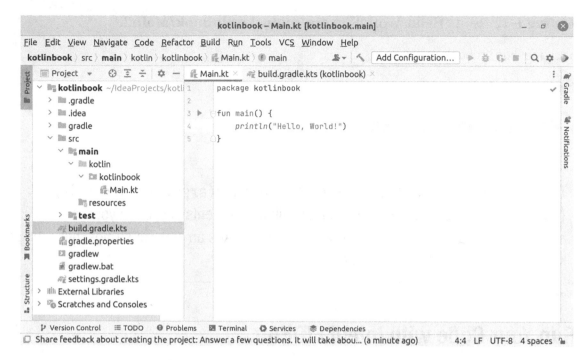

Figure 1-7. *A green play button next to the function name in IntelliJ IDEA shows a runnable function*

Run Your Code with Gradle

You can also configure Gradle to run your code. Later, you'll use Gradle to build deployable JAR (Java archive) files, and Gradle needs to know where your main function is to be able to build them. Additionally, even if you're not going to run the code with Gradle, developers unfamiliar with the project can look at the Gradle config to find the main function. This helps understand where the main entry point is in the project and is a good place to start reading code to become familiar with it.

You'll use the *application* plugin in Gradle to specify a runnable application with a main entry point. In the file *build.gradle.kts*, add the `application` plugin:

```
plugins {
  kotlin("jvm") version "..."
  application
}
```

The `application` plugin needs to know where to find the main function. At the top-level of *build.gradle.kts* (not inside the `plugins` block), declare the name of the main class:

```
application {
  mainClass.set("kotlinbook.MainKt")
}
```

Tip   Did you notice the leaky abstraction? The `application` plugin is not aware of Kotlin, and it needs to know the name of the compiled Java class file. To be compatible and interoperable with the Java platform at large, the Kotlin compiler turns `Main` into `MainKt`. A file *Foo.kt* that only declares the class Foo is compiled to *Foo.class*. Any other scenario will generate `FooKt.class`.

To run the function with Gradle, use either of the two following methods:

- In a terminal (either stand-alone or the Terminal tab at the bottom of IntelliJ), type `./gradlew application`.

- In the Gradle panel in IntelliJ (found in the rightmost sidebar), click *Tasks* ➤ *application* ➤ *run*.

You should now see the output of your application, either in your terminal or in the IntelliJ "Run" output panel.

IntelliJ IDEA Tips and Tricks

IntelliJ IDEA is a vast tool filled with features. This book is not about IntelliJ IDEA, and you might have chosen to use another editor entirely. But here are some tips that can help you become familiar with IntelliJ IDEA and avoid common beginner mistakes that pro IntelliJ IDEA users know how to avoid.

If you want to dig deeper and learn more about the vast world of IntelliJ IDEA, you should check out the book *Beginning IntelliJ IDEA* by Ted Hagos (`www.amazon.com/dp/1484274458`).

Look Out for the Progress Bar

IntelliJ IDEA will sometimes show a progress bar to the right in the bottom toolbar, as shown in Figure 1-8. When this progress bar is visible, IntelliJ IDEA is busy doing something important in the background.

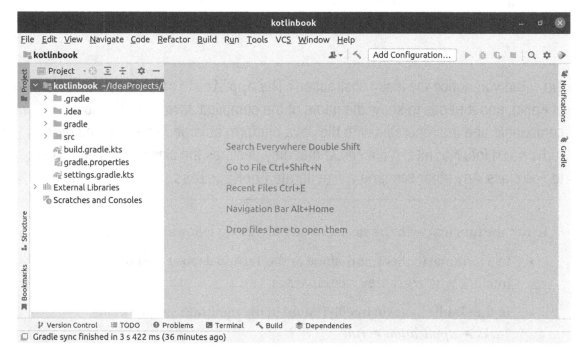

Figure 1-8. *IntelliJ IDEA is running background analysis of a project, shown by a blue progress bar to the right in the bottom toolbar*

When you see this progress bar, you should wait until it's gone before you start editing code.

IntelliJ IDEA knows a lot about your code. To gain that knowledge, it needs to analyze your code first. When you type in new code, this will happen automatically (and so quick you probably won't notice). But when you create a new project or open an existing project for the first time, IntelliJ IDEA might spend many minutes running analysis in the background.

The editor is still active while analysis is running, so you assume that IntelliJ IDEA is ready to go. But many core features won't be available until the analysis is complete.

When the progress bar is gone, IntelliJ IDEA is ready to go, and you can now edit code with all the features IntelliJ IDEA provides.

Remember to Refresh the Gradle Project in IntelliJ IDEA

As you grow your project, you will make changes to *build.gradle.kts*, such as adding additional third-party code as dependencies, configuring how to build JAR files for production, and so on.

IntelliJ IDEA has deep knowledge of the contents of *build.gradle.kts*. For example, IntelliJ IDEA will auto-complete functions from all third-party code added as dependencies to your Gradle project.

When you make changes to *build.gradle.kts*, IntelliJ IDEA requires that you refresh its knowledge of the Gradle project. If you make changes to *build.gradle.kts* and don't perform a refresh, you can easily end up in a situation where you pull your hair out in frustration, since IntelliJ IDEA's knowledge of your project doesn't match your expectations.

Fortunately, IntelliJ IDEA is here to help. When there are changes that are not refreshed yet, IntelliJ IDEA will display a small but vital button, shown in Figure 1-9. The button shows the Gradle logo and a small refresh arrow. Click this icon to perform a Gradle refresh.

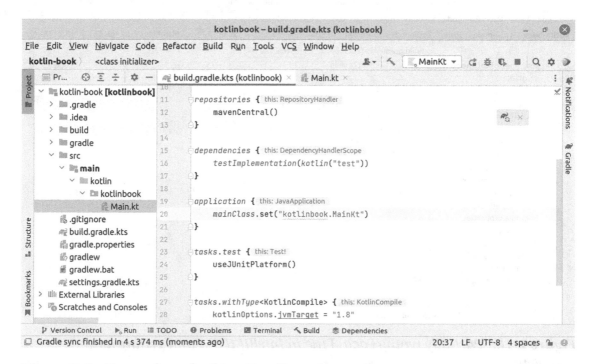

Figure 1-9. *Popup for refreshing Gradle project settings*

The icon will only be visible when there are changes made to *build.gradle.kts* that IntelliJ IDEA is not yet aware of. But it's easy to miss, so make sure you refresh your Gradle project in IntelliJ IDEA every time you change *build.gradle.kts*.

Embrace Auto-completion in IntelliJ IDEA

IntelliJ IDEA has powerful auto-completion features. Maybe you noticed it as you were typing in the main function earlier. As you type in code with your keyboard, a dropdown appears near your cursor. This dropdown contains all the viable symbols you can add at the location you're writing currently, limited to symbols that match what you're currently typing.

Auto-completion is particularly useful when combined with auto-importing, as seen in Figure 1-10 and 1-11. If you select an auto-completion in IntelliJ IDEA and your choice is not imported in the file you're editing, IntelliJ IDEA will import it for you automatically.

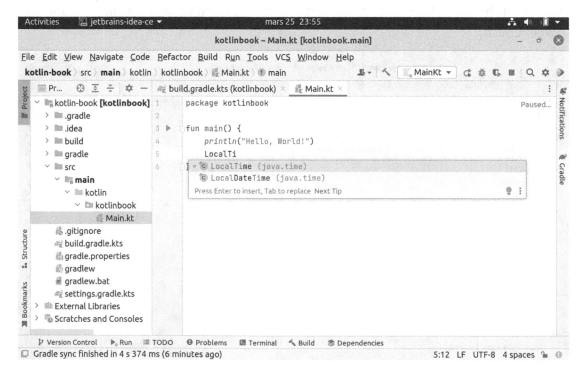

Figure 1-10. *Partially typing* LocalTime *in IntelliJ IDEA and getting auto-completion*

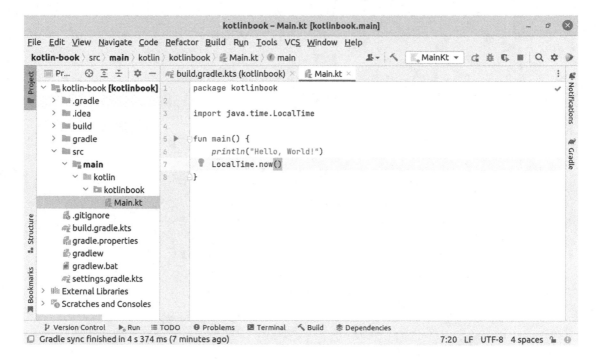

Figure 1-11. *Hit the Enter key, and the auto-completion will add the full class name and add an import automatically*

By embracing auto-completion, you'll save yourself from manually typing everything, as well as having to manually add import statements for code in other packages, be it from the standard library, third-party code, or your own modules.

CHAPTER 2

Setting Up the Web App Skeleton

Look at all the things I'm not doing!

—David Heinemeier Hansson

This chapter will give you superpowers. You will get all the way to a working web app with routing, views/templates, and logging. You'll set the stage for what's to come in later chapters. It will just be you and your IDE, no starter kits or frameworks.

If you're new to Kotlin, here are some language features you'll see examples of in this chapter:

- Lambdas
- Named arguments

Also in this chapter, you will learn the following about creating web apps:

- Setting up a web server, powered by Ktor, listening on port 4207
- Logging setup, using SLF4J and Logback, configurable with standard *logback.xml* setup
- Tweaking Ktor to display useful error messages when your application throws unexpected errors

You'll wire up all these things yourself, instead of having a framework do it for you. If you've only used frameworks before, I envy you. Prepare to be surprised how little manual wiring you need to do to get it done.

© August Lilleaas 2023
A. Lilleaas, *Pro Kotlin Web Apps from Scratch*, https://doi.org/10.1007/978-1-4842-9057-6_2

Web Server Hello, World!

In Chapter 1, you wrote a small program that printed "Hello, World!" It's time to take it to the next level: a full-fledged working web app that starts a server, sets up URL routing, and outputs "Hello, World!" over HTTP.

Choosing Ktor

You need a library to handle URL routing and to start up a web server to host your web app. In this book, you'll use Ktor. You can swap out Ktor for something else later if you want, and in Appendix A you'll learn how to use Jooby instead of Ktor. But in the rest of the book, all the code you'll write will use Ktor.

Ktor is one of the most popular libraries for web app routing in Kotlin. It has everything you need to build production-grade web apps, and it's written in Kotlin, so it's both convenient and powerful to use and makes use of all the relevant features that Kotlin has to offer for building web apps. It's also built to be highly scalable and performant and is battle proven across a large number of real-world web apps.

And, most importantly, Ktor is a library, not a framework. Frameworks, such as Spring Boot, typically start a web server automatically and use inversion of control to call your code, somewhere deep down in tens of thousands of lines of framework code. The point of this book is to learn how to do everything yourself, from scratch.

Interestingly, Ktor labels itself a framework. There aren't any widely accepted definitions of libraries vs. frameworks. The one I use in this book is that frameworks automatically and implicitly do things for you, whereas libraries do nothing unless you explicitly tell them to. Ktor nicely fits this definition of a library.

Add the Ktor Library

Add Ktor as a dependency in *build.gradle.kts*, inside the `dependencies` block. Ktor needs two dependencies to work: the server core, and the specific server implementation (Netty in this case):

```
dependencies {
  implementation("io.ktor:ktor-server-core:2.1.2")
  implementation("io.ktor:ktor-server-netty:2.1.2")
}
```

Tip   Remember to refresh the Gradle project in IntelliJ when you update `build.gradle.kts`. Use the small popup that appears when there are changes that Gradle hasn't refreshed yet or open the Gradle tab and click the refresh button.

Gradle automatically downloads the dependencies and makes them available to your own code.

Start a Web Server

You'll start the web server manually in the application entry point – the `main` function. Instead of just printing "Hello, World!", you'll change it to start a Ktor web server.

In Listing 2-1, you can see the full working main function needed to start it all up.

Listing 2-1. Start a web server in the application main function at **src/main/kotlinbook/Main.kt**

```
package kotlinbook

import io.ktor.server.application.*
import io.ktor.server.engine.*
import io.ktor.server.netty.*
import io.ktor.server.response.*
import io.ktor.server.routing.*

fun main() {
  embeddedServer(Netty, port = 4207) {
    routing {
      get("/") {
        call.respondText("Hello, World!")
      }
    }
  }.start(wait = true)
}
```

The code is plain and straightforward. You create an embedded Ktor server that is using Netty for the server implementation under the hood and starts at port 4207. You set up routing, which means HTTP verb and path matching. Each route has an implementation that generates a HTTP response. And finally, you start the embedded server.

You don't need to manually write the `import` statements. For example, when you write `embeddedSe` and pause, IntelliJ IDEA will suggest `embeddedServer`. If you choose the auto-completion from the dropdown, IntelliJ IDEA will also add an `import` statement.

For clarity, the code in Listing 2-1 contains all the import statements needed to make the code compile. For the remainder of this book, I'll omit them unless there are ambiguities (e.g., when there are two extension functions available with the same name, but in different packages.)

Tip Embedding a HTTP server is standard practice on the Java platform, even if you use a framework. A proxy such as Nginx or a cloud service like Azure Web Apps or Amazon Application Load Balancer will sit in front of the embedded HTTP server in your application and take care of SSL, load balancing, and other web server tasks. In Chapter 14 you will learn how to build a servlet-style WAR file that doesn't start its own server but is embedded into an application server container such as Tomcat.

Extracting to a Separate Function

Extracting your routes to a separate function is not strictly necessary at this point. But later in the book, you'll use your Ktor routing definitions in multiple separate places. So you need to have it available as a separate function that you can call from anywhere, instead of locking it into the `embeddedServer` call.

It's also common to separate the Ktor server configuration to a separate function in open source apps and in the Ktor documentation itself, so it's nice to follow the conventions in your own web app to make your code more readable.

Listing 2-2 shows how to set this up.

Listing 2-2. Configuring Ktor in a separate isolated function

```
fun main() {
  embeddedServer(Netty, port = 4207) {
    createKtorApplication()
  }.start(wait = true)
}

fun Application.createKtorApplication() {
  routing {
    get("/") {
      call.respondText("Hello, World!")
    }
  }
}
```

The function createKtorApplication is an extension function. You'll learn more about those in Chapter 3, but the gist of it is that the "this" inside the embeddedServer lambda is an instance of io.ktor.server.application.Application. And by making createKtorApplication() an extension function of Application, it will have the same "this" available when it's a separate function, as when it's in-line inside the embeddedServer lambda.

Using Lambdas

Lambdas are everywhere in Kotlin. In fact, you've already written a few of them. The functions embeddedServer, routing, and get all take lambdas as arguments.

Lambdas are blocks of code, just like functions. They are created using curly brackets, { and }. The main difference between lambdas and regular functions is that a lambda does not have a name, but a function does.

Tip   Another name for lambdas is *anonymous functions*. There are a few differences in syntax between lambdas and functions (you'll see more about that throughout the book), but logically they are identical.

There's a convention in Kotlin for functions that take a lambda as their last argument. Let's look at the function get to demonstrate. It takes two arguments: a string, denoting the path that triggers the route, and a lambda, which holds the code that should execute when the web app handles a request at that path. One way of calling get would be like this:

```
get("/", { ... })
```

Because it's so common in Kotlin for functions to take a lambda as their last argument, there's a more convenient way to pass them to functions. Instead of placing the lambda inside the parentheses of the function, you can place it after:

```
get("/") { ... }
```

This is particularly useful for functions that *only* take a lambda. An example of this is the routing function. It's nice to be able to skip the parentheses entirely.

It's common for Kotlin programmers to put the lambda outside the parentheses. In fact, IntelliJ IDEA will out of the box show a warning if you put a tailing lambda inside of the parentheses. You can disable this warning if you want to, but it's a good idea to follow this convention if you want to make your code as readable as possible to other programmers.

Named Arguments Instead of Magic Numbers and Booleans

The function start() takes a Boolean as its only argument. The function embeddedServer() takes the port number that the server should use. You can call both like this:

```
embeddedServer(Netty, 4207) {
  createKtorApplication()
}.start(true)
```

A common name for Booleans and numbers passed to functions in this manner is *magic Booleans* and *magic numbers*. It's not immediately obvious to the reader what a Boolean means when it's passed to the function start() and what a number means in the second argument passed to embeddedServer().

To make it easier to understand what these numbers and Booleans mean, you can pass them as *named arguments* instead:

```
embeddedServer(Netty, port = 4207) {
  createKtorApplication()
}.start(wait = true)
```

You can't name it anything you want. It must be the same as the name of the argument in the implementation of the function.

Run Your Web App

Run your application with IntelliJ IDEA or Gradle. Open *http://localhost:4207* in your browser, and you'll be politely greeted by your code. You should see results like those in Figure 2-1. Behold! You have a working web app.

Figure 2-1. *Your web app is up and running and responding to the port defined in your code*

Logging

High-quality logging is a vital component of production-grade web apps. It can make or break your ability to find out what happened when errors happen in production.

When you run your application, the console prints the error messages shown in Figure 2-2.

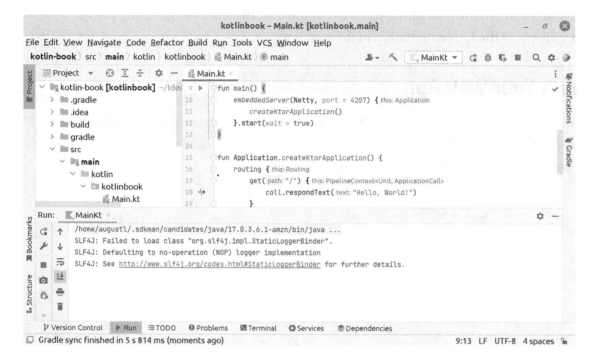

Figure 2-2. *SLF4J issues an error message when your application runs*

In this section, you'll learn about logging and configure your application to output useful information from third-party code, as well as logging from your own code.

Loggers on the Java Platform

There are several terms and concepts to be aware of when it comes to logging on the Java platform.

The error messages in Figure 2-2 mention something called "SLF4J." SLF4J is a *logging façade*. SLF4J is short for Simple Logging Façade for Java. A logging façade is not able to produce any actual log output; it's only able to receive log statements. When you start a Ktor server, Ktor tries to log information about the startup process, using instances of SLF4J loggers. But you haven't configured logging yet, so SLF4J prints the error messages seen in Figure 2-2 to let you know that SLF4J received log statements but isn't able to output them.

The Java platform has standardized on using SLF4J, and libraries and frameworks will pull in the SLF4J library and use it to perform its logging.

To see actual log output, you need to add a *logging implementation*. There are many different implementations available. The most widely used ones are Logback and Log4j.

SLF4J searches the *class path* for a logging implementation. The class path is where the Java platform runtime can find all compiled code from your own source code, as well as code from third-party dependencies. SLF4J will scan the class path for the class file *org/slf4j/impl/StaticLoggerBinder.class*. The logging implementation you choose will provide this file so that SLF4J can find it and wire it up. SLF4J will then forward all the log statements it receives to the logging implementation, so that the logging implementation can display the log messages.

Log levels are a hierarchy of severity levels. A logging statement always has a log level. The available log levels are trace, debug, info, warning, error, and fatal. The log levels separate debugging output and information about what your system is up to from important warnings and critical errors.

You can use log levels to differentiate output from distinct parts of your code. For example, you can tell the logging implementation to use the warning level for a given module. The log level hierarchy then dictates that it will hide all levels below warning (trace, debug, and info) and that the only visible log messages will be those at the warning level and above (warning, error, and fatal).

Configure Logging in Your Web App

To enable log output for your own code as well as third-party dependencies, you need to add a logging implementation. For this book, you'll use Logback. You also need to configure Logback, so that its output is as useful as possible.

To add Logback to your web app, add Logback and SLF4J as dependencies. In *build. gradle.kts*, add the following to the dependencies block that's already present:

```
dependencies {
  implementation("ch.qos.logback:logback-classic:1.4.4")
  implementation("org.slf4j:slf4j-api:2.0.3")
```

> **Tip**   You don't have to add SLF4J as a dependency. Ktor already depends on
> SLF4J, and the Gradle build system will make all *transitive dependencies* (i.e.,
> dependencies of dependencies) available to your own code as well. But later,
> you'll call code from SLF4J directly, and it's considered good hygiene to add direct
> dependencies in *build.gradle.kts* to all code you call directly.

When you restart your web app, you'll no longer see a warning from SLF4J. Instead, you'll see actual log output, like what you can see in Figure 2-3.

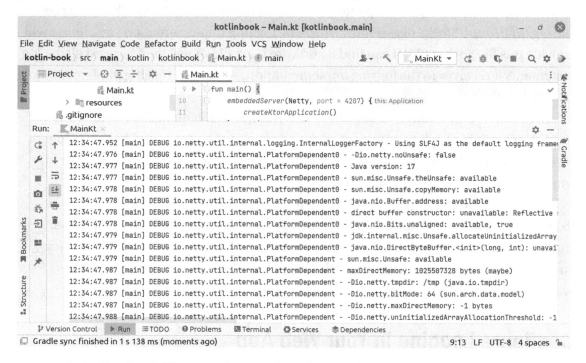

Figure 2-3. *Logback fills your logs with verbose information because you haven't configured Logback yet*

The log output visible in Figure 2-3 is from Netty, the server implementation used by Ktor. In other words, what you see is the log output from a dependency of a dependency, multiple steps away from your own code. The ability to investigate what *all* parts of the system are up to is what makes logging so useful.

The most common way to set up a logging implementation is to use the info level for all third-party code and the debug level for your own code. Debug log statements from third-party code are usually not relevant unless you're working on changes to that code or you're debugging an issue with an unknown cause. For your own code, the debug level log output is truly relevant, as you are in fact working actively on changing that code.

To configure Logback, you need to add an XML config file to *src/main/resources/ logback.xml*. Listing 2-3 shows an example of a valid Logback config file.

Listing 2-3. Logback configuration, stored in **src/main/resources/logback.xml**

```
<configuration>
  <appender
    name="STDOUT"
    class="ch.qos.logback.core.ConsoleAppender"
  >
    <encoder>
      <pattern>%d{YYYY-MM-dd HH:mm:ss.SSS} [%thread] %-5level %logger{36} -
      %msg%n</pattern>
    </encoder>
  </appender>
  <root level="INFO">
    <appender-ref ref="STDOUT"/>
  </root>

  <logger name="kotlinbook" level="DEBUG"/>
</configuration>
```

The `<appender>` in Listing 2-3 tells Logback where to write the log output. You can tell Logback to write to files and even send emails. Here, you configure Logback to simply write logging output to the console. This is the most common configuration for production setups as well, as most production environments will have facilities to make console output available to developers.

The `<root>` logger in Listing 2-3 is the default logger that Logback will use for all code – your own, as well as third-party dependencies – that does not have a specific logger configuration. It's set to the info level, which means Logback will only show statements at info, warn, error, and fatal.

The statement `<logger name="kotlinbook" level="DEBUG"/>` in Listing 2-3 overrides the `<root>` logger for all logging statements coming from `kotlinbook`. This means Logback will show all log statements for your own code at the debug level and above.

Figure 2-4 shows what the log output looks like, after you've added the Logback XML config file.

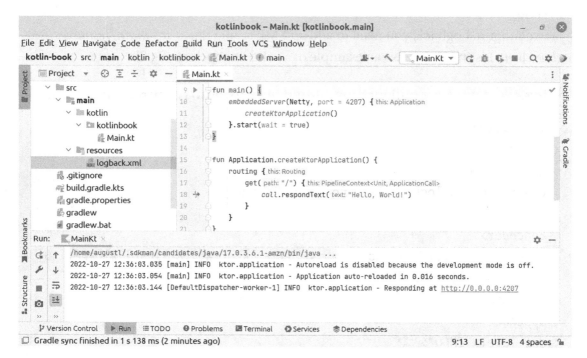

Figure 2-4. *Logback has much nicer output when you've configured it to only show info-level logs for third-party dependencies*

The addition of a config file drastically reduced the amount of log statements written to the console. Instead of verbose implementation details from Netty, you now only see two messages about the Ktor startup and an info message that lets you know that the web server is up and running. It even includes the full URL where your website is accessible, for your convenience.

Write to the Log from Your Own Code

You have a working logging setup for third-party code, as well as for your own code. But you haven't logged from your own code yet. To write to the log, you'll do exactly what Ktor, Netty, and other third-party code does – creating SLF4J logging façade instances.

You can create instances of loggers by invoking the SLF4J LoggerFactory class.

Listing 2-4. Create an instance of a logger and write to the log

```
import org.slf4j.LoggerFactory

private val log = LoggerFactory.getLogger("kotlinbook.Main")
log.debug("Testing my logger")
```

In the *logback.xml* configuration file, you specified that you want log output at the debug level for loggers that start with the name `kotlinbook`. You've named your own logger `kotlinbook.Main`, and your log statement is at the debug level, so when you add the code in Listing 2-4 to `Main.kt` and run your web app again, you should see your logging statement printed in the console, like what you see in Figure 2-5.

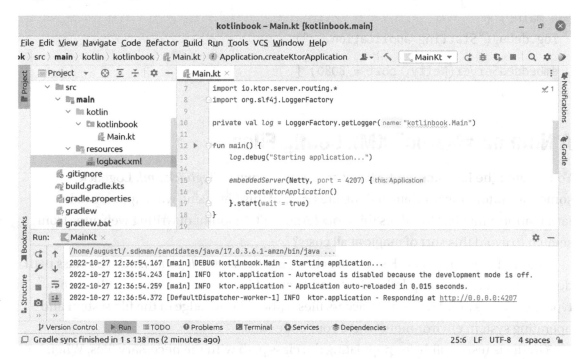

Figure 2-5. *Your logging configuration and your logging statement are set up so that you can see the log text in the log output*

You should always name your logger the same as the package name plus the name of the file where you create the logger. The name `kotlinbook.Main` follows this rule.

You typically create a single logger at the top of the file where you want to write to the log, below the import statements and before any function or class declarations.

In Listing 2-5, you can see a full example of what logging from your own code might look like in your existing main function.

Listing 2-5. Create a logger and write to the log from your main function in **src/main/kotlin/kotlinbook/Main.kt**

```
package kotlinbook

import ...
import org.slf4j.LoggerFactory

val log = LoggerFactory.getLogger("kotlinbook.Main")

fun main() {
  log.debug("Starting application...")

  embeddedServer(Netty, port = 8080) {
    // ...
```

A Note on "Magic" XML Config Files

You created the Logback config file at *src/main/resources/logback.xml*. Logback somehow automatically detected the presence of this file, using what appears to be Java platform magic. How does this work? And isn't the point of writing web apps from scratch to avoid this sort of magic at all costs?

Under the hood, Logback scans the class path for the file *logback.xml*. The class path doesn't just contain compiled code stored as class files. It can contain any file of any type and is a way for Java code to access files without knowledge of the file system and operating system environment where your code runs.

Gradle is responsible for populating the class path with the necessary files. When Gradle builds your web app, it will place all the files in *src/main/resources* in the class path. This is what lets Logback find the *logback.xml* config file. Logback simply asks the class path for the file *logback.xml* and receives it from the Java runtime.

Generally, I aim to keep the magic in this book to an absolute minimum. The logging config is as far as I'm willing to go. It's simply impractical to avoid it. Ktor and its dependencies are already using it. If you don't configure SLF4J and Logback, you can't access the log statements it creates, and you'll always see that warning you got in Figure 2-2, before you configured SLF4J and Logback.

Tip   If you for some reason don't want to access the logs from dependencies that use SLF4J, you can disable SLF4J entirely and suppress the error it logs on startup when it can't find a logging implementation. Add a dependency to `org.slf4j:slf4j-nop:1.7.36` in *build.gradle.kts*, and you won't hear from SLF4J again.

In my experience, SLF4J and Logback are so stable and mature that you'll never have problems with them. Magic can be infuriating when it stops working, but you'll be hard-pressed to bork your logging setup when you set it up as I've described it in this chapter. Logging is also one of those things that most programmers accept as being slightly magic and opaque. Even programmers in the Clojure community, which is probably the least magic-prone community on the Java platform, will often use Logback and XML config files in their projects.

You now have a full-fledged logging setup in your web app, with no boilerplate other than having to invoke the `LoggerFactory` in each file where you want to log, and you're using all the tools that the rest of the Java community is using. It's amazing what you can achieve without frameworks these days.

Useful Error Pages

Out of the box, Ktor will display a blank HTML page when your code throws an exception. It's much more practical to have Ktor display some information instead, such as the actual error message from the exception.

To handle exceptions in Ktor, you can use the `StatusPages` plugin. This plugin lets you hook into various parts of the Ktor lifecycle, such as when your code throws an unhandled exception.

To add the `StatusPages` plugin, you'll first need to add it as a dependency to *build.gradle.kts*. As always, add it to the existing `dependencies` block that's already present there:

```
dependencies {
  implementation("io.ktor:ktor-server-status-pages:2.1.2")
```

You configure Ktor plugins inside the `createKtorApplication` function, alongside the routing that's already there:

```
fun Application.createKtorApplication() {
  install(StatusPages) {
    // Configure the plugin here
  }

  routing {
    // Existing routing is here...
```

Listing 2-6 shows a full example of how you can use the exception handling hook in the `StatusPages` plugin to tell Ktor exactly what you want to happen when your code throws an unhandled exception.

Listing 2-6. Use the `StatusPages` plugin to make Ktor show useful info about errors, instead of a blank page

```
install(StatusPages) {
  exception<Throwable> { call, cause ->
    kotlinbook.log.error("An unknown error occurred", cause)

    call.respondText(
      text = "500: $cause",
      status = HttpStatusCode.InternalServerError
    )
  }
}
```

The Java platform has a class hierarchy of exceptions, and `Throwable` is at the top of that hierarchy. Specifying `exception<Throwable>` means that the `StatusPages` plugin will invoke the exception handler for *all* errors that can occur. You can add multiple exception handler blocks if you want to show different output for different errors. Ktor will use the most specific one that it can find for the thrown error.

The `call` parameter passed to the exception handler lambda is the same type as the `call` inside route handlers. This means that your error pages have the full power of Ktor available to them, and you can respond any way you like. It's a good idea to keep the exception handling as simple as possible, though. If your exception handling code is too complex, it can end up failing and throwing an exception of its own. If that happens, your exception handler won't be able to show any output, and Ktor will just show a blank page, as if you didn't configure an exception handler.

The `cause` parameter is the error object that represents the exception that occurred. Note the logging statement in Listing 2-6. It's useful to have the logs contain information about any errors that might occur. The SLF4J logger has a special implementation of the error log level, which takes the normal message text as well as the actual error object for the exception that was thrown. The logging implementation will print the message text and a nice, formatted version of the error object that includes the error message and the full stack trace.

CHAPTER 3

Configuration Files

All web apps need configuration files. Configuration files let you move things like database credentials, API keys, and which port to run the HTTP server on away from your source code and into a separate configuration file.

Your application will also run in at least three different environments: local development, automated testing, and production. Configuration files enable having different defaults in each environment, all checked into version control and easily reproducible.

You *could* get through the examples in this book without configuration files, but then you wouldn't learn how to build production-ready web apps from scratch.

If you're new to Kotlin, here are some language features you'll see examples of in this chapter:

- Defining classes with constructors
- Data classes
- let blocks
- The it shortcut for single-argument lambdas
- Null safety and nullable types
- Metaprogramming
- Regular expressions
- The Elvis operator
- Single-expression functions

© August Lilleaas 2023
A. Lilleaas, *Pro Kotlin Web Apps from Scratch*, https://doi.org/10.1007/978-1-4842-9057-6_3

Also in this chapter, you will learn the following about using configuration files in your web app:

- Making properties configurable instead of hard-coded

- Storing configuration in a configuration file that's checked into version control

- Having different default configuration values for different environments

- Providing secrets such as production password and API keys through environment variables, without checking them into version control

- Logging your config on application startup, for transparency and ease of debugging

Instead of hard-coding values in your source code, you'll place them in a configuration file. You'll use the Typesafe Config library to manage configuration. In Appendix B, you'll learn about how to replace Typesafe Config with Hoplite.

Create a Configuration File

As the title of this chapter indicates, you'll store your configuration in a configuration file. The first step is to create this file, store some configuration in it, and use values from the configuration file instead of hard-coding them into your source code.

The Configuration File Anatomy

What is a configuration file? What should it contain, and how do you write one?

The configuration file is a key/value lookup system. You'll write configuration properties in the file, assign values to them, load the configuration file into your web app, and fetch the assigned values.

The configuration file is using a format commonly referred to as HOCON. This format is a superset of JSON and supports typed values and nested properties. While JSON is great for parsing and outputting data to and from APIs, it's a cumbersome format to work with when typing configuration values into a file by hand.

Create your configuration file in *src/main/resources/app.conf*. For now, all you'll put in it is the HTTP port that the web app binds to. In Listing 3-1, you can see a full working example of such a configuration file.

Listing 3-1. The **app.conf** configuration file, specifying which HTTP port the web app will use

```
httpPort = 4207
```

The HOCON file format is very straightforward and readable. Each line consists of a config property name (`httpPort`), an equals sign (`=`), and the value to assign to that config property (`4207`).

Reading Values from Your Configuration File

To load and access the values in your configuration file, you'll use a library called Typesafe Config. It's a simple library that reads configuration files and provides a programmatic interface to read out the configuration file values.

You need to add Typesafe Config as a dependency to your web app. As seen in previous chapters, add the following to the `dependencies` block of *build.gradle.kts*:

```
implementation("com.typesafe:config:1.4.2")
```

To read your configuration file, you'll use the `ConfigurationFactory` class provided by Typesafe Config. It has a `load()` method that wires up your configuration and makes it accessible to your code:

```
ConfigFactory
  .parseResources("app.conf")
  .resolve()
```

This gives you a `Config` object, which has everything you need to access the properties you define in your configuration file. For example, to get the value of the configured HTTP port, you can call `config.getInt("httpPort")`.

The Config object has several methods available to get config values as a specific type. `getInt`, `getLong`, `getString`, `getBoolean`, etc. will all give you the configured value with the type you specify in the method call.

Tip   Use auto-completion to see which getters are available on the `Config` object. Type `config.get` in your code and then wait, and you'll see a popup that shows all the available methods on Config that start with `get`.

Typesafe Config will also perform validation and throw an exception if it's not able to convert to the type you want. For example, `config.getBoolean("httpPort")` will fail, as Typesafe Config doesn't know how to convert 4207 into a Boolean.

Listing 3-2 shows a full example of how to load and access configuration files in your application and how to use the `httpPort` from *app.conf* instead of hard-coding the port number in your Kotlin source code.

Listing 3-2. An example of using Typesafe Config to load your configuration file and use it to provide config values to your code

```
val config = ConfigFactory
  .parseResources("app.conf")
  .resolve()

embeddedServer(Netty, port = config.getInt("httpPort")) {
  // ...your existing code here
```

Make the Configuration Fail Early and Type-Safe

Using the raw `Config` object from Typesafe Config works fine. But using it has two issues that need to be addressed.

The first issue is that the Config object is *fail late*, but it should be *fail early*. Fail early is a pattern in programming where failures should occur as close to the cause of the failure as possible. For example, if you pass around a `Config` object and a property is either missing or set to the wrong type, it won't fail until you access configuration properties somewhere deep down in your code. You instead want it to fail as early as possible, ideally at the time where you read and load the configuration file into your web app.

The second issue is the limited type safety of the config property names. When you use strings to refer to the name of a config property, such as `config.getInt("httpPort")`, your code will compile fine even if you have a typo in the name of the property. To make the Kotlin compiler throw an error if you misspell a config property, you should be able to write something like `config.httpPort`.

You can resolve these issues by using a Kotlin *data class* to represent your configuration file.

Store Configuration in a Data Class

In general, it's nice to have the data in your system represented as just that – data – and not opaque objects with behaviors and error states. Data is transparent and immutable and carries no extra meaning or behaviors other than the data itself.

A *data class* in Kotlin is bridging the gap between objects and immutable data. You can think of data classes as restricted and typed hash maps. A data class only stores data and has no behavior associated with it. It comes with built-in *value semantics*: it's immutable, and it implements equality so that the Java platform considers two instances of the same data class containing the same data to be equal.

Listing 3-3 shows the initial data class representation of your config file. It only has one property for now, but you'll extend this later when you add more properties to your configuration file.

Listing 3-3. A data class to represent your configuration file

```
data class WebappConfig(
  val httpPort: Int
)
```

This looks just like a normal Kotlin class, except it starts with the keyword `data` to indicate that it's a data class and not a plain class.

The code inside the parentheses are the constructor arguments. By adding `val` before the name of the argument, you indicate to Kotlin that in addition to taking the `httpPort` as the first constructor argument, you also want to store it as a property on the class instances. `val` indicates an immutable property, whereas `var` makes it mutable.

To create an instance of this data class, you construct it like you would any other class in Kotlin:

```
WebappConfig(4207)
```

41

As you saw in Chapter 2, you can use named arguments so that people who read this code can understand what the number 4207 means. In fact, it's a convention in Kotlin to always use named arguments for data classes. This makes the code more readable, and when you have multiple constructor arguments, you don't have to pass them in the same order as they're defined in the data class:

```
WebappConfig(
    httpPort = 4207
)
```

Load Config into the Data Class

The next step is to convert the Config object from Typesafe Config to an instance of your own WebappConfig.

The simplest way of doing this is to do the mapping completely by hand:

```
WebappConfig(
  httpPort = config.getInt("httpPort")
)
```

Your configuration will now fail early. As you load the config and create the instance of WebappConfig, you'll immediately call getInt on config, which will fail if Typesafe Config is unable to cast it to an integer.

It's also type-safe on access. Kotlin knows that you named the config property httpPort. Typing config.getInt("http proot") would cause a runtime error, but config.httpProot will fail when you compile your code.

Kotlin Null Safety

Kotlin is strict about null safety. Kotlin will throw a compile error if you pass null to something that doesn't handle nulls.

WebappConfig uses the *non-nullable* type Int for the httpPort property. This means that if you try to do something like WebappConfig(httpPort = null), you'll get a compile error.

If you want to be able to set something to null, you should instead use a *nullable type*. Listing 3-4 shows an example of adding a nullable type, String?, to store the database password in your configuration.

Listing 3-4. A data class with a nullable and non-nullable type

```
data class WebappConfig(
  val httpPort: Int,
  val dbPassword: String?
)
```

You will still get a compile error if you try to set `httpPort` to `null`. But you can set `dbPassword` to `null`, such as `WebappConfig(httpPort = 4207, dbPassword = null)`. Data classes also let you omit nullable properties with `WebappConfig(httpPort = 4207)`, as a convenient shortcut for setting them to null.

Kotlin Platform Types

Kotlin has a concept called *platform types*. Java has a weaker type system than Kotlin, especially around nulls. Java allows any object reference to be `null` at any time. Typesafe Config is written in Java, which means that the Kotlin compiler can't guarantee compile-time that a Java method that returns an object is not `null`.

The Java method `config.getInt("...")` has the Java return type of `int` – a primitive integer value – and not the object type `Integer`. Primitives in Java can never be null, so Kotlin casts the type to the non-nullable `Int` type.

However, the Java method `config.getString("...")` has the Java return type of `String`, which is an object, and *can* be null. Kotlin does *not*, however, cast to the nullable type `String?`. Instead, it's casted to the *platform type* `String!`.

Platform types essentially mean "I'll allow you to pass this thing, which might be null, to a non-nullable type." Listing 3-5 shows how you can pass platform types to non-nullable types, even though the Kotlin compiler doesn't know at compile time whether the value is null.

Listing 3-5. Passing the platform type `String!` to the non-nullable type `String`

```
data class WebappConfig(
  val httpPort: Int,
  val dbUsername: String,
  val dbPassword: String?
)
```

```
WebappConfig(
  httpPort = 4207,
  dbUsername = config.getString("dbUsername")
)
```

If Kotlin allowed the creation of WebappConfig with dbUsername set to null, all the guarantees from the Kotlin type system would be out the window, and any code that reads dbUsername would be prone to null pointer exceptions.

Thankfully, Kotlin will fail early here as well. Kotlin adds runtime checks to all variable and property assignments where the type is non-nullable. You will get a null pointer exception, but you'll get it the moment your code tries to create an instance of WebappConfig with dbUsername set to null. This means that all places in your code that operate on non-nullable types will still continue to do so safely, as Kotlin didn't allow the creation of an invalid type in the runtime.

Use the Data Class in Your Web App

When your web app starts up, you should load the config file and create an instance of WebappConfig as soon as possible. Later, when you add more functionality, it will likely require the configuration properties to be readily accessible so that you can use them to wire up your web app. So wiring up configuration is often the first thing a web app does, and then it starts up.

Listing 3-6 shows how to create a function that first loads the configuration file and then creates an instance of WebappConfig, so that you have the configuration available for use.

Listing 3-6. Creating a function for loading configuration in your web app

```
fun createAppConfig(): WebappConfig {
  val rawConfig = ConfigFactory
    .parseResources("app.conf")
    .resolve()

  return WebappConfig(
    httpPort = rawConfig.getInt("httpPort")
  )
}
```

You now have the same WebappConfig as before, but you're storing the values in a config file, instead of hard-coded into your source code.

Use let Blocks to Avoid Intermediate Variables

Listing 3-6 has a problem that you should fix. You're only using the value rawConfig temporarily while creating your WebappConfig. rawConfig is now available to all the other code in this scope. And it makes the code harder to read, as it introduces an extra name your brain must understand and keep track of.

It's better to instead use a let block. Listing 3-7 shows an example of how you can use a let block to avoid the extra named variable rawConfig and return the WebappConfig instance directly in a single statement.

Listing 3-7. Create the WebappConfig using a let statement

```
fun createAppConfig() =
  ConfigFactory
    .parseResources("app.conf")
    .resolve()
    .let {
      WebappConfig(
        httpPort = it.getInt("httpPort")
      )
    }
```

A let block is not special or magical syntax. It's just a function, and you can call let on all types. let takes a single lambda and returns whatever the lambda returns. In this case, let returns an instance of WebappConfig, as Lambdas will return the last statement in them. You don't have to explicitly write return for a lambda to return something.

The lambda in let also gets a single argument passed to it, which is whatever object or value you called let on. In this case, you called let on ConfigFactory.load(), which returns a Config object from Typesafe Config. So the lambda in let gets this Config object passed to it.

A lambda with a single argument is so common that Kotlin has a shortcut for referring to that argument: it. You could write .let { myThing -> doSomething(myThing) }, but to save you some typing and to have a common name that's easy to recognize, you can also write .let { doSomething(it) }.

Also note that when a function body is a single statement, you don't have to specify the return type of the function, and you can replace the curly brackets and the `return` with an equals sign and the single statement that makes up the function body. Kotlin calls this a *single-expression function.*

Provide Different Default Values for Different Environments

Currently, your configuration file can define the `httpPort` where you want your web app to start. But what happens if you need a different `httpPort` in your production environment? Your configuration file needs a way to specify different defaults for different environments.

The ideal setup is to have a set of default config values that works for most environments. Then, you should be able to override specific config values for specific environments, such as binding a different HTTP port locally and in the production environment.

Environment-Specific Config Files

To group the different config properties for the different environments, you can create a separate file for each environment you need to support and use those files to override values in `app.conf`.

Typically, you'll need at least two extra config files:

- `app-local.conf`
- `app-production.conf`

These files override values for the local development environment and the live production environment, respectively.

This separation gives you full control of how you want to override defaults from `app.conf`.

For example, let's say you can enable or disable the actual sending of SMS messages in your web app. You can set it to disabled by default in `app.conf` and enable it in `app-production.conf`. This ensures that you don't send SMS messages by accident in your local test environment and that if you add an additional environment later, SMS delivery will be off by default.

Conversely, let's say you have a cumbersome but very secure way of logging into your web app. You can set this to enabled by default in app.conf and disable it in app-local.conf. This lets you implement a more convenient way of logging in for local development, but you won't accidentally turn off secure authentication in your production environment.

Define the Web App Environment

To support running your web app in different environments and with different config values, you need a way to specify which environment the web app is supposed to run in.

You can use operating system environment variables to do this. The default environment should be set to "local", and then an environment variable can be set to override it to whatever the environment variable specifies, such as "production". The code in Listing 3-8 shows how to read an environment variable and, if it's not set, use "local" instead. To make it easy to debug your web app, Listing 3-8 also logs the actual value of env that your web app is using.

Listing 3-8. Use environment variables to specify the environment your web app is running in

```
val env = System.getenv("KOTLINBOOK_ENV") ?: "local"
log.debug("Application runs in the environment ${env}")
```

This code uses the *Elvis operator*, which is a convenient way to specify a default value when something is null or false. The statement System.getenv("KOTLINBOOK_ENV") ?: "local" means that if the call to System.getenv() returns null, the statement will return "local", the value on the right side of the Elvis operator. This sets your config loading up so that you don't have to set the environment variable KOTLINBOOK_ENV for your code to work.

Override Defaults with Environment-Specific Config

Currently, your code only reads values from app.conf. You need to update it to override values in app.conf with values in app-[your environment].conf.

In Typesafe Config, you can do this with *fallback configs*. In Listing 3-8, you set the variable env to the environment your web app runs in. Instead of loading app.conf, you'll load "app-${env}.conf".

In Listing 3-9, you can see how to use `withFallback()` to tell Typesafe Config to load values from `app.conf` when you ask the `Config` object to get a value that isn't present in `"app-${env}.conf"`.

Listing 3-9. Load your environment-specific config file and fall back to `app.conf` for default values

```
fun createAppConfig(env: String) =
  ConfigFactory
    .parseResources("app-${env}.conf")
    .withFallback(ConfigFactory.parseResources("app.conf"))
    .resolve()
    .let {
      WebappConfig(
        httpPort = it.getInt("httpPort")
      )
    }

// In your main function:
val env = System.getenv("KOTLINBOOK_ENV") ?: "local"
val config = createAppConfig(env)
```

Make sure you create an empty `app-local.conf` before you run this code. The default environment is `"local"`, and the code will always try to load the environment-specific config file. Typesafe Config will fail if the file you specified isn't on the class path.

Secret Config Values

You should check the configuration files into version control. The checked-in config files should hold most of the config values in your system. But you also need a method for handling secret config values, like database passwords, that you should not check into version control.

Don't Store Secrets in Version Control

First, let's add some detail to why it's important to not store secrets in version control.

At first, it might seem convenient to store everything in a single file and have it checked into version control. Your source code probably isn't accessible to the public, and you already have a tight regime on who has access to the source code and the config files.

There are two big problems I want to highlight, though.

The first problem is accidental source code leaks. A simple click of a button is all it takes to make a repository on a hosting site like GitHub accessible to the public. If this happens, it's not just your source code that leaked to the public, but also all the secrets that you checked into version control. This can include API keys and signing secrets for verifying authenticity against third-party systems, as well as passwords for database access and so on.

The second problem is that everyone that has access to the source code also has access to all the secrets that you've checked into version control. In some scenarios, regulation such as GDPR or PSD2 in Europe mandates that only a subset of certified and vetted developers has access to personal identifiable information (PII) or financial transaction data. And for security reasons in general, it can be a good idea to restrict access to live production data. If you don't store secrets in version control, you don't have to vet and certify every developer who has access to the code source. These developers can instead develop and test against staging environments that contain fake PII and can't transfer real money.

Note that I am not a lawyer. You should confer with your lawyer for all legal issues. Don't take legal advice from a software developer.

You need a mechanism to provide secrets to your web app, other than the config files. Operating system environment variables are a great fit for this.

Typesafe Config has built-in support for reading from environment variables, so you don't have to change the code that loads your config files. Typesafe Config has a concept of *substitutions*. This means that your config file can contain the name of the environment variable you want to read from, instead of the actual raw value.

For example, if you want to read the web app HTTP port from an environment variable, you can replace `httpPort = 4207` with `httpPort = ${KOTLINBOOK_HTTP_PORT}`. It's common to use uppercase and underscores for environment variable names and to prefix the environment variables that you use with the name of your system. This makes `KOTLINBOOK_HTTP_PORT` a good name for an environment variable.

Listing 3-10 shows how `app.conf` can set the value of `httpPort` to 4207, like you've seen earlier in this chapter. Listing 3-11 shows how `app-production.conf` can override the `httpPort` property and set it to the value of an environment variable instead.

Listing 3-10. `app.conf` explicitly specifies the value of `httpPort`

```
httpPort = 4207
```

Listing 3-11. `app-production.conf` sets `httpPort` to the value of the environment variable `KOTLINBOOK_HTTP_PORT`

```
httpPort = ${KOTLINBOOK_HTTP_PORT}
```

This solution makes it easy to reason about how you mapped environment variables to config properties – it's right there in the config file. It also has the benefit of failing early if you inadvertently forgot to set the environment variable `KOTLINBOOK_HTTP_PORT` in production. Instead of falling back to your default setting, Typesafe Config will crash with a useful and informative error message if the environment variable for some reason isn't available to your web app process, as seen in Figure 3-1.

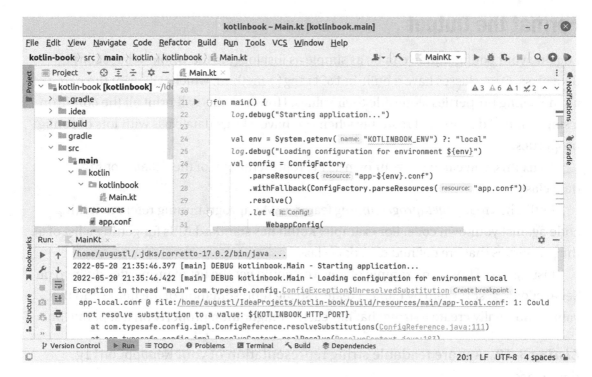

Figure 3-1. *Typesafe Config throws an error if it can't find a specified environment variable*

Note that while it's not a technical requirement, it's common to use uppercase and underscores for environment variable names. You should also prefix the environment variables with the name of your system, so that you avoid naming conflicts with other environment variables. This makes KOTLINBOOK_HTTP_PORT a good name for an environment variable.

Logging Config on Web App Startup

When you run your application in a production environment, you might find yourself asking the question: "But what is *actually* the config value set to?" This is particularly useful when you use a combination of config files and environment variables and you're fiddling around in your production environment, trying to figure out why a config property isn't set to what you thought it would be.

By logging the configuration when your web app starts, you can easily refer to the logs to see the actual values of all your configuration properties.

Format the Output

Logging your configuration can be as simple as just logging the whole WebappConfig data class. Data classes have a built-in toString() method, which will print the name of all the config properties alongside their values. However, this will print all the config on a single line and is not that readable when you have a large data class with lots of config properties.

To fix this, you can write your own string representation of the WebappConfig data class.

Kotlin has many *metaprogramming* features. Metaprogramming refers to writing code against your own code. For example, Kotlin has standard APIs for getting a list of all the properties that are defined on a data class.

Listing 3-12 shows an example of how you could get the list of properties defined on WebappConfig, sort them by name, create a string representation of the name and the value, and finally create a string that has each configuration property on a separate line.

Listing 3-12. A more readable string representation of your WebappConfig data class

```
WebappConfig::class.declaredMemberProperties
    .sortedBy { it.name }
    .map { "${it.name} = ${it.get(config)}" }
    .joinToString(separator = "\n")
```

This is a good example of functional programming in Kotlin. You start with a list of properties, call a function to sort them that returns the sorted list, map over the list to create a new version of it, and finally join it to create a string representation.

Masking Secrets

You don't want to log things like database passwords and API keys. Printing secrets to the log adds an attack vector for hackers to exploit, and you should take security seriously from the get-go.

Listing 3-12 contains a custom string representation of your WebappConfig. You can modify it so that properties that are likely to contain secrets will have the value masked out, instead of printed as is.

Listing 3-13 shows how you can use a regular expression to match config property names and avoid printing the full config value for config properties that contain secrets.

Listing 3-13. Filter out secrets from the string representation of WebappConfig

```
val secretsRegex = "password|secret|key"
  .toRegex(RegexOption.IGNORE_CASE)

WebappConfig::class.declaredMemberProperties
  .sortedBy { it.name }
  .map {
    if (secretsRegex.containsMatchIn(it.name)) {
      "${it.name} = ${it.get(config).toString().take(2)}*****"
    } else {
      "${it.name} = ${it.get(config)}"
    }
  }
  .joinToString(separator = "\n")
```

If your configuration file contains the property databasePassword, your output will be "databasePassword = 12*****" instead of "databasePassword = 1234".

The regular expression here is limited, and you should make sure to update and maintain it as your application grows.

Writing to the Log

You have a Config object from Typesafe Config, you create a WebappConfig data class, and you mask out secrets when printing. Now, all you need to do is to perform the logging.

Listing 3-14 shows the final version of how this might look in your web app.

Listing 3-14. A full working example of loading, logging, and using a configuration file

```
val config = createAppConfig(env)

val secretsRegex = "password|secret|key"
  .toRegex(RegexOption.IGNORE_CASE)
```

53

```
log.debug("Configuration loaded successfully: ${
  WebappConfig::class.declaredMemberProperties
    .sortedBy { it.name }
    .map {
      if (secretsRegex.containsMatchIn(it.name)) {
        "${it.name} = ${it.get(config).toString().take(2)}*****"
      } else {
        "${it.name} = ${it.get(config)}"
      }
    }
    .joinToString(separator = "\n")
}")

embeddedServer(Netty, port = config.httpPort) {
  // ...your existing code here
```

And that's it! You now have a full-fledged setup for reading config files, having different configurations for different environments, and printing your config on startup with secrets masked out.

CHAPTER 4

Decoupling Web Handlers from Specific Libraries

As your application grows, you'll have hundreds or even thousands of individual web handlers, for different combinations of HTTP verbs and URL paths. The purpose of these handlers is to run different pieces of business logic. In this chapter, you'll learn how to uncouple your business logic and web handlers from Ktor, so that you can use them in any context.

In later chapters, you'll run your web handlers in many different environments, not just Ktor. Uncoupling your web handlers from Ktor is a requirement to make that possible. For example, you'll see how to run the same web handlers you use in Ktor from a serverless environment in Chapter 10.

The implementation of the decoupling itself also serves as a nice opportunity to learn some important concepts about the Kotlin language.

Be aware, though. I would be careful with implementing this kind of decoupling in a real-world web app. It introduces complexity and abstraction. It's unlikely that your real-world web apps need to support multiple simultaneous libraries and/or deployment scenarios. So be careful, and exercise good judgment.

If you're new to Kotlin, here are some language features that you'll see examples of in this chapter:

- Sealed classes with abstract properties and functions
- Function overloading
- Functional data-driven programming with maps and lists
- Copying data classes
- Immutability
- Destructuring assignments

55

© August Lilleaas 2023
A. Lilleaas, *Pro Kotlin Web Apps from Scratch*, https://doi.org/10.1007/978-1-4842-9057-6_4

- Function types

- Extension functions

Also in this chapter, you will learn the following about decoupling web handlers from specific libraries in your web app:

- Creating abstractions and connecting them to libraries

- Why you should consider *not* decoupling your web handlers in real-world web apps

In addition to learning how to deploy your web handlers in a serverless environment in Chapter 12, Appendix A will teach you how to replace Ktor with Jersey.

Your Own HTTP Response Abstraction

So far, you've responded to HTTP requests by calling methods directly on the Ktor `call` API. To decouple from Ktor, you'll need to create your own abstraction that doesn't know anything about Ktor and `call`. You'll update all your web handlers to use your own abstraction, to make them independent and decoupled from Ktor.

Representing HTTP Responses

Ktor has a rich API to represent HTTP responses. Your own abstraction also needs to be able to represent any HTTP response, just like Ktor. Thankfully, you can boil down a HTTP response to a simple structure: a status code, some headers, and a response body.

You can represent HTTP response data using a simple data class:

```
data class WebResponse(
  val statusCode: Int,
  val headers: Map<String, List<String>>,
  val body: Any
)
```

You'll expand heavily on this data class throughout this chapter. For example, the type Any works, and it can be used to represent any (pun intended) HTTP response body. But it blocks the type system from having any (pun also intended) knowledge of the contents of the HTTP response. Kotlin has a rich and powerful type system, so you should avoid the type Any as much as you can.

Instead, you can alter `WebResponse` to take advantage of the fact that you can represent the status code and headers the same way for all your HTTP responses. You can update `WebResponse` to be a top-level class that doesn't know anything about the type or contents of the response body. Then, subclasses of `WebResponse` can implement the different body types you want to support.

Multiple Response Types

To support multiple response types, the top-level `WebResponse` will be a *sealed class*. A sealed class is an *abstract* class, meaning you can't create direct instances of it, and it can contain abstract properties that all the subclasses have to implement. It's also *sealed*, which means that the Kotlin type system knows about all the defined subclasses at compile time. This lets Kotlin treat sealed classes like enums, so that you can get help compile-time with things like ensuring that you don't forget to handle all your subclasses of `WebResponse` when you later write code that maps `WebResponse` to Ktor.

The Kotlin documentation has a page dedicated to sealed classes (`https://kotlinlang.org/docs/sealed-classes.html`) if you want to read more about them.

For this chapter, you'll write two child classes: `TextWebResponse` and `JsonWebResponse`. Listing 4-1 shows both, alongside a new implementation of `WebResponse` as a sealed class without the body property.

Listing 4-1. Two concrete classes, `TextWebResponse` and `JsonWebResponse`, that you'll use to represent HTTP responses

```
sealed class WebResponse {
  abstract val statusCode: Int
  abstract val headers: Map<String, List<String>>
}

data class TextWebResponse(
  val body: String,
  override val statusCode: Int = 200,
  override val headers: Map<String, List<String>> = mapOf()
) : WebResponse()
```

```
data class JsonWebResponse(
  val body: Any?,
  override val statusCode: Int = 200,
  override val headers: Map<String, List<String>> = mapOf()
) : WebResponse()
```

You need a little bit of boilerplate to make it work. Data classes in Kotlin aren't "smart," so you must specify all the properties you can pass to them – you can't set them via class inheritance. You need to set default status code of 200, as well as the default empty list of headers.

TextWebResponse defines a body property with the type String. When you create text-based HTTP responses, all you really need to define is that the content is an arbitrary string of text, and that's about it.

JsonWebResponse defines a body property with the type Any?. You could enhance this and create something like JsonMapWebResponse and JsonListWebResponse, with more specific types. But at the end of the day, most JSON serialization libraries don't encode JSON value types in the type system and encode the input as Object! or Any? anyway, opting to throw errors runtime if you pass it a value that can't be JSON encoded. So defining the exact value type of the JSON body won't net you any practical benefits.

You create instances of your response classes just like you create instances of any data class. Listing 4-2 shows some examples of how you can create WebResponse instances.

Listing 4-2. Valid response types of your TextWebResponse and JsonWebResponse classes

```
TextWebResponse("Hello, World!")
TextWebResponse("Oh noes", statusCode = 400)
JsonWebResponse(mapOf("foo" to "bar"))
JsonWebResponse(listOf(1, 2, 3), headers = mapOf(
  "Set-Cookie" to listOf("myCookie=123abc")
))
```

You now have the basics in place for representing HTTP responses in your web handlers, without any coupling to Ktor.

Convenience Functions for Headers

The current API you've created for building HTTP responses is a little bit cumbersome to work with. To be compliant with the HTTP spec, you've encoded header values as List<String>, not a plain String. It's rare to need multiple values for the same header. But the HTTP spec allows it, and it can be practical in some cases, such as responding with multiple Set-Cookie headers.

You could opt to represent your headers as a String instead of a List<String>, so that you don't have to wrap all your header values in listOf to create a list, as seen in Listing 4-2. But you can also update WebResponse to make it more convenient to work with multi-valued headers.

You can do this by adding two methods to WebResponse for appending header values:

```
sealed class WebResponse {
  fun header(headerName: String, headerValue: String) =
  ...

  fun header(headerName: String, headerValue: List<String>) =
  ...
}
```

This is an example of *function overloading*. Kotlin lets you write multiple implementations of functions with the same name. Kotlin looks at which arguments you pass to the function and determines which function to run. In this case, the difference between them is that headerValue can either be a string or a list of strings. Both methods append headers to the response. The only difference between them is that one takes a single header and the other takes a list of headers, covering both use cases for your convenience.

The implementation of header(String, String) is straightforward – it just defers to the function header(String, List<String>) and wraps the header you provided in a list:

```
fun header(headerName: String, headerValue: String) =
    header(headerName, listOf(headerValue))
```

At first glance, this might look like an infinite loop, as the header function does nothing but call the header function. But the different argument types (single string vs. list of strings) mean they are two distinct functions and no infinite loop occurs.

The code that does the heavy lifting will reside in header(String, List<String>). It will need to do two things: All the properties of WebResponse are immutable, so we must create a new instance of WebResponse with new values. Additionally, the headers map is also immutable, so we need to create a new headers value with the new list of headers appended.

To create a new instance of WebResponse, we can lean on the copy function that is built into all data classes. The WebResponse class itself is not a data class, so it does not have a built-in copy function. But WebResponse is the class that implements header(String, List<String>) and therefore needs access to a method that can create a new copy. You can implement this using an abstract function on WebResponse, which has no implementation, but returns a new instance of WebResponse and defers the implementation to the child classes:

```
sealed class WebResponse {
  abstract fun copyResponse(
    statusCode: Int,
    headers: Map<String, List<String>>)
  : WebResponse
}
```

You'll now get a compile error for TextWebResponse and JsonWebResponse, as they do not implement the new abstract function. Listing 4-3 shows the full implementation of TextWebResponse with copyResponse implemented by calling the built-in copy function on data classes.

Listing 4-3. An implementation of TextWebResponse with the abstract function copyResponse from WebResponse implemented

```
data class TextWebResponse(
  val body: String,
  override val statusCode: Int = 200,
  override val headers: Map<String, List<String>> = mapOf()
) : WebResponse() {

  override fun copyResponse(
    statusCode: Int,
    headers: Map<String, List<String>>
  ) =
```

```
    copy(body, statusCode, headers)

}
```

The order of the arguments for copy is the same as the order of the arguments in the constructor of the data class. If you prefer, you can also name the arguments, such as copy(body = body, statusCode = statusCode, ...). But it saves you some typing to omit the names. And the implementation of copy lives right next to the constructor itself in the source code, so it's easy to locate the actual ordering of arguments by just looking at the code right there.

All that's left is to create the actual implementation of header(String, List<String>) in WebResponse:

```
sealed class WebResponse {
  fun header(headerName: String, headerValue: List<String>) =
    copyResponse(
      statusCode,
      headers.plus(Pair(
        headerName,
        headers.getOrDefault(headerName, listOf())
          .plus(headerValue)
      ))
    )
}
```

This implementation calls the copyResponse function we created earlier. It passes in the statusCode as is. For the headers, it needs to handle duplicates of headerName. If we pass a headerName that's already present in headers, the plus will replace any existing value with the new one. So we ask headers for the existing value of headerName, or an empty list if there is none, and append the list of headers to this list instead of replacing it altogether.

You now have everything you need to create a finished implementation.
Listing 4-4 shows a full implementation of header(String, String), header(String, List<String), as well as the copyResponse functionality to create new instances under the hood.

Listing 4-4. The full implementations of WebResponse, TextWebResponse, and JsonWebResponse

```
sealed class WebResponse {
  abstract val statusCode: Int
  abstract val headers: Map<String, List<String>>

  abstract fun copyResponse(
    statusCode: Int,
    headers: Map<String, List<String>>)
  : WebResponse

  fun header(headerName: String, headerValue: String) =
    header(headerName, listOf(headerValue))

  fun header(headerName: String, headerValue: List<String>) =
    copyResponse(
      statusCode,
      headers.plus(Pair(
        headerName,
        headers.getOrDefault(headerName, listOf())
          .plus(headerValue)
      ))
    )
}

data class TextWebResponse(
  val body: String,
  override val statusCode: Int = 200,
  override val headers: Map<String, List<String>> = mapOf()
) : WebResponse() {

  override fun copyResponse(
    statusCode: Int,
    headers: Map<String, List<String>>
  ) =
    copy(body, statusCode, headers)

}
```

```
data class JsonWebResponse(
    val body: Any?,
    override val statusCode: Int = 200,
    override val headers: Map<String, List<String>> = mapOf()
) : WebResponse() {

  override fun copyResponse(
    statusCode: Int,
    headers: Map<String, List<String>>
  ) =
    copy(body, statusCode, headers)

}
```

You can now use this code to append headers using convenient functions instead of manually creating maps and lists for the headers:

```
// Before
TextWebResponse("Hello, World!", headers = mapof(
  "X-Whatever" to listOf("someValue")
))
JsonWebResponse(listOf(1, 2, 3), headers = mapOf(
  "Set-Cookie" to listOf(
    "myCookie=123abc",
    "myOtherCookie=456def"
  )
))

// After
TextWebResponse("Hello, World!")
  .header("X-Whatever", "someValue")

JsonWebResponse(listOf(1, 2, 3))
  .header("Set-Cookie", "myCookie=123abc")
  .header("Set-Cookie", "myOtherCookie=456def")
```

The implementation of WebResponse appends header values on each call, so it's up to you if you want to call header(String, String) multiple times or do a single (or multiple) call to header(String, List<String>).

Case-Insensitive Headers

To make headers even easier to work with, you can update WebResponse to handle headers in a case-insensitive way. Specifically, this lets you add "set-cookie" and "Set-Cookie" and combine them into the same header value, even though one is all lowercase and the other is Camel-Case.

You can achieve this by leaving the existing code as is and storing the headers in multiple casings in the headers map. Then you can add a new function that creates a version of the headers where they're all lowercased.

The headers map is just data, and Kotlin has plenty of facilities for transforming data (commonly called functional programming or data-oriented programming), so that's how you'll implement this new function.

The first step is to convert the headers map to a list of pairs and lowercase the keys:

```
headers
  .map { it.key.lowercase() to it.value }
```

The call to map turns this map of type Map<String, List<String>>

```
mapOf(
  "foo" to listOf("bar"),
  "Foo" to listOf("baz")
)
```

to this list of type List<Pair<String, List<String>>>:

```
listOf(
  "foo" to listOf("bar"),
  "foo" to listOf("baz")
)
```

Notice the subtle difference in casing here. The original map contained the keys "foo" (lowercased) and "Foo" (capitalized), which Kotlin considers two different keys. But you will be lowercasing the keys so that they're both "foo" (lowercased), and Kotlin maps can't contain two different values for the same key. But calling the map function on a map data structure will turn it into a list of Pair. And a list can contain duplicates. So the final list will contain multiple pairs with the same lowercased key "foo".

Listing 4-5. A headers() function on WebResponse with all header names in lowercase

```
sealed class WebResponse {
  fun headers(): Map<String, List<String>> =
    headers
      .map { it.key.lowercase() to it.value }
      .fold(mapOf()) { res, (k, v) ->
        res.plus(Pair(
          k,
          res.getOrDefault(k, listOf()).plus(v)
        ))
      }
}
```

The headers() function in Listing 4-5 returns a new map that has all the header names in lowercase. Just like the function header(String, List<String>) for adding new header values in Listing 4-4, the headers() function in Listing 4-5 uses getOrDefault to merge the values of headers where the names are identical when lowercased, so that you don't end up replacing the values in "foo" (lowercased) with the values of "Foo" (capitalized).

The fold Function

Sit back, take a deep breath, and clear your mind, as I attempt to do the impossible: explain how functional programming works.

fold is at the core of all list transformations in functional programming. You can use fold to implement other functional transformations, like map, filter, forEach, max, take, etc. This makes fold useful in cases where your list transformation needs some extra rules and isn't just a plain map or filter.

In the implementation of headers() in WebResponse in Listing 4-5, fold is on a list and passes an initial value mapOf() (an empty map) and a lambda. fold then calls the lambda and passes the initial value you provided, res, and the first value in the list, (k, v). Then, fold calls the lambda again with whatever the lambda returned the first time fold called the lambda and the second value in the list. Then, this process repeats for each item in the list, calling the lambda for each subsequent item in the list, with whatever the lambda returned the last time fold called the lambda, as well as the list item itself.

The initial empty map is an *accumulator*. You start with the initial value and accumulate new values into it each time fold calls the lambda. fold does not care what type of value the accumulator is. It can be a list, a map, a number, or anything else you might want to accumulate over.

Destructuring Assignment

(k, v) is a *destructuring assignment*. Many entities in Kotlin, such as data classes and Pair, implement componentN() functions. You can access the key of Pair as it.key, but also as it.component1(). Similarly, you can access the value of a Pair as it.value, but also as it.component2(). For all entities that implement componentN() functions, you can destructure them. This is a convenient way to directly refer to components of an entity, without having to create explicit named variables for them. Listing 4-6 shows how destructuring and explicit variables are identical in functionality.

Listing 4-6. Comparing the destructuring syntax with manual variable assignment

```
val it = Pair("foo" to "bar")

// Using destructuring
val (k, v) = it

// Using normal functions
val k = it.key
val v = it.value

// Using manual variable declaration
val k = it.component1()
val v = it.component2()
```

Destructuring assignment can save you from some manual typing, and they are particularly useful when destructuring arguments passed to functions or lambdas, as seen in Listing 4-5.

Connecting to Ktor

You now have a full stand-alone representation of HTTP responses, which has no knowledge of Ktor or any other library. However, your web app does use Ktor. So you need to tie the two together and make Ktor handle your `WebResponse` classes.

Ktor Route Mapping

The first step is to make it possible to have Ktor routes, like `get("/")` and `post("/products")`, interact with `WebResponse` instances returned by your own code.

To see what the result should look like, Listing 4-7 compares the current way you handle routing with what it will look like when you've finished wiring up Ktor to WebResponse.

Listing 4-7. Comparison of the current Ktor APIs with the desired result

```
// Raw calls to the Ktor APIs
get("/") {
  call.respondText("Hello, World!")
}
// The end result of connecting Ktor and WebResponse
get("/", webResponse { req ->
  TextWebResponse("Hello, World!")
})
```

There are two main differences between the two examples in Listing 4-7. First, there's no direct interaction with the Ktor `call` API in the handlers. Second, the Ktor `call` API is imperative in that you invoke methods on it imperatively and in succession. The `WebResponse` API is functional in nature, meaning that the only point of interaction is the immutable value `WebResponse` that's returned from your own handlers, with no imperative method invocations.

The first step is to create a function that creates and returns a new lambda. The function `get` in Ktor has the (simplified) signature `get(path: String, body: ApplicationCall.() -> Unit)`. In other words, the second argument is an *extension function* on `ApplicationCall`, with no return value.

Extension Functions

The first step is to create the function webResponse as seen in Listing 4-7. The return value of webResponse is passed as the second argument to get and needs to match that type signature. The type signature of get is get(path: String, body: ApplicationCall.() -> Unit). So webResponse needs to return something that matches the type ApplicationCall.() -> Unit.

This is a *function type* with a *receiver type*. In the original call to get in Listing 4-7, you pass a lambda as the second argument. Function types are, among other things, how you set up a Kotlin function to receive lambdas. In other words, lambdas are valid function types.

The *receiver type* is ApplicationCall. Lambdas with receiver types are lambdas where you customize what this refers to inside the lambda.

Extension functions are just like lambdas with receiver types, where you can customize what this refers to inside the function body, but are full-fledged named functions instead of anonymous lambdas.

In object-oriented programming, there's always an implicit this that refers to the instance you called the method on. Extension functions are a hybrid between instance methods and plain stand-alone functions. You don't define extension functions inside classes or interfaces. Instead, you define them anywhere you want in your code, for any type that you want.

In Listing 4-8, an example demonstrates an extension function on String. The function uses this to refer to the string that you called the function on. You invoke the function as if it were a method defined on the String class itself.

Listing 4-8. A demonstration of an extension function on String

```
fun String.getRandomLetter() =
  this[Random.nextInt(this.length)]

"FooBarBaz".getRandomLetter() // "z"
"FooBarBaz".getRandomLetter() // "B"
```

Lambdas with receiver types are like extension functions, except they are just lambdas and not named functions defined on a type. You can only call a lambda with a receiver type as if it were a method defined on an instance of that receiver type. Listing 4-9 shows an example of implementing and calling a lambda with a receiver type.

Listing 4-9. A demonstration of a lambda with a receiver type

```
fun String.transformRandomLetter(
  body: String.() -> String
): String {
  val range = Random.nextInt(this.length).let {
    it.rangeTo(it)
  }

  return this.replaceRange(
    range,
    this.substring(range).body()
  )
}

"FooBarBaz".transformRandomLetter {
  "***${this.uppercase()}***"
}
// "FooB***A***rBaz
```

The argument body represents the lambda. Like extension functions, you call body directly on an instance of String, as if it's a method implemented on String itself.

To read more about extension functions, you can read more about them in the official Kotlin documentation: https://kotlinlang.org/docs/extensions.html.

Functions Returning Functions

As a quick reminder, webResponse needs to return something that matches the type ApplicationCall.() -> Unit. In other words, webResponse needs to return a function or a lambda, so that the types are matching.

You can see a first empty skeleton version of the webResponse implementation in Listing 4-10. For now, it doesn't do anything, and it's just a starting point.

Listing 4-10. The initial empty skeleton for webResponse

```
fun webResponse(
  handler: suspend PipelineContext<Unit, ApplicationCall>.(
  ) -> WebResponse
```

```
): PipelineInterceptor<Unit, ApplicationCall> {
  return {
  }
}
```

As previously mentioned, the type `ApplicationCall(). -> Unit` is a simplification. The actual type you need to return from `webResponse` is `PipelineInterceptor<Unit, ApplicationCall>`, which is an alias for the type `suspend PipelineContext< Unit, ApplicationCall >.( Unit) -> Unit`. The type of your `handler` lambda is almost identical, except it returns a `WebResponse` instance instead of nothing (`Unit`). The goal of `webResponse` is to call `handler` and use the `WebResponse` instance that `handler` returns and finally map it to Ktor.

Tip   The keyword `suspend` will be explained in detail in Chapter 8. For now, all you need to know is that it is a part of the type for Kotlin handlers and that it's related to coroutines. Some of the APIs on the `ApplicationCall` from Ktor require a `suspend` keyword to work properly.

`webResponse` returns a lambda. You don't need to annotate the lambda itself with types, as Kotlin has everything it needs to infer the type from the fact you return the lambda and that you've defined a return type for `webResponse`. Kotlin automatically turns it into a lambda that matches `PipelineInterceptor<Unit, ApplicationCall>`.

Map Headers

The lambda that's returned by `webResponse` should contain all the mapping code between Ktor and the `WebResponse` class. All instances of `WebResponse` have a map of headers, so that's a good place to start.

You can find an updated version of `webResponse` in Listing 4-11 that reads the headers from the `WebResponse` instance and maps them to Ktor.

Listing 4-11. Mapping the `WebResponse` headers to Ktor

```
fun webResponse(
  handler: suspend PipelineContext<Unit, ApplicationCall>.(
  ) -> WebResponse
```

```
): PipelineInterceptor<Unit, ApplicationCall> {
  return {
    val resp = this.handler()
    for ((name, values) in resp.headers())
      for (value in values)
        call.response.header(name, value)
  }
}
```

You obtain the instance of WebResponse by invoking the handler() lambda. The mapping code does not care about the contents and details of how you created that WebResponse. All it cares about is mapping arbitrary WebResponse instances to Ktor.

You call handler as an extension function. The type of this matches the receiver type of handler, which is why you can call this.handler() as if handler was a method on the object this represents.

The headers() function returns a map where the key is the header name and the value is a list of header values for that header name. So all you need to do is to iterate through them and invoke call.response.header for each header value.

Remember: The lambda you return from webResponse has the (simplified) signature of ApplicationCall.() -> Unit. This is what makes call available to it.

Map TextWebResponse and Status Code

The next step is to map the individual response types so that you do something more useful than just setting headers and use all the data in your WebResponse instances and pass them on to Ktor.

Listing 4-12 shows an updated version of webResponse that checks the type of the WebResponse instance and handles TextWebResponse.

Listing 4-12. Mapping TextWebResponse and JsonWebResponse to Ktor

```
fun webResponse(
  handler: suspend PipelineContext<Unit, ApplicationCall>.(
  ) -> WebResponse
): PipelineInterceptor<Unit, ApplicationCall> {
  return {
    val resp = this.handler()
```

```
  for ((name, values) in resp.headers())
    for (value in values)
      call.response.header(name, value)

  val statusCode = HttpStatusCode.fromValue(
    resp.statusCode
  )

  when (resp) {
    is TextWebResponse -> {
      call.respondText(
        text = resp.body,
        status = statusCode
      )
    }
  }
}
```

WebResponse has a statusCode field that's defined as an Int. Ktor needs an instance of HttpStatusCode. Thankfully, Ktor has the function HttpStatusCode.fromValue to convert a valid Int to a HttpStatusCode.

You can use a when statement to map the individual types of WebResponse to Ktor. when is like switch in other languages, where each statement defines how you want to handle various cases. For now, all you have is TextWebResponse, but you'll add more types later, so you can use a when statement right away.

Map JsonWebResponse

Mapping JsonWebResponse requires a few extra steps compared with mapping TextWebResponse. You need to add a third-party JSON serializer (something that takes data and writes JSON strings), and you need to add an implementation of the Ktor interface OutgoingContent to map a string containing JSON to Ktor.

There are many JSON serializers available. For this book, you'll use Gson, a Java library made by Google. Gson is one of the fastest JSON libraries out there (www. overops.com/blog/the-ultimate-json-library-json-simple-vs-gson-vs-jackson-vs-json/). It's also easy to use it in a data-oriented style, so that you don't have to create mapping classes and annotations to use it, which some other JSON libraries on the Java platform require. It works with plan lists and maps for serializing data and for parsing JSON in later chapters.

Add Gson as a dependency by adding the following to the dependencies block of *build.gradle.kts*:

```
implementation("com.google.code.gson:gson:2.10")
```

Next, you'll need an OutgoingContent implementation, as seen in Listing 4-13, which takes your JSON content from JsonWebResponse and maps it to Ktor.

Listing 4-13. An implementation of OutgoingContent for JSON serialization in Ktor

```
import com.google.gson.Gson

class KtorJsonWebResponse (
  val body: Any?,
  override val status: HttpStatusCode = HttpStatusCode.OK
) : OutgoingContent.ByteArrayContent() {

  override val contentType: ContentType =
    ContentType.Application.Json.withCharset(Charsets.UTF_8)

  override fun bytes() = Gson().toJson(body).toByteArray(
    Charsets.UTF_8
  )
}
```

This new class KtorJsonWebResponse takes the JSON data in body and an optional status code in status and maps them all to Ktor by overriding key functions in OutgoingContent. You can make it more flexible if you want, by enhancing it to pass in your own ContentType instance that lets you choose other content types and charsets. But for most cases, it should be enough to be able to hard-code it to the default application/json and a hard-coded encoding (UTF-8 in this case).

Finally, you need to use an instance of KtorJsonWebResponse in your implementation of webResponse, where currently you're only handling TextWebResponse. Listing 4-14 shows an updated when statement from webResponse, where you handle both JsonWebResponse and TextWebResponse.

Listing 4-14. Handle both TextWebResponse and JsonWebResponse inside the when statement in webResponse

```
when (resp) {
  is TextWebResponse -> {
    call.respondText(
      text = resp.body,
      status = statusCode
    )
  }
  is JsonWebResponse -> {
    call.respond(KtorJsonWebResponse (
      body = resp.body,
      status = statusCode
    ))
  }
}
```

The meat of the mapping resides inside KtorJsonWebResponse, so all you need to do is to add a case in the when statement for JsonWebResponse and pass an instance of KtorJsonWebResponse to call.respond.

Using the New Mapping

You have now fully mapped WebResponse to Ktor, and you can start using it in your handlers.

Currently, you only have one route: a GET to / returns a plain text response that says "Hello, World!" This route uses the Ktor API directly. You can change it to use WebResponse instead. Listing 4-15 shows how to do this, as it also shows how you can add some extra routes while you're at it.

Listing 4-15. Add routes to Ktor using WebResponse, inside the routing block of your Ktor application

```
get("/", webResponse {
  TextWebResponse("Hello, world!")
})
```

```
get("/param_test", webResponse {
  TextWebResponse(
    "The param is: ${call.request.queryParameters["foo"]}"
  )
})

get("/json_test", webResponse {
  JsonWebResponse(mapOf("foo" to "bar"))
})

get("/json_test_with_header", webResponse {
  JsonWebResponse(mapOf("foo" to "bar"))
    .header("X-Test-Header", "Just a test!")
})
```

Start your application and try to open all the new paths and see what happens!

A Note on Overengineering

There's a lot of handling of various edge cases in this stand-alone representation of HTTP responses. Do you really need all this extra code?

I've never actually done something like this in real-world web apps. This is because I've never written a web app that runs both on Ktor and in a serverless environment. I have done rewrites where I switched from one web framework to another. But you don't need to abstract away your web framework up front to make rewrites possible – you can just do the rewrite, like any other rewrite. I'm not a fan of using an abstraction solely to ease potential rewrites later in the project.

In the context of this book, the abstraction makes sense, as I want to show you later how you can easily replace Ktor with Jersey and others and how to run your handlers in a serverless environment. This is almost trivial to do when you have WebResponse between your business logic and the web routing library.

Additionally, WebResponse isn't all that complex. And I personally prefer my web handlers to be functional in style, which WebResponse is. So I think the trade-off is worth it. The next time I create a Kotlin web app from scratch, I'll probably introduce something like WebResponse to the code base, just because I like the functional style of it.

But it's all this handling of all kinds of use cases that you may or may not use that makes frameworks so big and complicated. `WebResponse` is just a micro example of this issue. A framework needs to handle hundreds of thousands of cases like this and provide APIs and interfaces to allow for all of them, in any combination. Frameworks must therefore contain mountains of abstractions and code that you won't ever need, and in turn this is what makes frameworks unapproachable as a unit in your system. If something goes wrong in the framework you use, you must dig deep into the caves of Mount Framework that contains hundreds of thousands of lines of code and multiple layers of abstraction, which can be a daunting task, to say the least.

This, of course, is also the value of frameworks. There's already a solution available to you in the framework when you need to do something. And having a standardized way of doing things makes it easier to work on different code bases, where they all do things the same way, following framework conventions.

All abstractions have a cost. I think `WebResponse` is worth it. But be careful. Don't abstract away a library just for the sake of abstracting away a library.

PART II

Libraries and Solutions

CHAPTER 5

Connecting to and Migrating SQL Databases

Your web app needs somewhere to store and read data. By far the most common place to do that is in a SQL database. This chapter goes through all the wiring you need to connect to your database with a connection pool, how to set up the initial schema, and how to maintain changes to your database schema over time, as requirements inevitably change.

If you're new to Kotlin, here are some language features that you'll see examples of in this chapter:

- Closing and cleaning up resources with `use`

- `AutoCloseable` and `Closeable` objects

- Avoiding intermediate variables with `also`

- Using functions as lambdas with function references

Also in this chapter, you will learn the following about migrating and querying SQL databases:

- Using Flyway to manage the initial schema and schema changes over time

- Using JDBC connection pools to connect to the SQL database

- Generating seed data for pre-populating your database with required data

In Chapter 6, you'll learn more about executing queries against your database.

© August Lilleaas 2023
A. Lilleaas, *Pro Kotlin Web Apps from Scratch*, https://doi.org/10.1007/978-1-4842-9057-6_5

Connecting to a SQL Database

You can't do anything with a SQL database unless you connect to it. There are some exceptions, including managed cloud databases such as AWS Aurora Serverless. But that's the exception, not the rule. So the first step is to figure out how to manage connections to your database.

The Connection Pool

The first step when connecting to a SQL database from a web app is to set up a connection pool. Your web app is likely to have to handle tens or hundreds (or even thousands) of simultaneous requests. A connection pool is a tool that manages multiple simultaneous connections. PostgreSQL is one of the most popular and scalable SQL databases out there, but out of the box, PostgreSQL supports a maximum of 100 simultaneous connections.

It's possible to create connections by hand. For example, you could just create one connection and have your web app use that connection for everything. But a connection can't handle multiple simultaneous transactions, for example. So you should set up your web app to create multiple simultaneous database connections from the get-go.

Instead, you should use a connection pool. You set up a connection pool by giving it the credentials for connecting to your database. In your web app, when you want to execute queries in your database, you ask the connection pool to give you a connection. If the pool has a connection available, you'll get it right away. If all the connections in the pool are busy, it creates a new one. If the pool has reached the maximum number of allowed simultaneous connections, the connection pool will wait until the current number of simultaneous connections is lower than the maximum and only then give you a connection.

You can also optimize performance via the connection pool. I won't go into the many intricate details of scaling a SQL database here. But benchmarks and real-world experience have shown that in some cases, you'll get more performance out of your database if you limit the maximum allowed number of simultaneous connections to about half the maximum of what the database supports.

Additionally, in a deployment scenario where you have multiple instances of your web app running, you can tell the connection pool to only create a maximum number of 25 connections. That way, you can have four instances of your web app running simultaneously, and your database won't have more than 100 simultaneous connections across all the running instances.

In addition to being a useful tool for your own code, you'll often encounter third-party libraries that expect to be handed a connection pool instead of a direct connection as well. Using a connection pool from the get-go prepares your code for that eventuality.

Installing the Database Driver

To connect to a database, you need a database driver for the database you're connecting to. There are plenty of SQL databases to choose from, like PostgreSQL, MariaDB, Oracle DB, and many more. For convenience, this book will use H2, an embedded SQL database for the Java platform. H2 is a full-featured SQL database, and since it's embedded, you don't need to spend additional time installing and setting it up.

Tip   You can use another database than H2 if you want to. Make sure you also alter the SQL to match your database. Most of the SQL in this book is straightforward and should work outside of H2, but some things like CREATE TABLE statements and the data types are usually different between the SQL databases.

You also need a library for creating the connection pool, and the library you'll be using is HikariCP. It's a generic library that implements the JDBC DataSource interface for connection pools and is a tried-and-true production-grade library that I've used in plenty of real-world projects, in Clojure, Groovy, and Kotlin.

To install H2 and HikariCP, add them as dependencies to the dependencies block in *build.gradle.kts*:

```
implementation("com.zaxxer:HikariCP:5.0.1")
implementation("com.h2database:h2:2.1.214")
```

The H2 dependency includes the database driver, as well as the actual implementation of the H2 database. Normally, the database driver only contains what's necessary to connect to an external database. But H2 is an embedded database and therefore includes both driver and server in one convenient package.

Setting Up H2

When you connect to any database, you give the connection pool a URL that it connects to. H2 is an embedded database, so the connection URL is also where you configure H2 and how it operates.

H2 has two main modes of operation: in-memory and with file system persistence. The in-memory mode means that H2 completely wipes out the database when you restart your web app. To make H2 use the in-memory mode, you set it up using the URL `jdbc:h2:mem:mydbname`.

In this book, you'll use the file system mode, though. While the in-memory mode can be convenient, the goal is to learn how to set up real-world web apps using databases like PostgreSQL and MariaDB, where data is persisted through restarts. The file system mode makes H2 behave more like those databases. To make H2 use the file system mode, you set it up using the URL `jdbc:h2:path/to/file`.

A good location in the file system to place your H2 database is `./build/local`. This places the database file in the `build` folder, which is the directory that Gradle already uses to store its build output. If you run the Gradle `clean` task, it'll wipe out the entire build `directory`, including your database. If you want to make sure Gradle never touches your database, place it somewhere else. But you shouldn't be storing important data in your local development database anyway.

You'll also set two flags in the connection URL, `MODE=PostgreSQL` and `DATABASE_TO_ LOWER=TRUE`. Setting these two flags makes H2 easier to work with, and it makes H2 not care about whether you spell table and column names in uppercase or lowercase, among other things.

Updating WebappConfig

You already have a system in place for storing configuration for your web app from Chapter 3, and config files are the perfect place to store database connection credentials.

You also need to set up your configuration file to contain the credentials that the connection pool will use to connect to your database. H2 doesn't require a username and a password. But you'll set it up with full credentials anyway, to mimic what you would do in a real-world web app.

First, add the required properties to your configuration files. Your main configuration file in *src/main/resources/app.conf* should contain default or empty versions of all the configuration properties in your system. Listing 5-1 shows the properties you need to add.

Listing 5-1. Add default empty values to **src/main/resources/app.conf**

```
httpPort = 4207
dbUser = null
dbPassword = null
dbUrl = null
```

You also need to specify the values you'll be using in your local development environment, which you do in the config file *src/main/resources/app-local.conf*. H2 accepts empty strings for the database username and password. All you need to do, shown in Listing 5-2, is to set the database URL so that HikariCP knows that it should use H2.

Listing 5-2. Configure your local dev environment to use H2, in **src/main/resources/app-local.conf**

```
dbUser = ""
dbPassword = ""
dbUrl = "jdbc:h2:./build/local;MODE=PostgreSQL;DATABASE_TO_LOWER=TRUE;"
```

Finally, you need to update your configuration data class to extract and store the database connection values. Listing 5-3 shows how to add the required properties to the data class and extract them from the config file.

Listing 5-3. Extract database config from the config files and store it in the config data class

```
data class WebappConfig(
  val httpPort: Int,
  val dbUser: String,
  val dbPassword: String,
  val dbUrl: String
)
```

```
// Instantiation when reading the config file
WebappConfig(
  httpPort = it.getInt("httpPort"),
  dbUser = it.getString("dbUser"),
  dbPassword = it.getString("dbPassword"),
  dbUrl = it.getString("dbUrl")
)
```

This sets you up with a `WebappConfig` that's populated with the database connection credentials required when you want to connect.

Set Up the Connection Pool

To create a connection, you need to set up a HikariCP connection pool with the credentials to your database and then obtain a connection from the HikariCP connection pool.

Tip *Data source* and *connection pool* are both terms that refer to the same thing. The Java platform names the API for using connection pools `javax.sql.DataSource`. Any time you see an API that requires a data source to work, you can pass it your HikariCP connection pool.

Later in this book, you'll be using the connection pool in multiple places, so you'll create a function for setting up the connection pool. Listing 5-4 shows how to call HikariCP and pass on the relevant details from your `WebappConfig`.

Listing 5-4. Set up a HikariCP connection pool

```
fun createDataSource(config: WebappConfig) =
  HikariDataSource().apply {
    jdbcUrl = config.dbUrl
    username = config.dbUser
    password = config.dbPassword
  }
```

Creating a Connection

To test that everything works correctly, create a connection pool in your web app initialization, and try to run a query. Listing 5-5 shows how to use the JDBC API to perform a simple test query.

Listing 5-5. A query to test that your database connection works

```
val dataSource = createDataSource(config)

dataSource.getConnection().use { conn ->
  conn.createStatement().use { stmt ->
    stmt.executeQuery("SELECT 1")
  }
}
```

SELECT 1 is a good query to test that everything is up and running. It works for empty databases without any tables. If executeQuery runs without throwing any exceptions, it means HikariCP was able to create a connection and that the query executed successfully inside the H2 database engine.

getConnection() is the API on connection pools to obtain a connection you can use for executing queries. createStatement() is the function on a connection to create a JDBC query statement. Finally, executeQuery() is the function to execute arbitrary SQL queries against your database.

Database connections implement the interface java.lang.AutoCloseable. AutoCloseable, and its sibling Closeable, represents objects on the Java platform that hold on to external resources and have a close() method. The object will hold on to the external resources potentially forever, until you call close(), so it's important to remember to call that method on any closeable objects. For a raw database connection, calling close() disconnects it. For connections provided by a connection pool, calling close() just means that you won't be using that connection more from your code and that you've released it back to the pool. Whether or not the connection pool closes the actual database connection is up to the connection pool implementation.

use() is a scope function on java.lang.AutoCloseable that automatically calls close() on the object after the lambda finishes executing. You could manually call close() on the connection, but using use() has the added benefit of wrapping the whole operation in a try/catch block so that you close the connection even if control flow breaks due to your code throwing an exception.

The Initial Schema

To do anything useful with a SQL database, you need to set up and maintain a database schema.

You *could* just use the SQL console and manually run CREATE TABLE statements. But this quickly degrades into a mess of conflicts and lack of traceability. Instead, you'll set up a schema migration library from the get-go.

When you use a schema migration library, you'll store all the changes to the SQL database over time as files, checked into version control. The schema migration library will automatically run new migration files that you add, so you never forget to run an important SQL migration that causes your database and code to be in an inconsistent state.

Installing Flyway

The library you'll use for managing database schema migrations is Flyway (https://flywaydb.org/). Flyway is an industry-standard library, used by JVM developers everywhere. It's what I've been using for the last ten or so years in real-world projects. Just like HikariCP, I've been using it from Gradle and Clojure as well as from Kotlin.

There are other libraries available, such as Liquibase (www.liquibase.org/). I've also used Liquibase in real-world projects, and it's a solid and stable library. The reason I prefer Flyway is that you can use plain SQL files for migrations without any boilerplate and XML configuration files. I don't like DSLs that attempt to wrap the SQL to make it database agnostic; I prefer to write SQL that's specific to the database engine my web app is using. I also like the way Flyway supports versioned and repeatable migrations based on simple file name conventions, instead of having to set config flags and write XML.

To install Flyway, add it as a dependency to the dependencies block in *build.gradle.kts*:

```
implementation("org.flywaydb:flyway-core:9.5.1")
```

Running Flyway During Startup

The ideal time to run Flyway migrations is when your application starts up. This is because your database schema and your code are tightly coupled. Your code will refer to the tables and columns added by your migration scripts, so you don't want your code to start executing until Flyway has finished running the schema migrations and added the new fields and tables.

Just like `createDataSource()`, you'll need to run Flyway in later chapters in this book. So you'll create two separate functions for running it. Listing 5-6 shows how to create those functions.

Listing 5-6. Functions for creating a migrated data source and for running the actual migrations

```
fun migrateDataSource(dataSource: DataSource) {
  Flyway.configure()
    .dataSource(dataSource)
    .locations("db/migration")
    .table("flyway_schema_history")
    .load()
    .migrate()
}

fun createAndMigrateDataSource(config: WebappConfig) =
  createDataSource(config).also(::migrateDataSource)
```

Call this function as soon as possible in your `main()` function, preferably right after you create your `WebappConfig`. If you already have a call to `createDataSource`, replace it with `createAndMigrateDataSource`.

You use Flyway by passing it the data source, the location of your database migration files, and the name of the table where Flyway stores its own metadata. Flyway uses the metadata table to keep track of its own internal state. You'll see more about that state later in this chapter.

Tip   You can omit the `locations` and `table` method calls in Listing 5-6, as they are set to their default values. I included them in the listing because they are important properties you need to be aware of to understand how Flyway operates.

The `also` function is another scope function like `let`, `use`, and `apply`. The goal of `createAndMigrateDataSource()` in Listing 5-6 is to create the data source, run the migrations, and then finally return the newly created data source. This is exactly what `also` does. `also` first runs the lambda and passes the object that you called `also` on to that lambda (dataSource in this case). When the lambda has finished executing, also returns the object you called it on initially. This saves you from creating an intermediate variable and lets you write the whole operation as a single statement.

The syntax ::migrateDataSource is called a *function reference*. You could have written .also { migrateDataSource(it) }, which would wrap the migrateDataSource function in a lambda. But you can skip that extra step and just pass in the function directly. Kotlin doesn't care if you pass a lambda or a function reference to an argument that's a function type, and function references and lambdas with the same arguments and return types are logically equivalent.

Creating the Initial Schema

Flyway now executes when you start your web app. But you haven't added any migration scripts yet, so Flyway logs *No migrations found. Are your locations set up correctly?* at the warning level.

To create the initial schema, you need to add your first migration script to Flyway. Initializing the database to the base schema is not a special operation in Flyway. The initial schema is simply the first (and, so far, only) migration in your system.

Flyway migration files are numbered. Flyway runs the migrations in ascending order, from the lowest to the highest number. It's up to you if you want your numbers to be an incrementing sequence or a timestamp or something else.

Flyway also has a naming convention that migration files should follow. The format is *V{number}__{myFileName).sql*. That's an uppercase V, the version number of the migration, two underscores, the name of your migration, and a *.sql* suffix.

In this book I'll use an incrementing number. This means you should place your initial migration file in *src/main/resources/db/migration/V1__initial.sql*. Listing 5-7 shows what you're going to put in this file.

Listing 5-7. The contents of your initial schema setup in **src/main/resources/ db/migration/V1__initial.sql**

```
CREATE TABLE user_t (
  id BIGSERIAL PRIMARY KEY,
  created_at TIMESTAMP WITH TIME ZONE DEFAULT now(),
  updated_at TIMESTAMP WITH TIME ZONE DEFAULT now(),
```

```
  email VARCHAR(255) NOT NULL UNIQUE,
  password_hash BYTEA NOT NULL
);
```

If you run your web app, you'll see log output from Flyway saying, *Migrating schema "PUBLIC" to version "1 - initial"*. This means that Flyway successfully ran the SQL file and registered the migration as successfully completed. If you rerun your web app, Flyway will now log, *Current version of schema "PUBLIC": 1* and *Schema "PUBLIC" is up to date. No migration necessary*, indicating that the migration file you created has already run successfully and Flyway didn't write any changes to the database.

Managing Schema Changes

As your web app grows, you'll add more tables and columns to your database. And as requirements change and you uncover more knowledge about your web app and its details, you'll want to make changes to the database schema. Flyway has everything you need to make this happen.

Don't Edit Migrations After Run

You can't edit migrations that have already run when you want to make additional changes to your database schema. If you try to do that, Flyway will throw an error:

```
Exception in thread "main" org.flywaydb.core.api.exception.
FlywayValidateException: Validate failed: Migrations have failed validation
Migration checksum mismatch for migration version 1
-> Applied to database : 299127514
-> Resolved locally    : -1989839469
Either revert the changes to the migration, or run repair to update the
schema history.
```

Flyway treats changes to migration files that have already run as a critical error. That's why it throws an exception instead of just informing about it in the log. You should not catch this exception; it's better if you leave it as it is so that your main() function throws and stops your web app from starting when your migration files are in an invalid state.

Flyway keeps track of which migrations it has successfully run and which it hasn't. Flyway does this at the level of the migration file version. Flyway is not able to detect which changes you've made to the migration file and only run those changes.

This makes sense, as Flyway can't know how to handle changes automatically. Let's say you changed the name of a column. Should Flyway delete the old column and create a new one? Should it rename the column? Or something else?

Instead of having "magic" handling of all these cases, Flyway gives up and treats it as a user error if you change a migration file after it's executed successfully.

Adding More Schema

In Listing 5-7 you created a table. If you want to add more tables to your web app, it's as simple as creating yet another migration file.

To create a new migration, just create a new migration file inside *src/main/resources/db/migration*. You've already used version number 1 for the initial migration, so you should name it something like *V2__add_name_to_user.sql*. Listing 5-8 shows an example of what that might look like.

Listing 5-8. A second migration, which adds a new column to the existing user_t table

```
ALTER TABLE user_t ADD COLUMN name VARCHAR(255);
```

If you rerun your app, Flyway will see the new V2 file, detect that it hasn't executed it yet, and execute it.

Adding Non-nullable Columns

Adding the name column to user_t was easy, because you didn't tag it with NOT NULL. Any existing rows in the table would get the new name column set to NULL when you run the V2 migration in Listing 5-8. What do you do if you want to add a new NOT NULL column to user_t?

If your database is empty, adding a NOT NULL column will work fine. But if you have data in user_t and create a new *V3* migration and put something like ALTER TABLE user_t ADD COLUMN tos_accepted BOOLEAN NOT NULL in it, you'll get an error from Flyway saying that the migration is failing and an error from H2 saying NULL not allowed for column "TOS_ACCEPTED".

This is because the SQL database doesn't know what to do with the existing rows in the table. It can't set them to NULL, because you disallowed NULL for that column.

There are two ways to solve this. The first is to set a default value for that column. This means that when you create new rows in that table and don't set that column, it'll be set to the default value you specified. Additionally, this tells the SQL database that when it creates the column, it can set it to the default value for existing rows in the database. Listing 5-9 shows what that migration file looks like.

Listing 5-9. Add **V3** migration with a non-nullable column with a default value

```
ALTER TABLE user_t
  ADD COLUMN tos_accepted BOOLEAN
  NOT NULL
  DEFAULT false;
```

The second way of solving this, which is my preferred way, is to do the change in multiple steps. What if you don't want to have a default value? I prefer to have default values in my business logic, not in my database. If I forget to set tos_accepted from my code, I want the operation to fail.

You can do this by splitting the operation to three steps: add the column and allow nulls, run an UPDATE statement that sets the column to the preferred value, and then update the column with a NOT NULL constraint. Listing 5-10 shows how to write that migration.

Listing 5-10. Add **V3** migration with a non-nullable column in multiple steps, with no default value

```
ALTER TABLE user_t
  ADD COLUMN tos_accepted BOOLEAN;

UPDATE user_t SET tos_accepted = false;

ALTER TABLE user_t
  ALTER COLUMN tos_accepted
  SET NOT NULL;
```

This way, your database ends up in the desired state. New inserts will fail if you don't set tos_accepted. And existing records get the new tos_accepted column set to false.

Backward-Compatible Migrations

It's common to run your web app in blue/green deployments, meaning that when you deploy the latest version of your code, you keep the previous version up and running until the process with your new code has started up and is fully initialized. Then, your deployment setup directs all incoming requests to the latest version and only then shuts down the previous version.

The consequence of this is that for some time, the previous version of your code is running while the latest version of your code is starting up and running the database migrations. So the previous version of your code is now running against the latest version of the database schema.

If you're not careful, you'll make changes to your database schema that are incompatible with the previous version of the code. Therefore, it's helpful to write your database migrations to be backward compatible with the previous version of your code.

The migration in Listing 5-10 is not backward compatible. It runs successfully, but it also makes a change to the database that causes the previous version of the code to fail. If the previous version of the code tries to insert a new user, the operation will fail as it has no knowledge of the new `tos_accepted` column and doesn't set it.

You can solve this by leaning on the fact that you have blue/green deployments and that deploying the latest version of your code does not incur any downtime on your system. Listing 5-11 shows an updated version of the V3 migration, where all you do is to add the new column.

Listing 5-11. An updated **V3** migration that's backward compatible

```
ALTER TABLE user_t
  ADD COLUMN tos_accepted BOOLEAN;
```

Deploy this version first and wait until it's completed. Remember, when you deploy in a blue/green environment, the previous version of the code runs only temporarily, and the blue/green deployment shuts the old code down before the deployment is complete. The next step is to create a new *V4* migration, which finishes the job. The previous version of the code is no longer running in production, and the current code in production knows about the `tos_accepted` column. Listing 5-12 shows the new *V4* migration, which contains the remaining changes to mark the new column as NOT NULL.

Listing 5-12. A **V4** migration that marks the new column from V3 as non-nullable

```
UPDATE user_t SET tos_accepted = false;

ALTER TABLE user_t
  ALTER COLUMN tos_accepted
  SET NOT NULL;
```

If you look at the V3 and V4 migrations from Listings 5-11 and 5-12, you can see that they are identical in content to the original V3 migration from Listing 5-10 that did the entire operation in one step. So the only change that you made was to run it in two steps, instead of one, to make sure that your migrations are always compatible with the current and previous versions of code that are running in your production environment.

Be aware, though. This migration was easy to make backward compatible. But this is not always the case. The larger your change, the more complex your backward-compatible migrations can become, compared with writing it in a non-backward-compatible way. You should consider whether to make a migration backward compatible on a case-by-case basis. If the cost is too high, risking some downtime or exceptions in productions might be acceptable.

Insert Seed Data

You can also use Flyway to generate *seed data*. Seed data is data that your web app expects to always be in the database. For example, if you build a web app for scheduling and delivering packages, you might store the types of packages your system supports in a table. But this table shouldn't contain arbitrary packages. Your code only supports the package types that the table lists, and you don't provide any user interface for adding more package types.

Repeatable Migrations

A good place for static seed data is *repeatable migrations*. This is a special type of migration that Flyway will always run every time you ask Flyway to execute your migrations. Flyway runs them after all the schema change migrations have finished running, so they will always operate on the latest version of the schema.

Repeatable migrations are just like normal migrations – they're a SQL file that runs some operations on your database. To create a repeatable migration, you put it alongside your normal migrations in *src/main/resources/db/migration*. But instead of naming the file *V{number}__{myFileName}.sql,* you name it *R__{myFileName}.sql.* Repeatable migrations do not have a version number, as Flyway doesn't need one. The migration always runs.

You also need to make sure that the actual SQL script is repeatable. Flyway doesn't do anything smart or magic when it runs a repeatable migration. If your repeatable migration is full of `INSERT INTO` statements, you'll get duplicated rows in your database every time Flyway runs your repeatable migration.

How you'll handle this varies from database to database. PostgreSQL has upsert statements, Oracle has merge statements, and so on. Listing 5-13 shows an example of how to write a merge statement in H2 that will either insert a new row or update an existing row, making the SQL statement safe to put in a repeatable migration.

Listing 5-13. A SQL statement that can run multiple times but will insert one row, making it safe for repeatable migrations

```
MERGE INTO user_t
(email, password_hash, name, tos_accepted)
KEY (email)
VALUES
('august@crud.business', '456def', 'August Lilleaas', true);
```

H2 will check if a row exists with the provided email. If H2 can't find it, it will insert a new row. If H2 finds a match, it will update that row instead of inserting a new one.

Updating Repeatable Migrations

You can't change normal versioned migrations after Flyway has run them. But you can change repeatable migrations as much as you want. And Flyway will run the latest updated version every time your run your migrations.

The whole point of a repeatable migration is that it contains SQL statements that put your database in the state you require it to be. This required state can (and likely will) change over time. So you can update your repeatable migration, and Flyway will run the latest version, making sure that your database is always up to date with the latest required seed data for your web app.

Note that if you remove a SQL statement, Flyway won't try to be smart and delete data that's no longer present in your repeatable migration. How you solve that is up to you. You're free to add DELETE statements to your repeatable migration if you want. Or you can just remove the statement that inserts the data and manually delete it yourself.

Handling Failed Migrations

Despite your best efforts, migrations can and will fail in production. Hopefully, they are a rare occurrence. But when they happen, you need to know how to handle them.

Failed Migrations Locally

If a migration fails locally, you have more options at hand. The data in your local development environment isn't critical to anyone and is (or should be) completely dispensable.

When a migration fails locally, what I typically do is to just wipe out the entire local database and create a new one. When you use H2, it's as simple as deleting the database files in the *build/* folder, namely, *build/local.mv.db* and *build/local.trace.db*.

All the core data in your system should be in a repeatable migration, and if you restart your web app, the migrations will run from scratch and create a new database with all the tables and data you need to work with the web app.

Failed Migrations in Production

If migrations fail in production, you need to be more careful about how you approach things.

Ideally, your failed migration was backward compatible. So even if it failed, and the latest version of the code didn't deploy, the previous version of the code that's now still in production will work fine.

If it wasn't backward compatible, you probably have a sweaty forehead and a high pulse, because production is now *down* and you're the cause.

I won't get into the exact kinds of operations you need to do to fix the borked migration. What you need to do to fix it depends entirely on your business logic, the contents of your migrations, and at what step of the migration the error occurred.

Rerunning Failed Migration

In general, there are two ways of solving it. The first is to make Flyway believe that it has never attempted to execute the new migration.

The first step is to make any necessary manual changes to the database, by inputting SQL commands in the database by hand. Then, you make any changes needed to the migration file that failed.

When that's done, you restart your web app, which makes Flyway run the failed migration again.

To make Flyway believe a migration never ran, you update the `flyway_schema_history` table (configured in Listing 5-6) that Flyway uses for bookkeeping. Assuming the migration that failed was *V5*, you can run `DELETE FROM flyway_schema_history WHERE version = 5` to make Flyway rerun the migration from scratch next time you start your web app.

Manually Performing Migration

The second way to solve a failed migration is to finish the migration completely by hand and make Flyway believe the migration has already run.

The first step is to manually run SQL commands against your database to make the database end up in a desirable state. Make sure you really think through what you're doing here, and write your SQLs with care, as it's possible for your database to end up in a state that's different from what the Flyway migration specifies.

To make Flyway believe a migration has executed successfully, you update the `flyway_schema_history` table and flag the migration as being successful. Assuming the migration that failed is still *v5*, you can run `UPDATE flyway_schema_history SET success = true WHERE version = 5`.

The next time you run your web app, Flyway will see that according to its own tables, the migration is successful, so it won't try to rerun it.

CHAPTER 6

Querying a SQL Database

In Chapter 5, you set up a data source for managing connections to your database, and you configured Flyway to manage your database schema so that you have some tables in which you can execute queries. In this chapter, you'll learn how to execute those queries.

If you're new to Kotlin, here are some language features that you'll see examples of in this chapter:

- Null-safe casting and type checks of dynamic data

- Companion objects in data classes

- Generic types in plain Kotlin functions

Also in this chapter, you will learn the following about querying SQL databases:

- How to use SQL directly, instead of a database mapping library

- Best practices for executing queries in production-grade web apps

- How to structure your web app to get the highest amount of type safety and convenience

- How to manage transactions

I'm hard-pressed to think of a web app that doesn't use a database. There are many databases out there, and SQL is not the best fit for all cases. But most web apps use SQL databases, so that's what you'll learn in this book.

Setting Up Querying

Building on the connection pool and schema management capabilities of Chapter 5, you need a few more things to be able to comfortably execute queries. In Chapter 5, you ran a small query using JDBC directly. But the JDBC API is full of boilerplate and is not that comfortable to work with. So you need a library to sit between you and JDBC and make your life better.

© August Lilleaas 2023
A. Lilleaas, *Pro Kotlin Web Apps from Scratch*, https://doi.org/10.1007/978-1-4842-9057-6_6

Use SQL Directly

To execute queries, you'll write SQL directly. Before you'll set that up, I want to explain why.

Some developers prefer to use a mapping library, so that you can express your queries as Kotlin code. Exposed (`https://github.com/JetBrains/Exposed`) and Ktorm (`www.ktorm.org/`) are popular Kotlin libraries, and you can also use Java libraries such as Hibernate (`https://hibernate.org/`) and MyBatis (`https://mybatis.org/mybatis-3/`) and many more. Common between them all is that they let you create classes that represent tables, with a type-safe mapping layer between your code and the database tables. You can set up object graphs (hence the name Object-Relational Mapper, or ORM) that define the relationships between the tables. You don't write any SQL queries. Instead, you interact with the mapping classes and use them to express inserts, queries, groupings, and so on.

All of this sounds good. The smartest people in our industry make these libraries and frameworks, and lots of developers use them, in both small and large projects. So what's the catch?

I consider the database to be an integral part of any web app. I want my code to be as close as possible to the actual database that I use in the web app I build. This is the case no matter which language I use, be it Node.js, Groovy, Clojure, and of course Kotlin. The intricate details of how my code and the database interact always end up being important, especially as the application grows. An ORM hides these details from you by design. So, for the way you'll write web apps in this book, the ORM becomes an anti-pattern.

And being able to use all the features of a SQL database without having to worry if it's possible to map it using an ORM or express it using a SQL wrapper is a plus.

One benefit of ORMs is that they can generate efficient SQL queries automatically. But an ORM can also generate inefficient queries. So you need to have a deep understanding of SQL if you're using an ORM, to be able to handle these situations. There's no escaping knowledge of SQL. With that in mind, I prefer to just write the SQL directly.

I'm not saying you should never use an ORM. But I personally never use them, for the reasons mentioned previously, so I avoid them in this book.

Installing Kotliquery

You'll use Kotliquery to execute queries. Kotliquery is a small wrapper library around JDBC, and it helps you solve the problem of boilerplate and uncomfortable APIs in JDBC.

Note that using Kotliquery doesn't limit you from calling JDBC directly if you should need that later. The benefit of a library like Kotliquery is that you can mix and match; there's no lock-in.

To install Kotliquery, add it as a dependency to the `dependencies` block in *build. gradle.kts*:

```
implementation("com.github.seratch:kotliquery:1.9.0")
```

Kotliquery is a well-designed library that has all the features you'll need to build a production-grade web app. It's not a popular library, if you judge it by the number of GitHub stars. But popularity is a vanity metric. I've used Kotliquery successfully in large production systems.

Mapping Query Results

A row mapper is a function that Kotliquery uses to extract row data and turn it into a data structure of your liking. This row mapper is a function that takes a raw Kotliquery Row object and converts it into useful data.

Listing 6-1 shows how to create a row mapper function that you can use later when you execute queries with Kotliquery.

Listing 6-1. A function that maps Kotliquery Row objects to plain maps

```
import kotliquery.Row

fun mapFromRow(row: Row): Map<String, Any?> {
  return row.underlying.metaData
    .let { (1..it.columnCount).map(it::getColumnName) }
    .map { it to row.anyOrNull(it) }
    .toMap()
}
```

There are several interesting things happening in this code. Inside the let block, you create a *range* from 1 to the `metaData.columnCount` of the query results. You can think of ranges as a list of the numbers in that range, so `1..5` is the equivalent of listOf(1, 2, 3, 4, 5). Then, you map over that range and use a *function reference* to get the column name. map(it::getColumnName) is equivalent to map { colIdx -> it.getColumnName(colIdx) }. It's the same as if you called getColumnName on the metaData object (it) with the column index from the range passed as the first argument. Then, the list of column names are mapped over to return a pair of the column name and the value of that column with row.anyOrNull(it). At this point, all you're doing is extracting the raw data from the query; you don't do any type checking or casting. Finally, you convert the list of pairs to a map with toMap(). The result is that you've converted the Kotliquery Row object to a plain map of column name to column value.

Execute SQL Queries

Kotliquery is now set up and ready to go. It's time to execute some queries!

Creating a Session

To execute queries with Kotliquery, you need the row mapper you just created and a Kotliquery session.

You create a session by calling the Kotliquery function sessionOf with your connection pool. A Kotliquery session is a small wrapper around a raw database connection. The session has methods that you call to execute queries, and Listing 6-2 shows how you can use single to fetch a single row.

Listing 6-2. Create a Kotliquery session and execute a query

```
import kotliquery.sessionOf

sessionOf(dataSource).use { dbSess ->
  dbSess.single(queryOf("SELECT 1", ::mapFromRow))
  // {?column?=1}
}
```

Just like in Listing 5-5 in the previous chapter, a Kotliquery session implements java. io.Closeable, and you must remember to call close() when you're finished using it. use will call close() for you, and Kotliquery will in turn close the underlying connection it got from the data source when you created the session.

Querying for Single Rows

You've already seen how you can use `single()` on a Kotliquery session to fetch a single row, in Listing 6-2. `single()` is an optimization that will only ever return one row from the query. This allows Kotliquery to make some assumptions under the hood, such as not even trying to your database for multiple rows. And the return type (via the row mapper) is `Map<String, Any?>?`, meaning it will return `null` or a single row. Listing 6-3 has some additional examples of the output from `single()`.

Listing 6-3. Examples of output from `single()`

```
dbSess.single(queryOf("SELECT 1"), ::mapFromRow)
// {?column?=1}
```

```
dbSess.single(queryOf("SELECT 1 as foo"), ::mapFromRow)
// {foo=1}
```

```
dbSess.single(queryOf(
  "SELECT * from (VALUES (1, 'a'), (2, 'b')) t1 (x, y)"
), ::mapFromRow)
// {x=1, y=a}
```

The last query selects from two rows, but you only get the first row back from `single()`. No special magic happens here; it just relies on whatever ordering of the result set that the database engine returns.

Querying for Multiple Rows

You can use `list()` just the same way you use `single()`, except `list()` will give you all the rows that the query returns. `list()` has the return type (via the row mapper) of `List<Map<String, Any?>>`. Listing 6-4 shows some examples of querying for multiple rows.

Listing 6-4. Examples of output from `list()`

```
dbSess.list(queryOf("SELECT 1 as foo"), ::mapFromRow)
// [{foo=1}]

dbSess.list(queryOf(
  "SELECT * from (VALUES (1, 'a'), (2, 'b')) t1 (x, y)"
), ::mapFromRow)
// [{x=1, y=a}, {x=2, y=b}]

dbSess.list(queryOf(
  """
  SELECT * from (VALUES (1, 'a'), (2, 'b')) t1 (x, y)
  WHERE x = 42
  """
), ::mapFromRow)
// []
```

You'll always get a list of rows in return, even for queries that match a single row. You'll also get a list if there are zero matching rows. You never need to check that the return value of `list()` is `null` (as the Kotlin type system also tells you).

You can also use `forEach()` when your query loads in vast amounts of data. `forEach()` will yield data row by row, whereas `list()` will accumulate all the results into a list before it yields the data to your code. Memory usage and performance will be much better if you use `forEach()` when you expect your query to return either a high number of rows or rows that contain columns of binary blobs or other arbitrarily sized items. Listing 6-5 shows an example of how to use `forEach()`.

Listing 6-5. Example of using `forEach` to avoid loading the entire result set into memory

```
dbSess.forEach(queryOf(
  "SELECT * from (VALUES (1, 'a'), (2, 'b')) t1 (x, y)"
)) { rowObject ->
  val row = mapFromRow(rowObject)
  println(row)
}
```

```
// {x=1, y=a}
// {x=2, y=b}
```

forEach() calls the lambda once for each row that your query yields. It's the raw Kotliquery Row object that's passed to the lambda. You can use the same mapFromRow() function that you use for single() and list() to convert this structure to a plain map.

Inserting Rows

To insert rows, you'll use the updateAndReturnGeneratedKey() function on the Kotliquery session. You also need to create the session correctly by setting the flag returnGeneratedKey to true. Listing 6-6 shows how to create a session and execute an insert correctly. If you don't set this up correctly, you won't be able to access the ID of the inserted row that the database generated automatically when it inserted the row.

Listing 6-6. Create a session that lets you get the ID of an inserted row

```
sessionOf(dataSource, returnGeneratedKey = true)
  .use { dbSess ->
    dbSess.updateAndReturnGeneratedKey(queryOf(
      """
      INSERT INTO user_t
      (email, password_hash, name, tos_accepted)
      VALUES
      (?, ?, ?, ?)
      """,
      "august@augustl.com",
      "123abc",
      "August Lilleaas",
      true)
    )
    // 2
  }
```

If you've followed the examples in this book one by one so far, the ID you'll get when you run this insert is 2. That's because you already created a user using a repeatable migration in the previous chapter, as seen in Listing 5-13.

Updating and Deleting

To run update and delete SQL statements, you'll use the update() function. This function doesn't really care what the actual SQL statement does. But it returns the number of rows that the query affected. That can be particularly useful for sanity checks, by checking that the query affected more than zero rows. Listing 6-7 shows examples of running UPDATE and DELETE SQL statements.

Listing 6-7. Examples of executing UPDATE and DELETE statements

```
dbSess.update(queryOf(
  "UPDATE user_t SET name = ? WHERE id = ?",
  "August Lilleaas",
  2
))
// 1

dbSess.update(queryOf("DELETE FROM user_t"))
// 2
```

The UPDATE statement returns 1, as it updated one specific row matched by row ID. The DELETE statement returns 2, as it deleted both the user rows in the user_t table.

Positional vs. Named Parameters

So far, your code uses question mark symbols to refer to SQL query parameters. Kotliquery has another syntax for those arguments, which allows you to name them.

Naming the arguments is useful for two reasons: it makes your code more readable if you have queries with many arguments, and it lets you reuse the same arguments multiple times without having to pass them twice or more. Listing 6-8 shows an example of the update statement from Listing 6-7, using named parameters instead of positional parameters.

Listing 6-8. Pass query parameters using named parameters

```
dbSess.update(queryOf(
  "UPDATE user_t SET name = :name WHERE id = :id",
  mapOf(
```

```
    "name" to "August Lilleaas",
    "id" to 2
)))
```

This lets you refer to the parameters by name, and it also has the added benefit of naming the inputs, so you don't have to count the position of the parameter in the list of parameters to figure out what goes where.

Additional Operations

As you can see, Kotliquery has everything you need to perform queries and inserts. Compared with working with JDBC directly, the Kotliquery API is much simpler and makes it easy to convert your queries to data and pass in parameters to your queries.

You can find detailed documentation and API references to the parameters and methods available in Kotliquery at the project GitHub page: `https://github.com/seratch/kotliquery`.

Querying from Web Handlers

You'll be running most of your queries from your web handlers. It's convenient to have a helper function that you can use to make your web handlers prepare and manage a Kotliquery session automatically.

Creating a Helper Function

To make it easy to query in your web handlers, you'll create a version of `webResponse` from Chapter 4 named `webResponseDb`. This function does everything `webResponse` does, but also creates and manages a Kotliquery session. This makes it easy and convenient to run queries in your web handlers. Listing 6-9 shows the implementation of `webResponseDb`.

Listing 6-9. webResponseDb – wrap webResponse and add database querying capabilities

```
import kotliquery.Session

fun webResponseDb(
  dataSource: DataSource,
  handler: suspend PipelineContext<Unit, ApplicationCall>.(
    dbSess: Session
  ) -> WebResponse
) = webResponse {
  sessionOf(
    dataSource,
    returnGeneratedKey = true
  ).use { dbSess ->
    handler(dbSess)
  }
}
```

The signature of webResponseDb is like that of webResponse, except it adds a dbSess argument that points to a Kotliquery session. You also must pass a data source when invoking it. Additionally, returnGeneratedKey is always set to true, to ensure that your web handlers can access auto-generated row IDs from your database. Listing 6-10 shows an example of how you can invoke webResponseDb from your Ktor route mapping.

Listing 6-10. An example of creating a Ktor route that executes a database query

```
get("/db_test", webResponseDb(dataSource) { dbSess ->
  JsonWebResponse(
    dbSess.single(queryOf("SELECT 1"), ::mapFromRow)
  )
})
```

In a real-world web app, most web handlers need a database connection. So it's very convenient to have a helper like webResponseDb to create web handlers with all the database connection stuff and resource management handled in one place.

A Note on Architecture

Many frameworks and architectures contain patterns to separate and isolate different concerns in your web app. For example, the typical hexagonal architecture aims to loosely couple the components of your web app and make them interchangeable.

For web handlers, such as the one in Listing 6-10, I don't do much separation. The purpose of a web handler is to interact with the database and implement business logic around it. I consider the database to be a core part of this interaction. You can separate it out and hide the database from the business logic, but that has the trade-off of adding opaqueness and friction to understanding what's going on in the system.

If I do separate a web handler into multiple parts, it's with the functional core, imperative shell pattern. By analogy, you can think of it as a president deciding what to do and signing documents (functional core) and an executive branch that executes the orders (imperative shell). Something like 90% of the code ends up in the functional data-driven core, and that's where all the business logic resides. Then, the imperative shell is "dumb" and executes the commands based on the data generated by the functional core, without any business logic.

When it makes sense, I use queues to separate operational concerns. If one part of your system writes to a queue and another part of your system reads from a queue, they're architecturally and operationally separate and completely decoupled.

I'm adamant about separating business logic from user interface rendering logic. The top level of the user interface code fetches data and massages it to render a "dumb" GUI that has no business logic, and the user interface code just renders based on the data it receives.

In general, I try to avoid overarchitecting my code. I prefer "dumb" plain functions and SQL and data that's easy to trace and follow along with over firewalling isolation between all components of my web app.

Avoid Long-Running Connections

When you wrap your entire web handler in a Kotliquery session, you need to be aware that you should consider alternatives if your web handler includes calls to external APIs.

A Kotliquery session is just a small wrapper over a database connection. And as mentioned previously, a database connection is an expensive resource. If your web handler keeps a Kotliquery session open while it executes long-running operations (such as call to external APIs) that are unrelated to the database, you're wasting resources. The connection is not available to other web handlers from the connection pool. And the database server maintains the connection while you're not really using it.

Sometimes, there's no way to avoid this situation. For example, maybe you need to open a transaction that first writes some data to the database, then performs a potentially long-running call to an external API, and then writes some more data to the database in the same transaction. If that's the case, then you simply must accept the fact that you need to maintain an idle database connection for the duration of the external API call.

You can also avoid this in many cases by redesigning your business logic, though. For example, you can write a temporary item to the database that's flagged so that your application knows to ignore it in queries. Then you can perform your external API call. Finally, you can ask Kotliquery for a new session and finalize the operation by unflagging the temporary item and executing whatever extra operations you need to do against the database. That way, you avoid holding on to a database connection for the duration of the external API call.

Also note that if you expect your web app to only handle lower volumes of traffic, keeping database connections open will not cause problems. If you expect your web app to handle hundreds or thousands of requests per second, though, you need to take this into consideration.

Maps vs. Data Classes

When you execute queries, the row mapper converts row data to plain maps. Why doesn't it convert query results directly to more type-safe data classes? To understand why, let's look at what you can do with the maps returned from the row mapper you're using now.

Regardless of what you end up doing, it's better to stick to returning the raw query data as maps and then write code that checks the shape of the data and transforms it accordingly according to your business logic and requirements.

Passing Around Maps

Sooner or later, you'll end up passing data from query results to functions in your web app that implement business logic. One way to handle this is to just pass the maps you get from your query results directly to your business logic, with no extra treatment of the data. Listing 6-11 shows an example of what this would look like.

Listing 6-11. Passing raw maps around to business logic

```
def sendEmailToUser(userRow: Map<String, Any?>) {
  deliverEmail(
    "Welcome, ${user["name"] ?: user["email"]}",
    user["email"] as String
  )
}

def handleSignup() {
  val userRow = createUser(...)
  sendEmailToUser(userRow)
}
```

I rarely do this in real-world web apps. If you spell a property wrong, you'll get a `null` instead of an actual value. You could cast with `as`, which will throw an error if the type is wrong or if the value is `null`. But then you will have to litter your business logic with this type of casting. And you'll get an error deep down in your system somewhere far away from the code that fetches data from your database.

Passing Individual Properties

Another option when passing data from query results to your business logic is to extract properties from the plain maps and pass them as individual arguments to various business logic functions. Listing 6-12 shows an example of what this would look like.

Listing 6-12. Passing individual properties to business logic

```
def sendEmailToUser(userName: String?, userEmail: String) {
  deliverEmail(
    "Welcome, ${userName)}",
    userEmail
  )
}

def handleSignup() {
  val userRow = createUser(...)
  sendEmailToUser(
```

```
    userRow.get("name") as? String,
    userRow.get("email") as String
  )
}
```

This is something I do more often. This way, the business logic is not dependent on the database structure. All casting happens close to where you extract the data from the query, so you don't have to put type casts all over your business logic. And the casting is now "fail fast," meaning that you'll get the cast error sooner and closer to the code that executes the database query.

Mapping to a Data Class

You can also represent query result rows as data classes. This is something I typically do for simpler queries where I select all columns of a table and I can reuse the same data class for multiple queries where the output is similar. Listing 6-13 shows an example of a data class that maps query results from the table user_t.

Listing 6-13. Mapping query results to a data class

```
data class User(
  val id: Long,
  val createdAt: ZonedDateTime,
  val updatedAt: ZonedDateTime,
  val email: String,
  val tosAccepted: Boolean,
  val name: String?,
  val passwordHash: ByteBuffer
) {
  companion object {
    fun fromRow(row: Map<String, Any?>) = User(
      id = row["id"] as Long,
      createdAt = (row["created_at"] as OffsetDateTime)
        .toZonedDateTime(),
      updatedAt = (row["updated_at"] as OffsetDateTime)
        .toZonedDateTime(),
      email = row["email"] as String,
```

110

```
      name = row["name"] as? String,
      tosAccepted = row["tos_accepted"] as Boolean,
      passwordHash = ByteBuffer.wrap(
        row["password_hash"] as ByteArray
      )
    )
  }
}

dbSess.single(
  queryOf("SELECT * FROM user_t"),
  ::mapFromRow
)?.let(User::fromRow)

// User(
//   id=1,
//   createdAt=2022-07-27T16:40:44.410258+02:00,
//   updatedAt=2022-07-27T16:40:44.410258+02:00,
//   email=august@crud.business,
//   tosAccepted=true,
//   name=August Lilleaas,
//   passwordHash=java.nio.HeapByteBuffer[pos=0 lim=6 cap=6]
// )
```

The data class uses a companion object to define the function fromRow that creates an instance of User from a query result row. You could define fromRow as a stand-alone function, but it's nice to be able to write User.fromRow(...). It's a common pattern in Kotlin to place various helper functions and constructor functions on companion objects. You can think of it as Kotlin's version of static methods in Java.

You call User.fromRow on the return value of single(). This is a good example of how you can use the let scope function combined with function references to save you from some typing and creation of intermediate variables. By calling ?.let() instead of .let(), you handle the case of single() returning null if no matching row is found. User.fromRow(...) takes a single argument, the row data. The scope function let also takes a single argument, which is the object you called let on. So, in this case, you can use a function reference to User::fromRow instead of a lambda.

Mapping tables to data classes is something I do rarely, but it depends on the circumstances. Usually, I take a hybrid approach. Listing 6-14 shows examples of both alternatives.

Listing 6-14. How to combine a query result data class with business logic

```
def sendEmailToUserA(user: User) {
  deliverEmail(
    "Welcome, ${user["name"] ?: user["email"]}",
    user["email"] as String
  )
}

def sendEmailToUserB(userName: String?, userEmail: String) {
  deliverEmail(
    "Welcome, ${userName)}",
    userEmail
  )
}

def handleSignup() {
  val user = createUser(...).let(User::fromRow)
  sendEmailToUserA(user)
  sendEmailToUserB(user.name, user.email)
}
```

The issue with sendEmailToUserA is that anyone who wants to call that function must construct a full User object with all properties, when all that's really required to call sendEmailToUserA is the name and the email. You could make most of the properties on the User data class nullable, but then it would no longer represent a valid user, as a user without an ID does not make sense.

Instead, I prefer to write functions like sendEmailToUserB. That way, the function does not care about aggregates and just operates on the individual data points it requires to execute.

Use your judgment here, though. Sometimes, passing on the full data class is advantageous, and it's difficult to make a general rule for deciding when to do what.

Database Transactions

Transactions are a hallmark feature of SQL databases. I'll assume some prior knowledge, and I won't go into the many intricate details of modeling business logic around transactions. You need to learn how to create, commit, and roll back transactions, though.

Creating Transactions

Kotliquery sessions are not transactional. When you want to execute your database operations in a transaction, you must explicitly create a transaction by hand.

To create a transaction, you call the `transaction` function on your Kotliquery session and pass a lambda to it. The lambda executes inside the transaction. Kotliquery commits the transaction when the lambda has finished running or rolls it back if your code in the lambda threw an exception. Listing 6-15 shows how that works.

Listing 6-15. Create a transaction and execute SQL statements

```
dbSess.transaction { txSess ->
  txSess.update(queryOf("INSERT INTO ..."))
  txSess.update(queryOf("INSERT INTO ..."))
}
```

`txSess` represents the open transaction, and it has the exact same methods available as the normal Kotliquery session, such as `single`, `list`, `update`, `forEach`, etc. If both the INSERT statements in Listing 6-15 succeed, the transaction is committed. If, on the other hand, one of them fails, the `update` function will throw an exception, which the Kotliquery transaction handling code catches, and it rolls back the transaction instead of committing it.

`ByteBuffer` is from `java.nio.ByteBuffer`. The password hash is a raw byte array, and on the Java platform, byte arrays don't implement equality. So you'll get a warning from the Kotlin compiler if you try to store `ByteArray` values directly on a data class. By wrapping the byte array in a `ByteBuffer`, the Kotlin data class can correctly compare two separate byte values to see if they're equal.

You can also throw an exception by hand if you want to roll back. Or you can call `txSess.connection.rollback()` directly.

113

Transactions in Web Handlers

In my experience, most web apps will require most or all of database-related code to run in a transaction. So it's convenient to have a helper function for creating a web handler that also creates a transaction.

You can do this by creating yet another version of webResponse, called webResponseTx. This function is just like webResponseDb, but in addition to creating a Kotliquery session, it also starts a transaction that wraps the entire web handler. Listing 6-16 contains an implementation of the webResponseTx function.

Listing 6-16. webResponseTx, a version of webResponseDb that also creates a transaction

```
fun webResponseTx(
  dataSource: DataSource,
  handler: suspend PipelineContext<Unit, ApplicationCall>.(
    dbSess: TransactionalSession
  ) -> WebResponse) = webResponseDb(dataSource) { dbSess ->
  dbSess.transaction { txSess ->
    handler(txSess)
  }
}
```

Tip   Originally, Kotliquery did not support transactions inside suspend functions. transaction was not itself a suspend function, so the handler inside the lambda did not have access to the suspend scope. I submitted a pull request to fix it, and version 1.9 was released with that fix included. Open source FTW! See the pull request here: https://github.com/seratch/kotliquery/pull/57.

You call this function the same way as webResponseDb you created in Listing 6-9. The only difference between webResponseTx and webResponseDb is that the type of the session is TransactionalSession and Session, respectively.

Type-Safe Transactional Business Logic

Some of your business logic will require a transaction to work. For example, you might have a function that executes two inserts, and it's vital to your web app that either none or both succeed. You'll solve this problem by wrapping the function in a transaction.

But what if you somehow forget to create a transaction?

You can alleviate this issue by making sure that your business logic requires a Kotliquery session of the correct type. As mentioned previously, Kotliquery yields a `Session` for non-transactional sessions and a `TransactionalSession` for transactional sessions. So, if you write your business logic function to take a `TransactionalSession` as the type, you'll get a compile error if you try to call your business logic that requires a transaction to operate correctly from a context that doesn't have a transaction available. Listing 6-17 shows an example of how you can structure your business logic in this way.

Listing 6-17. Require transactions in business logic

```
fun createUserAndProfile(
  txSess: TransactionalSession,
  userName: String,
  bio: String
) {
  txSess.update(queryOf("INSERT INTO user_t ..."))
  txSess.update(queryOf("INSERT INTO profile_t ..."))
}

sessionOf(dataSource).use { dbSess ->
  // This code won't compile - dbSess has wrong type
  createUserAndProfile(
    dbSess,
    "august1",
    "Important author")

  dbSess.transaction { txSess ->
    // This code compiles fine - txSess has the correct type
    createUserAndProfile(
      dbSess,
      "august1",
```

```
        "Important author")
  }
}
```

This might seem like a small detail, but it can really save the day. It's easy to make a mistake and end up passing a non-transactional Kotliquery session to a function that requires transactions to operate correctly. By ensuring that those functions in your business logic that require transactions take a `TransactionalSession`, you'll get help from the type system and avoid this type of mistake (pun intended).

Nested Transactions

SQL databases don't support nested transactions. But you can use *save points* to mimic them.

Kotliquery does not have built-in functionality for save points, but it's easy to create your own small wrapper. This is also a good opportunity to see how Kotliquery implements the `transaction` function, as your function for creating save points will behave similarly. Listing 6-18 shows how you can implement a `dbSavePoint` function that creates a save point and makes it act like a transaction.

Listing 6-18. Create a save point, inspired by how Kotliquery creates transactions

```
fun <A>dbSavePoint(dbSess: Session, body: () -> A): A {
  val sp = dbSess.connection.underlying.setSavepoint()
  return try {
    body().also {
      dbSess.connection.underlying.releaseSavepoint(sp)
    }
  } catch (e: Exception) {
    dbSess.connection.underlying.rollback(sp)
    throw e
  }
}
```

```
sessionOf(dataSource).use { dbSess ->
  dbSess.transaction { txSess ->
    // Create a save point
    dbSavePoint(txSess) {
      txSess.update(queryOf("INSERT INTO ..."))
    }

    // Execute more database operations here
  }
}
```

The code inside the dbSavePoint lambda will act as if it runs in its own nested transaction.

A save point is a named entity. If you call setSavePoint without your own name for it, JDBC will auto-generate a name. You wrap the execution of the lambda body in try/catch. If the lambda throws an exception, you roll the save point back. If the lambda didn't throw any exceptions, you release the save point. You're using the scope function also to achieve this. also will return the object you called it on, but before it returns, it executes the code in the lambda. This makes also a convenient way to avoid having to create and name an intermediate variable for the return value of the body lambda.

You also see an example of how you can use generics in plain Kotlin functions. The A generic represents the return value of the lambda body. This means that dbSavePoint will pass on the return value of the body lambda, so that you can maintain a functional coding style while still wrapping your code in lambdas.

CHAPTER 7

Automated Tests with jUnit 5

You now have all the pieces of the web app puzzle assembled. But before you implement business logic on your own, you'll learn how to write automated tests.

If you're new to Kotlin, here are some language features that you'll see examples of in this chapter:

- Implementing test cases and assertions with `kotlin.test`

- Null safety with the unsafe cast operator `!!`

- Inline functions

Also in this chapter, you will learn the following about writing automated tests with jUnit 5:

- The basics of Test-Driven Development (TDD)

- Writing tests that interact with your database

- Isolating individual test cases to avoid inter-test dependencies

In Appendix C, you'll learn how to use the Kotlin test framework, instead of `kotlin.test`.

Setting Up Your Environment

jUnit 5 is an industry-standard library for writing and running automated tests and is the one you'll use in this book. Most automated testing libraries for Kotlin use jUnit 5 under the hood, as jUnit 5 includes everything you need to run tests efficiently on your own machine, as well as in an automated CI (continuous integration) build environment.

© August Lilleaas 2023
A. Lilleaas, *Pro Kotlin Web Apps from Scratch*, https://doi.org/10.1007/978-1-4842-9057-6_7

There are many alternative libraries available. A popular alternative in the Kotlin community is Kotest (*https://kotest.io/*), which is full of useful features and even sophisticated features such as property-based testing, which automatically generates tests based on boundaries and specifications. I tend to prefer "dumb" testing libraries, though, and the standard kotlin.test and jUnit 5 style assertions are simple to use and familiar. Additionally, I've never actually used Kotest in a real-world project. So you'll learn how to use jUnit 5 and kotlin.test in this book.

Adding jUnit 5 and kotlin.test

You need two things in your project to run tests: jUnit 5 for executing your tests and kotlin.test for writing your test cases.

kotlin.test is a wrapper library you'll use to write the test cases themselves. It contains annotations for defining something as a test class, assertions to compare values, and so on. kotlin.test includes a mapping to jUnit 5. jUnit 5 picks up the kotlin.test test cases and executes them.

So far, you've added third-party dependencies in the dependencies block in *build.gradle.kts*. You could do that for jUnit and kotlin.test as well. But for test running, you need more than just a dependency – you also need to tell Gradle how it should execute your tests, as well as mapping between jUnit 5 and kotlin.test. The easiest way to get all of that done is to use the built-in support for test running that comes with Gradle with the Kotlin plugin installed. Listing 7-1 shows what you need to add to your Gradle config to add support for jUnit 5, kotlin.test, and Gradle tasks for executing your tests.

Listing 7-1. Add support for kotlin.test and jUnit 5 in build.gradle.kts

```
dependencies {
  // ...

  testImplementation(kotlin("test"))
}

tasks.test {
  useJUnitPlatform()
}
```

Note that if you followed along with the book and created your Kotlin project using IntelliJ IDEA, you might already have these properties set, as IntelliJ IDEA generates projects with pre-configured jUnit 5 support.

Writing a Failing Test

To check that you configured everything correctly, you'll implement the automated test equivalent of printing `Hello, World`.

Notifying you of errors is a vital part of a correctly configured automated testing setup. So the first step is to deliberately write a failing test and verify that your programming environment notifies you of failing tests. Listing 7-2 shows how you'll write a failing test.

Listing 7-2. A test class in **src/test/kotlin/kotlinbook/UserTest.kt** with one test case that fails on purpose

```
package kotlinbook

import kotlin.test.Test
import kotlin.test.assertEquals

class UserTest {
    @Test
    fun testHelloWorld() {
        assertEquals(1, 2)
    }
}
```

Your test uses `assertEquals` with two different values to ensure a failed test. 1 is never equal to 2, so your test should fail.

Also, remember to put all your tests in *src/test/...* and not in *src/main/....*

Running a Failing Test

Now that you have a test case with a test that deliberately fails, the next step is to run your test.

There are two main ways of running tests. The first is to run a single test directly from IntelliJ IDEA. To do that, click the green arrow next to the name of the test class, and IntelliJ IDEA will execute it, as seen in Figure 7-1.

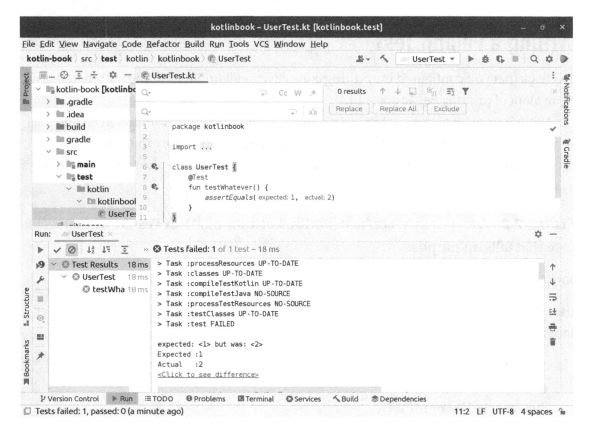

Figure 7-1. *Output from running a single test class with IntelliJ IDEA*

Running a single test class like this is particularly useful when your test suite has grown to hundreds or thousands of tests, but you only want to run the specific one that you're working on right now.

Also note that you can run a single test function, by clicking the green arrow next to it, for complete granular control of which tests you want to run.

It's also vital to know how to run all your tests in one go. Before you push code to production, you should run all the tests first, to verify that you didn't break anything. An automated build environment will also typically run all your tests every time someone pushes new code.

To run all your tests in one go, open the Gradle control panel in the right sidebar, and navigate to *kotlinbook* ➤ *Tasks* ➤ *verification* ➤ *test*. Double-click to run that task and execute all the tests in your test suite, as seen in Figure 7-2.

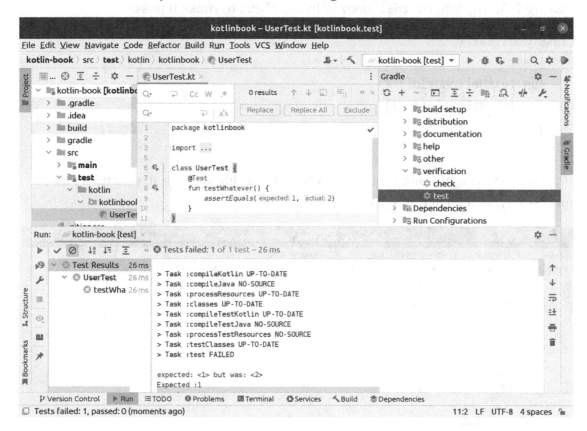

Figure 7-2. *Output from running your entire test suite with Gradle*

As Figures 7-1 and 7-2 signify, you've now verified successfully that your setup lets you know when a test is failing.

Making the Test Pass

The next step is to make the test pass. You've asserted that 1 is equal to 2, and while it can be useful to rethink fundamentals every now and then, Russell and Whitehead carefully concluded in Principia Mathematica, after 379 pages of dense mathematical notation, that $1 + 1 = 2$ and noted that "The above proposition is occasionally useful." So we'll let Kotlin have the win on this one and move forward with the assumption that 1 is indeed not equal to 2.

To make the test pass, update it to contain two values that are equal. Listing 7-3 shows an example of how to do that.

Listing 7-3. Update `testHelloWorld` in `UserTest` to make it pass

```kotlin
class UserTest {
    @Test
    fun testHelloWorld() {
        assertEquals(1, 1)
    }
}
```

Run the tests again, and you'll see IntelliJ IDEA telling you that all your tests passed successfully, as seen in Figure 7-3.

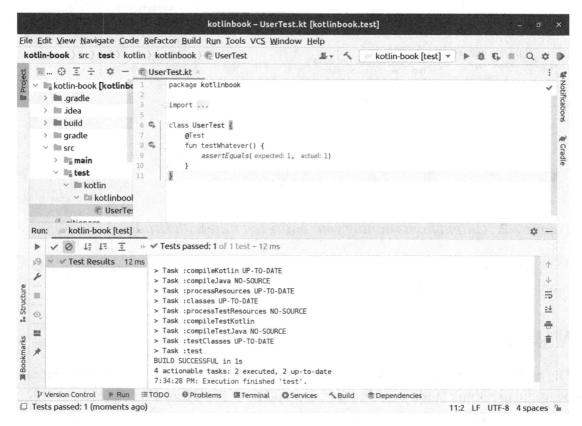

Figure 7-3. *Output from running your test suite with no failed assertions*

IntelliJ IDEA makes it easy to see that no tests failed, as it only lists failed tests. So, when the test output panel only shows "Test Results" and a green check mark, you know that everything is good and that all of your tests ran successfully, without any assertion errors.

Writing Web App Tests

Verifying that 1 is indeed equal to 1 has limited value in the context of writing web apps. You'll now write some tests that help ensure that your web app works correctly.

Setting Up the Basics

The goal of an automated test is to invoke your business logic with specific given parameters and specific given contexts and assert that your system ends up in a desired state. For most of your business logic to work, you need two things: a WebappConfig object and a database connection pool.

The simplest way to make your config and your database connection pool available to your tests is to declare them as top-level variables. In Kotlin, you can place val statements outside of classes and function implementations, at the top level. These values will be available to all functions from all contexts in that file and even to other files unless you explicitly tag them as private. Listing 7-4 shows an example of how to create a config object and a database connection pool this way.

Listing 7-4. Top-level declarations of config and a database connection pool for use in automated tests

```
val testAppConfig = createAppConfig("test")
val testDataSource = createAndMigrateDataSource(testAppConfig)
```

As you already have functions available for creating new instances of your config and connection pool, there's nothing special you need to do when you create them for your tests. You simply invoke them, and you get what you need.

Before you run this code, you need to add a missing config file. When you invoke createAppConfig with "test", it expects to find the file *src/main/resources/app-test. conf* and uses it to load config values. Listing 7-5 shows what this file should look like and what it needs to contain for your tests to run correctly.

Listing 7-5. The contents of the file **src/main/resources/app-test.conf**

```
dbUser = ""
dbPassword = ""
dbUrl = "jdbc:h2:mem:kotlinbook;MODE=PostgreSQL;DATABASE_TO_LOWER=TRUE;"
```

Note that the purpose of using the PostgreSQL mode is not to perfectly emulate PostgreSQL. H2 is not able to do that, and you can't expect your H2 SQLs to run perfectly in PostgreSQL. The purpose of setting the PostgreSQL mode is to set a collection of properties in one fell swoop and make H2 more convenient to work with than it is out of the box in the vanilla mode.

This config file contains the same as `app-local.conf`, which is database config that sets your data source up to use an in-memory H2 database. In a real-world web app, it's likely that you'll run against a real database, so it's useful to be able to separate the config for your local development database and the database that your automated tests will use.

Writing a Failing Test

Your first test case will test a function you'll implement for creating users. The test will be as simple as possible. It will create the user and check that we got the ID of the newly created user in return.

The first step is to write a failing test. To avoid failing at compilation due to a missing function, you'll create an empty implementation. Later, you'll return to this function and implement it. Listing 7-6 shows the signature and the empty implementation.

Listing 7-6. An empty implementation of the new function to create a user

```
fun createUser(
  dbSession: Session,
  email: String,
  name: String,
  passwordText: String,
  tosAccepted: Boolean = false
): Long {
    return -1
}
```

With this empty implementation in hand, you can now write a test case. You could write a test that creates the user and use assertNotNull to check that you get a valid user ID and not null back. But the type system already verifies that, as the return type is Long, not Long?. Instead, a more useful test could be to create two different users and check that they get a distinct ID. Listing 7-7 shows what that test case looks like.

Listing 7-7. A test case in **src/test/kotlinbook/UserTest.kt** that checks if createUser works and returns a distinct user ID

```
@Test
fun testCreateUser() {
  sessionOf(
    testDataSource,
    returnGeneratedKey = true)
  .use { dbSess ->
    val userAId = createUser(dbSess,
      email = "augustlilleaas@me.com",
      name = "August Lilleaas",
      passwordText = "1234"
    )

    val userBId = createUser(dbSess,
      email = "august@august1.com",
      name = "August Lilleaas",
      passwordText = "1234"
    )

    assertNotEquals(userAId, userBId)
  }
}
```

Try to run this test and notice how it fails. You hard-coded createUser to return -1, which means that the IDs of both the users you created are -1. And your test expects that when you create two users, they each get a separate and distinct ID assigned to them.

Making the Test Pass

The only thing left to do to make your test pass is to implement createUser and have it interact with the database and create the user and return the ID of the user that was created.

You already know how to create a user, as you wrote a function in Chapter 6 that inserts a user and returns the generated user ID. Listing 7-8 shows an implementation of createUser that does everything you need it to.

Listing 7-8. A working implementation of createUser

```
fun createUser(
  dbSession: Session,
  email: String,
  name: String,
  passwordText: String,
  tosAccepted: Boolean = false
): Long {
  val userId = dbSession.updateAndReturnGeneratedKey(
    queryOf(
      """
      INSERT INTO user_t
      (email, name, tos_accepted, password_hash)
      VALUES (:email, :name, :tosAccepted, :passwordHash)
      """,
      mapOf(
        "email" to email,
        "name" to name,
        "tosAccepted" to tosAccepted,
        "passwordHash" to passwordText
          .toByteArray(Charsets.UTF_8)
      )
    )
  )

  return userId!!
}
```

Run your tests again, and they should pass. The user ID of both users that you created in the test was the same before, as `createUser` was hard-coded to return `-1`. But with a real implementation that creates users and returns their distinct ID, the test passes.

The double exclamation mark is an unsafe cast operator. The type of `updateAndReturnGeneratedKey` from Kotliquery is `Long?`. This is because it's technically possible to write a SQL statement that doesn't insert any rows, so Kotliquery has to encode that possibility into the type system. In this case, though, a plain insert that succeeds and does not throw any exceptions will always return a `Long`. So it's safe to cast it from `Long?` to `Long` using `!!`.

If it for some extraordinary reason ends up actually being null, Kotlin will throw a `NullPointerException` at the point where you used the unsafe cast operator `!!`. So the rest of your program is still type-safe, as Kotlin will never return a null from a function with a non-null return type.

Avoiding Leaky Tests

Currently, you only have a single test case. But as your test suite grows, you want to make sure that each individual test case runs in isolation and that data does not leak between them.

Leaky Tests

To demonstrate the problem with leaky tests, you can write another test that also creates a user, `testCreateAnotherUser()`:

```
@Test
fun testCreateAnotherUser() {
  sessionOf(
    testDataSource,
    returnGeneratedKey = true)
  .use { dbSess ->
    val userId = createUser(dbSess,
      email = "augustlilleaas@me.com",
      name = "August Lilleaas",
```

```
        passwordText = "1234"
    )

    // ... write some assertions here ...
  }
}
```

If you try to run this test now, you'll get an error caused by a conflict between the test you wrote in Listing 7-7, `testCreateUser`, and the new test you just added. The tests both create a user with the email *augustlilleaas@me.com*. The `user_t` table has a uniqueness constraint added for the email column, and thus one of the tests fails with the following error message:

```
Unique index or primary key violation: "public.CONSTRAINT_CE_INDEX_1
ON public.user_t(email NULLS FIRST) VALUES ( /* 2 */ 'augustlilleaas@
me.com' )"
```

Your tests run against an in-memory database, but this database stays alive for the full test run. So all your tests run against the same database, and any data that a test leaves behind in the database after it runs is visible to subsequent tests.

Also note that currently, you use an in-memory database that resets between every test run. In a real-world project, you're likely to connect to an actual database where data is persisted. In that case, you'll run into issues even with a single test case, as data from the previous test run is still in the database and causes conflicts on subsequent test runs.

Avoiding Leaks with Transactions

To avoid data leaking between your test cases, you can use database transactions. By wrapping each test case in a transaction, you ensure that your database rolls back all the changes made by a test case when it finishes running.

The easiest way to make this work is to create a helper function that you can use in your tests, which replaces your call to `sessionOf` that you currently use. This function needs to do two things: it needs to create a session against the `testDataSource`, just like you do manually now, and it needs to start a transaction that it rolls back when the test has finished executing. Listing 7-9 shows an implementation of that function.

Listing 7-9. A helper function that wraps a test case in a database transaction

```
fun testTx(handler: (dbSess: TransactionalSession) -> Unit) {
  sessionOf(
    testDataSource,
    returnGeneratedKey = true
  ).use { dbSess ->
    dbSess.transaction { dbSessTx ->
      try {
        handler(dbSessTx)
      } finally {
        dbSessTx.connection.rollback()
      }
    }
  }
}
```

By placing the call to rollback() inside the finally block, you ensure that no matter what happens in your test, your database always rolls back any changes that you made to the database in your test case.

You also need to update your test cases to use the new testTx helper function. Listing 7-10 shows how you can write your tests and wrap them in testTx so that you don't get any leakage between your tests.

Listing 7-10. Wrap your test cases at **src/test/kotlinbook/UserTest.kt** in testTx to avoid data leaks between individual test cases

```
@Test
fun testCreateUser() {
  testTx { dbSess ->
    val userAId = createUser(dbSess,
      email = "augustlilleaas@me.com",
      name = "August Lilleaas",
      passwordText = "1234"
    )
```

```
    val userBId = createUser(dbSess,
      email = "august@august1.com",
      name = "August Lilleaas",
      passwordText = "1234"
    )

    assertNotEquals(userAId, userBId)
  }
}

@Test
fun testCreateAnotherUser() {
  testTx { dbSess ->
    val userId = createUser(dbSess,
      email = "augustlilleaas@me.com",
      name = "August Lilleaas",
      passwordText = "1234"
    )

    // ... write some assertions here ...
  }
}
```

Run your tests again, and you won't get an error. That's because testTx rolls back the writes in each test before the other ones run, so even though you create both users with the same email, there's no conflict.

I also prefer to explicitly write testTx for every test that needs that functionality, instead of figuring out some clever way to automatically wrap all test cases in a database transaction. It adds some boilerplate, but you also gain the ability to easily see what goes on in your tests and how your tests interact with the database. Additionally, you might encounter cases in real-world projects where you want to write a test that you don't wrap in a transaction. For example, you might want to test how two different transactions might interact with one another in your business logic. All you must do in those cases is to simply not use testTx and instead do what's appropriate for that specific test case.

Avoiding Leaks with Relative Asserts

To demonstrate another issue with automated tests, absolute asserts, you'll implement a function that lists all the users in your web app.

For some type of tests, it might make sense to make absolute asserts. For example, next up, you'll implement and test a function that lists all the users in the system. Listing 7-11 shows the implementation of that listing function.

Listing 7-11. A function to list all users in the system

```
fun listUsers(dbSession: Session) =
  dbSession
    .list(queryOf("SELECT * FROM user_t"), ::mapFromRow)
    .map(User::fromRow)
```

You can then write a test, seen in Listing 7-12, that inserts two users in the system and asserts that it contains the two users you created and that the number of users it returns is 2.

Listing 7-12. A test with absolute asserts for creating and listing users

```
@Test
fun testListUsers() {
  testTx { dbSess ->
    val userAId = createUser(dbSess,
      email = "augustlilleaas@me.com",
      name = "August Lilleaas",
      passwordText = "1234")

    val userBId = createUser(dbSess,
      email = "august@augustl.com",
      name = "August Lilleaas",
      passwordText = "1234")

    val users = listUsers(dbSess)
    assertEquals(2, users.size)
    assertNotNull(users.find { it.id == userAId })
    assertNotNull(users.find { it.id == userBId })
  }
}
```

You might be surprised to see that this test does not pass. In Chapter 6, you wrote a repeatable migration that inserts a user into user_t. So the number of users in your system after you insert two users is 3, not 2.

One way to solve this is to simply remove assertEquals(2, users.size). You assert that userAId and userBId are both present in the result of listUsers() and you can argue that that's enough.

Another way of solving this is to use relative asserts. You could argue that you don't care that listUsers() returns exactly two results. Another correct definition of listUsers() is that the number of users returned should increase by 2 after you create two users. Listing 7-13 updates the test from Listing 7-12 with a check for the relative difference before and after you create the users.

Listing 7-13. A test with relative asserts for creating and listing users

```
@Test
fun testListUsers() {
  testTx { dbSess ->
    val usersBefore = listUsers(dbSess)

    val userAId = createUser(dbSess,
      email = "augustlilleaas@me.com",
      name = "August Lilleaas",
      passwordText = "1234")

    val userBId = createUser(dbSess,
      email = "august@augustl.com",
      name = "August Lilleaas",
      passwordText = "1234")

    val users = listUsers(dbSess)
    assertEquals(2, users.size - usersBefore.size)
    assertNotNull(users.find { it.id == userAId })
    assertNotNull(users.find { it.id == userBId })
  }
}
```

With this change, the test only cares about the changes it made to the system and is not dependent on the specific state of the system before the test started running.

Test-Driven Development

So far in this chapter, you've written tests using Test-Driven Development (TDD). That means that you've first written a test that failed and then you updated your implementation and finally made the test pass successfully.

Design and Verification

Test-Driven Development has two main benefits: it helps with the design of your system, and it verifies that your tests are doing useful things.

By writing the tests first, alongside your implementation code, you gain an extra tool for making sure that your code is well-structured. The design of your tests directly informs the design of your implementation code. Writing tests becomes cumbersome if you must wire up too many dependencies and state before you can interact with your classes and functions. So, by writing the tests first, as you work with your implementation, you're almost forced to make your code modular and reusable, reducing complexity and increasing maintainability.

Tests also have the fundamental problem "Who tests my tests?" Having tests to verify that your system works is good, but how do you know that your tests do useful things? Writing a failing test first helps solve this issue. That way, you make sure that all your test cases have a valid failure state and will fail if your implementation does not work as expected. If your test passes on the first invocation, you know that your test doesn't verify anything.

There are entire books written about the TDD methodology, so I won't go into more detail here. If you're interested in learning more, I recommend Kent Beck's book *Test-Driven Development by Example*, originally published all the way back in 2002. It's a timeless classic, and you'll learn a lot about software development practices by reading it or anything else Kent Beck has produced.

Writing a Failing Test

To make the TDD pattern easy to recognize, you'll do another TDD cycle by adding a function to get a user by its ID.

The first step is to write a failing test and an empty initial implementation. Without the empty implementation, your test code simply won't compile, so you're not actually testing your test that way. Listing 7-14 shows the test as well as the empty implementation.

Listing 7-14. A failing test with an empty implementation

```
// Code
fun getUser(dbSess: Session, id: Long): User? {
  return null
}

// Test
@Test
fun testGetUser() {
  testTx { dbSess ->
    val userId = createUser(dbSess,
      email = "augustlilleaas@me.com",
      name = "August Lilleaas",
      passwordText = "1234",
      tosAccepted = true
    )

    assertNull(getUser(dbSess, -9000))

    val user = getUser(dbSess, userId)
    assertNotNull(user)
    assertEquals(user.email, "augustlilleaas@me.com")
  }
}
```

Make sure you put the code somewhere in *src/main/kotlin/kotlinbook* and the test in *src/test/kotlin/kotlinbook/UserTest.kt*.

This test will fail. The initial assertNull will run successfully. You don't have a user with the ID -9000 in your system. In fact, you'll never have users with negative IDs. So this test successfully verifies that calling getUser with a nonexisting user returns null. But the later assertNotNull will fail. Your end goal is for that test to pass successfully, as the user ID returned by createUser should always correspond with a user fetched by getUser. But getUser is currently hard-coded to return null.

Making the Test Pass

To make the test pass, you'll need to implement the getUser function.

You already have all the facilities you need to implement it. You've set up Kotliquery to run queries, your test passes a Kotliquery session to getUser, and you have a data class with mapping from table data to the User? type that getUser returns. Listing 7-15 shows how to implement it correctly.

Listing 7-15. A working implementation of getUser

```
fun getUser(dbSess: Session, id: Long): User? {
  return dbSess
    .single(
      queryOf("SELECT * FROM user_t WHERE id = ?", id),
      ::mapFromRow
    )
    ?.let(User::fromRow)
}
```

If you rerun your test, it should run without any assertion errors. You've now verified that if you haven't implemented getUser correctly, the test will fail. And by writing the test first, you made sure that it was easy to invoke getUser without any context other than database state and a Kotliquery session.

Notes on Methodology

You now have everything you need to write and run tests that execute your business logic code and assert that they yielded the expected and required outputs. For the remainder of this chapter, you'll learn more about the methodologies of testing and the thoughts behind why you're doing what you're doing.

What About Front-End Tests?

I'm not covering the world of JavaScript and front-end development in any depth in this book.

In Chapter 9, you'll learn how to build traditional web apps with HTML and CSS. And in Chapter 10, you'll learn how to set up front ends that are powered by Kotlin-backed APIs. But the actual implementation of your front end is outside of the scope of this book, which focuses on the server-side aspects of writing production-grade web apps with Kotlin.

Real Database Writes vs. Mocks

In your tests, you're doing real database writes against a real database. What about mocks, stubs, and other patterns?

Mocks and stubs let you run your business logic code in isolation, without relying on big stateful systems like databases and other external systems. Personally, I almost never use mocks and stubs. I prefer to test as close to the "edges" of the system as possible – that is, invoke the business logic in my web handlers directly. That way, your tests will reflect how your web handlers call your code in production, but you don't have to start a full web server and perform HTTP requests – you can just invoke the functions that make up your business logic. Another name for this type of testing is "black box tests," signifying that your tests have as little knowledge as possible about the inner workings of the system under test.

The biggest issue with stubs and mocks is that you end up with lots of logic in your tests that replicate the logic of other parts of your code or that of third-party systems. This has a high long-term maintenance cost, spent on coordinating your mocks with your actual implementation. It can also lead to false positives, where your code runs fine against mocks in your tests but doesn't work when you run your web app in production.

Note that there are plenty of smart and productive developers who are proponents of mocks and stubs. But if you want to learn more about that, you should listen to them, not me.

If you want to judge it based on my experience, most of the people I've collaborated with on real-world projects, and who have used mocks before, made a big mess of it and now mostly avoid using mocks and stubs.

Unit vs. Integration Tests

It's likely that you'll encounter discussions of unit tests, integration tests, and the difference between them. So I'll briefly discuss that subject here, so you know what to make of it.

I've seen entire talks at conferences discussing the definition of unit vs. integration tests, so I won't be able to go into full detail here. For example, Martin Fowler has an in-depth discussion about this in a 2021 blog post: *https://martinfowler.com/ articles/2021-test-shapes.html*. The tests you're writing in this book are unit tests, by my estimation. Your tests invoke various functions – units – in your business logic and assert what they return and which state they caused the system to end up in.

But what is an integration test?

The difference between unit vs. integration tests is clearer when you test user interface code. There, a unit test is a small and isolated test that typically only tests the underlying data model and business logic for the user interface, not the actual rendering. Integration tests are "full-featured" tests, which open your iPhone app or website in a simulator or a browser and perform user-like operations where buttons are clicked and forms filled in, testing that everything "actually" works.

When you work on real-world web apps, I've found that the distinction between unit tests and integration tests is unimportant, and you can instead just write tests like those in this chapter and refer to them as unit tests (or just tests), and everyone on your team will be happy.

CHAPTER 8

Parallelizing Service Calls with Coroutines

In this chapter, you'll learn how to perform service calls (i.e., call external APIs) and how to do so efficiently. Few web apps operate in isolation, and most real-world web apps use a combination of a database and calls to external services to do their work.

If you're new to Kotlin, here are some language features that you'll see examples of in this chapter:

- Using coroutines from different contexts

- The difference between `kotlin.coroutines` and `kotlinx.coroutines`

Also in this chapter, you will learn the following about parallelizing service calls with coroutines:

- The difference between blocking and non-blocking code

- Handling race conditions

Efficiently calling external services is extra useful if your web app runs in an environment with a micro-service architecture. In those cases, you quickly end up in a situation where you do hundreds of parallel calls, using outputs from some calls as inputs to other calls and so on.

Preparing Your Web App

The goal of this chapter is to write web handlers that use coroutines to perform parallelized calls to external services. These handlers will perform actual calls using a HTTP client. So you'll need an actual HTTP server that you can execute your calls against.

© August Lilleaas 2023
A. Lilleaas, *Pro Kotlin Web Apps from Scratch*, https://doi.org/10.1007/978-1-4842-9057-6_8

Implementing a Fake Service

There are plenty of public and open APIs around that you could use. But you never know when a public API shuts down or is updated in a way that breaks backward compatibility. It's also common for most APIs to require a personal API key, so that the owner of the API can limit abuse.

For the sake of future-proofing this book and making it as stand-alone as possible, you'll make your own fake service that you can invoke.

To make the fake service as realistic as possible, you'll create a separate HTTP API, running on a separate HTTP server, on a separate port. That way, you can invoke your fake service as if it was an external HTTP API. Technically speaking you could just invoke it directly, as it is running inside the same process as your main web app. But since it's also available over HTTP, that's what you'll use when invoking it.

Adding a Second Server

You'll run your fake service as a stand-alone HTTP server that runs alongside the HTTP server that runs your actual web app.

One of the benefits of using libraries is that it's easy to step outside of the box. That's because there is no box. You have full access to everything and full control of how everything starts up. You already know how to start a HTTP server from your Kotlin code, as that's what you already do for your existing web app. Adding a second server is as simple as adding a second call to Ktor's `embeddedServer()` somewhere in your existing `main()` function.

The actual implementation of the server will contain three routes: one route that picks a random number between 200 and 2000 and waits for that number of milliseconds and returns the number, another route that just returns the text `"pong"`, and one route that returns whatever you posted to it and reverses it. Listing 8-1 contains the code you need to set all this up.

Listing 8-1. A fake service with some route handlers that you'll use to demonstrate coroutines

```
embeddedServer(Netty, port = 9876) {
  routing {
    get("/random_number", webResponse {
      val num = (200L..2000L).random()
      delay(num)
      TextWebResponse(num.toString())
    })

    get("/ping", webResponse {
      TextWebResponse("pong")
    })

    post("/reverse", webResponse {
      TextWebResponse(call.receiveText().reversed())
    })
  }
}.start(wait = false)
```

200L..2000L is a range, and you've used ranges before when you implemented mapFromRow() back in Chapter 6 (see Listing 6-1). The built-in extension function on Range, random(), is a convenient way to get a bounded random number.

Notice how your new "fake" server is started with .start(wait = false). Be sure to place this before the existing call to your "real" embeddedServer(). The "real" server is set to wait (.start(wait = true)), meaning that it will cause the main() function to block forever, listening for new incoming connections. Without this blocking/ waiting of your "real" web app, the main() function would just exit immediately. The consequence of that is that any code you put below your "real" embeddedServer() starting will not run until your server shuts down. So start your "fake" server first, and set it to not wait/block. That way, your "fake" server will start, and then your "real" server will start, and your main() function will block and listen for incoming connections on both servers.

Understanding Coroutines

Before you start implementing parallelized service calls to coroutines, you should know a little bit about what a coroutine does and what makes them tick.

The `delay` Coroutine

You've already written your first coroutine. Did you notice?

In Listing 8-1, you wrote a web handler that generates a random number, and before it returns that number as text, it calls a function `delay()` with that random number. `delay()` is a coroutine!

`delay()` is a special function that only works inside a coroutine context. If you try to call `delay()` at the top level or just inside your `main()` function, you'll get an error, shown in Listing 8-2.

Listing 8-2. The error message you get when attempting to call a coroutine from a non-coroutine context

```
Suspend function 'delay' should be called only from a coroutine or another
suspend function
```

Why is it that you're allowed to write `delay()` inside your web handlers, but not everywhere in your code? And why are you using `delay()` in the first place, instead of more familiar functions such as `Thread.sleep()`?

The Problem with Threads

The whole point of suspend functions and coroutines in Kotlin is to limit and control the use of threads, particularly sleeping threads.

In the old days of Java platform web apps, the canonical architecture was for each HTTP request to take up one full thread, for the full duration of the handling of that request. If you got a new request incoming while another request was running, the web server would create a second thread to handle that request and so on. The web server would use a pool of threads to avoid having to create a new thread from scratch for each request. But fundamentally, a single thread handled a single request.

The consequence of that is that for some (or even most) of the time, threads were idle and not doing any work. For example, if your web server queried a database, the thread that handled that request was sleeping while it waited for a response from the database server.

This is a problem, because of the way threads work under the hood. A thread in Java creates a thread in the underlying operating system. An operating system thread is a relatively expensive resource. Each thread requires its own full call stack, and switching between threads also incurs an overhead.

You can get quite far on modern operating systems, as they are much better at handling tens of thousands of threads now than back in the early 2000s when the Java platform became popular. But it's usually a good idea to avoid creating a near-infinite number of threads and instead rely on other mechanisms for concurrency.

Suspending Instead of Locking

To avoid idle and sleeping threads, Kotlin has the concept of *suspension*.

Suspension, in short, means that Kotlin knows how to suspend execution of your code at specific points and continue execution later. When your code reaches a point of suspension, Kotlin knows that it can use the thread where your code ran to do other things. Later, when the suspended code is ready to continue running, execution will continue, potentially on another thread.

This is what the `delay()` function does. As soon as you call `delay()`, Kotlin suspends execution of your function. Later, when the internal scheduler triggers after the desired number of milliseconds (Kotlin uses a `ScheduledThreadPoolExecutor` for this on the Java platform), Kotlin resumes execution of your function.

If you call `Thread.sleep()`, the Java runtime will block the entire thread for the duration you specify. If you use `delay()`, you let Kotlin take control of the thread management. You should use `delay()` and coroutines where you can and let the Kotlin runtime take control of thread management.

Coroutine Contexts

You can only call suspend functions from two places: coroutine contexts or functions tagged with `suspend`.

The error message you got from Listing 8-2 indicates this requirement. Kotlin can't just suspend execution at arbitrary points in your code, as the Java platform does not allow for that. Listing 8-3 shows how you can create a suspend function and call `delay()` inside it.

Listing 8-3. An example of a suspend function

```
suspend fun myCoroutineFunction() {
  println("Hello, ...")
  delay(500)
  println("...world!")
}
```

This function, however, begs the question: How do you call *that* function inside your existing `main()`? If you try to invoke it there, as seen in Listing 8-4, you'll get the same error message from Listing 8-2 again.

Listing 8-4. Invoking a suspend function from inside main and getting an error message

```
fun main() {
  log.debug("Starting application...")

  myCoroutineFunction()
  // Error: Suspend function 'myCoroutineFunction'
  // should be called only from a coroutine or another
  // suspend function
```

One way to solve this is to tag the `main()` function itself with `suspend`. The Kotlin compiler will do what's necessary under the hood and bridge a plain Java platform main function with a separate coroutine-scoped main function that Kotlin will call under the hood.

Another way is to explicitly create a coroutine context yourself. Kotlin has the function `runBlocking` to bridge the gap between normal execution and coroutines. Listing 8-5 shows an example of how you can use it to invoke suspend functions from a non-coroutine context.

Listing 8-5. Use `runBlocking` to invoke coroutines from `main()`

```
suspend fun myFancyCoroutineFunction(): Number {
    val num = (100L..500L).random()
    delay(num)
    return num
}

fun main() {
    log.debug("Starting application...")

    val waitedFor = runBlocking {
        myFancyCoroutineFunction()
    }
    println("Waited ${waitedFor}ms")
    // Waited 427ms
```

`runBlocking` blocks the calling thread until the coroutine has finished executing. The purpose of `runBlocking` is to bridge the gap between the world of threads and the world of coroutines, which is why it blocks the calling thread. `runBlocking` returns the value of the lambda running in the coroutine context to the non-coroutine context, which in this case means that `waitedFor` represents the num inside `myFancyCoroutineFunction()`.

Coroutines in Ktor

With all that explanation out of the way, you can now return to the `delay()` in your "fake" external service that you wrote in Listing 8-1.

The reason you can write `delay()` inside your web handlers is that Ktor handlers already run in a coroutine context. Ktor was written from scratch with Kotlin in mind and uses coroutines extensively under the hood. Since most of the code in Ktor runs in a coroutine context already, it exposes this coroutine context to your web handlers so that you can start using coroutines in Ktor without any extra setup.

Under the hood, Ktor supports many different server implementations. In this book, you've used Netty, which is built on top of the non-blocking NIO (new I/O) API added to the Java platform way back in Java 1.4. The mapping between Netty and Ktor leans heavily on the non-blocking nature of Netty and makes for an efficient pairing where almost no thread blocking needs to happen.

147

Additionally, when you implemented `webResponse` in Chapter 4, you included the `suspend` keyword on the `handler` lambda where you build and return your `WebResponse` instances. The Ktor type `PipelineContext<Unit, ApplicationCall>` that is the receiver type of your `handler` lambda implements the built-in interface `coroutineScope`, which is what tells Kotlin that your web response handler lambdas have a coroutine scope available to them. And since the `handler` lambda function type includes `suspend`, you have everything you need to invoke coroutines from inside your `webHandler` wrapped Ktor handlers.

Parallelizing Service Calls

You now have a "fake" web server that you can use as if it was an external service, and you understand the basics of what coroutines do and why they are useful. You're now ready to write some parallelized service calls.

Adding Dependencies

You need two dependencies before you can perform external service calls: you need a HTTP client to invoke the "fake" server and you need a dependency to the Kotlin coroutine library itself.

There are plenty of HTTP clients available for the Java platform. For this book, you'll use Ktor's own HTTP client. The Ktor HTTP client has no direct coupling to the Ktor HTTP server. The reason you're using it is that it's fundamentally based on coroutines. So it's a good fit for Ktor web apps where you use coroutines.

Listing 8-6 shows what you need to add to make everything work.

Listing 8-6. Adding the coroutine library as a dependency in **build.gradle.kts**

```
implementation("io.ktor:ktor-client-core:2.1.2")
implementation("io.ktor:ktor-client-cio:2.1.2")
```

Like the Ktor server, the Ktor client supports multiple different back ends. The CIO (coroutine I/O) back end is the coroutine-based one that you'll use in this book.

Performing Parallelized Calls

To perform a parallelized service call, you'll write a new Ktor web handler that does a mix and match of parallel calls and using results of parallel calls to perform additional parallel calls.

This type of a la carte parallelization can be very tricky to write if you don't have something like coroutines available. A huge benefit of coroutines is that writing parallelized service calls is almost as easy as writing synchronous and sequential service calls.

In Listing 8-7, you can see an example of everything but the kitchen sink. There are several things happening there, which I'll explain in detail in the following.

Listing 8-7. A function that performs multiple parallel calls to external services

```
suspend fun handleCoroutineTest(
  dbSess: Session
) = coroutineScope {
  val client = HttpClient(CIO)

  val randomNumberRequest = async {
    client.get("http://localhost:9876/random_number")
      .bodyAsText()
  }

  val reverseRequest = async {
    client.post("http://localhost:9876/reverse") {
      setBody(randomNumberRequest.await())
    }.bodyAsText()
  }

  val queryOperation = async {
    val pingPong = client.get("http://localhost:9876/ping")
      .bodyAsText()
```

```
    dbSess.single(
      queryOf(
        "SELECT count(*) c from user_t WHERE email != ?",
        pingPong
      ),
      ::mapFromRow)
  }

  TextWebResponse("""
    Random number: ${randomNumberRequest.await()}
    Reversed: ${reverseRequest.await()}
    Query: ${queryOperation.await()}
  """)
}
```

At the core, this is just like any other web handler function. You pass in some parameters, namely, a Kotliquery database session, and you return a WebResponse. The main difference comes from the fact that it's a suspend function and that it's wrapped in coroutineScope.

async() is the main workhorse when you want to perform multiple parallelized service calls. The code you wrap in async() runs immediately, but asynchronously. When you perform the request to /random_number, your code does not halt and wait for a return value. Instead, it continues to the next statement, which starts a request to /reverse. Similarly, the code does not wait for that request to finish, and it moves directly on to the next statement, which starts yet another async block that performs a request to /ping and uses that return value as input to a database query.

The asynchronous magic happens when you call await(). The return value of async() is Deferred<T>, and calling await() on a Deferred<T> causes that code to suspend (not block). When the result is ready, your code will continue executing, and the value of your Deferred<T> will just be the T – in other words, the raw value that the async() block returned.

async() also requires a coroutine scope to function. Wrapping your function body in coroutineScope ensures that a coroutine scope is available. When you call handleCoroutineTest() from a Ktor web handler, it will inherit the already existing context. So there is no extra overhead created by wrapping your function in coroutineScope like this.

Handling Race Conditions

One of the main difficulties in writing non-blocking and parallelized code is that you have no control of the order the operations you initiate complete. When you start operations A, B, and C, they might finish in that order, or C might finish first and then B, or B might finish first, or any other permutation.

For example, Listing 8-7 fires off `randomNumberRequest, reverseRequest,` and `queryOperation` in parallel. So they all start executing immediately, without waiting for one another. But `reverseRequest` is dependent on the return value of `randomNumberRequest`. There's potential for *race conditions* here. A race condition is the name for an unexpected order of events that rarely occurs. Perhaps `randomNumberRequest` usually finishes before `reverseRequest` actually executes, due to implementation details under the hood. But in some rare cases, `reverseRequest` executes first and potentially fails because the return value of `randomNumberRequest` is not available yet.

When you use coroutines, race conditions like these are a nonissue. The code in `reverseRequest` uses `randomNumberRequest.await()`, which means that the coroutine runtime will always wait until `randomNumberRequest` has finished before it continues executing `reverseRequest`. The ability to combine `async()` and `await()` is what makes parallelization with coroutines so powerful. You don't have to manage the order in which requests happen, and you don't have to manually handle all combinations of when asynchronous operations complete. All you need to do is to start the asynchronous operation and simply `await()` on the value you need, and it will all work out as expected.

Adding to Ktor

To test this function, you can create a new Ktor route handler and invoke the `handleCoroutineTest()` function from Listing 8-7.

To do this, all you need to do is to add a new route handler in your Ktor `routes` block and, as seen in Listing 8-8, invoke the function there.

Listing 8-8. Invoking `handleCoroutineTest()` in a web handler

```
get("/coroutine_test", webResponseDb(dataSource) { dbSess ->
  handleCoroutineTest(dbSess)
})
```

Go ahead and test it now! The actual numbers you get are random by design, so this is the randomized output I got when I ran the code as I'm writing this book:

```
Random number: 1599
Reversed: 9951
Query: {c=1}
```

Mixing Coroutines and Blocking Calls

There are plenty of calls on the Java platform that block the current thread while waiting for an asynchronous operation to complete. You should avoid placing these blocking calls directly in your coroutines and instead wrap them appropriately to make Kotlin manage resources more efficiently.

Wrapping Blocking Calls

In Listing 8-7, you already broke the rule of wrapping blocking calls. The Ktor HTTP client is based on coroutines and isn't blocking. But JDBC and Kotliquery do block while they wait for the database to return:

```
val queryOperation = async {
  val pingPong = client.get("http://localhost:9876/ping")
    .bodyAsText()

  dbSess.single(
    queryOf(
      "SELECT count(*) c from user_t WHERE email != ?",
      pingPong
    ),
    ::mapFromRow)
}
```

To fix this issue, you should wrap all blocking calls using withContext and make sure that the blocking calls run on the built-in Dispatchers.IO context. Listing 8-9 demonstrates how to make the code in Listing 8-7 properly handle blocking calls in coroutines.

Listing 8-9. Appropriately handle blocking calls in coroutines

```
val queryOperation = async {
  val pingPong = client.get("http://localhost:9876/ping")
    .bodyAsText()

  withContext(Dispatchers.IO) {
    dbSess.single(
      queryOf(
        "SELECT count(*) c from user_t WHERE email != ?",
        pingPong
      ),
      ::mapFromRow)
  }
}
```

With this minor change, you allow the coroutine runtime to execute the blocking call in a separate thread pool, designated for long-running blocking I/O operations such as database queries.

In your main web handlers, wrapping your database access calls is not that important. The typical web handler does one or a handful of sequential database queries and doesn't really do any parallelization. But for heavily parallelized coroutine code, you should keep this in mind and try to remember to wrap all blocking calls in `withContext(Dispatchers.IO)`.

Coroutine Internals

In this chapter, you've already learned some details about what goes on under the hood of coroutines. In this section, I'll explain some even deeper details of how coroutines work. Let's go under the hood of the hood!

Kotlin vs. KotlinX

To avoid confusion, I've deliberately been sloppy with the terminology so far. There are actually two types of coroutines in Kotlin: the built-in `kotlin.coroutines` and the library `kotlinx.coroutines` that is not in the standard library and needs to be added as a dependency in *build.gradle.kts*.

The coroutines you've written so far are `kotlinx.coroutines`. You didn't add a dependency to that library in your *build.gradle.kts*, but you don't need to. Ktor adds that dependency transitively, and you can use the version of `kotlinx.coroutines` that comes bundled with Ktor from your own code as well.

`kotlinx.coroutines` builds on the built-in and low-level `kotlin.coroutines`. The low-level `kotlin.coroutines` library is what is part of the core language syntax and adds the keyword `suspend` to functions and causes compile errors when you try to call a `suspend` function from a non-coroutine context. A `suspend` function returns a *continuation,* which is a built-in state machine that the Kotlin runtime has intimate knowledge of. Kotlin leverages continuation suspend functions to be able to run code until it encounters a suspension point and later use the continuation to continue execution at that same suspension point.

Comparing with Arrow

Parallelization with `kotlinx.coroutines` is just one of the uses of `kotlin.coroutines` and continuations in Kotlin. Another prominent use of continuations is the Arrow library.

You'll use Arrow to learn more about coroutines in this chapter, but you'll also use it to validate data in later chapters. So add it as a dependency to *build.gradle.kts*:

```
implementation("io.arrow-kt:arrow-fx-coroutines:1.1.2")
implementation("io.arrow-kt:arrow-fx-stm:1.1.2")
```

Arrow enables sophisticated functional programming constructs, like what you can find in languages such as Scala and Haskell. Arrow does *not* use coroutines and continuations to allow for asynchronous programming and parallelization of service calls. Instead, Arrow uses them to implement deep non-tail recursion, computational DSLs like the `Either` and `Effect`, and more.

Explaining monadic functional programming with strong types using Arrow is outside of the scope of this book. But Arrow provides a good ground for demonstrating how useful continuations are to library developers.

One of the many features Arrow provides is completely functional error handling. Instead of throwing an exception to interrupt the flow of execution when an error happens, Arrow uses `kotlin.coroutines` and continuations to short-circuit the execution of your code so that the code after the error doesn't run. Listing 8-10 shows a full example of how to do this type of data validation with Arrow.

Listing 8-10. Using Arrow to write functional error handling

```kotlin
data class ValidationError(val error: String) {}
data class MyUser(val email: String, val password: String)

fun validateEmail(email: Any?): Either<ValidationError, String> {
  if (email !is String) {
    return ValidationError("E-mail must be set").left()
  }

  if (!email.contains("@")) {
    return ValidationError("Invalid e-mail").left()
  }

  return email.right()
}

fun validatePassword(password: Any?): Either<ValidationError, String> {
  if (password !is String) {
    return ValidationError("Password must be set").left()
  }

  if (password == "1234") {
    return ValidationError("Insecure password").left()
  }

  return password.right()
}

suspend fun signUpUser(
  email: String,
  password: String
): Either<ValidationError, MyUser> =
  either {
    val validEmail = validateEmail(email).bind()
    val validPassword = validatePassword(password).bind()
```

```
  MyUser(
    email = validEmail,
    password = validPassword
  )
}
```

The magic happens in the `either` block in `signUpUser`. `validateEmail` and `validatePassword` both have the return type `Either<ValidationError, MyUser>`, and `left()` and `right()` are extension functions that resolve to either (pun intended) the left or the right side of the `Either`. When you call `bind()` on the `Either` instance, you enable the short-circuiting. If the `Either` returns a left value, Arrow short-circuits using a continuation under the hood and stops execution of the `either` block. It also returns that left value where execution was short-circuited. On the other hand (pun also intended), if it returns a right value, that value is bound to the statement, and execution continues to the next line.

To extract the actual value from an Either, you can use fold, which calls separate lambdas depending on the result. Listing 8-11 demonstrates the output of a few different calls to `signUpUser()`.

Listing 8-11. Using `fold` to extract values from `Either`

```
signUpUser("foo@bar.com", "test")
  .fold({ err -> println(err)}, { user -> println(user)})

// MyUser(email=foo@bar.com, password=test)

signUpUser("foo", "test")
  .fold({ err -> println(err)}, { user -> println(user)})

// ValidationError(error=Invalid e-mail)

signUpUser("foo@bar.com", "1234")
  .fold({ err -> println(err)}, { user -> println(user)})

// ValidationError(error=Insecure password)
```

By leveraging low-level Kotlin continuations, Arrow can control the execution of the code and halt and continue execution as it sees fit, at any point where Arrow sees fit in their APIs.

Using Low-Level Continuations

To further demonstrate what kotlinx.coroutines and Arrow do under the hood, you can directly invoke the lowest-level coroutine and continuation APIs in Kotlin.

The kotlin.coroutines APIs are public, stable, and documented, and you can use them to build powerful language extensions. They are typically not useful for writing web apps and are better suited for authors of third-party Kotlin libraries. But it's nice to know what goes on under the hood. Listing 8-12 shows an example of using the raw low-level continuation APIs in kotlin.coroutines to manually manage suspension and execution of code.

Listing 8-12. Using low-level continuations to control execution of code

```
import kotlin.coroutines.intrinsics.*

suspend fun haltHere() =
  suspendCoroutineUninterceptedOrReturn<Unit> { cont ->
    COROUTINE_SUSPENDED
  }

fun createContinuation(): suspend () -> Unit {
  return {
    println("a")
    haltHere()
    println("b")
    println("c")
    haltHere()
    println("d")
  }
}

val cont = createContinuation()
  .createCoroutineUnintercepted(
    Continuation(EmptyCoroutineContext, {}))
```

```
cont.resume(Unit)
// a

cont.resume(Unit)
// b
// c

cont.resume(Unit)
// d

cont.resume(Unit)
// d
```

Notice how the first call to resume the continuation prints "a", but nothing else. That's because haltHere uses the low-level continuation APIs to indicate to Kotlin that it should suspend execution at this point. After you've executed this first step, it's completely optional to continue execution of the coroutine.

When you invoke cont.resume(Unit) for the second time, the second part of the code runs, and it prints "b" and "c". Then, simply by the way continuations function in Kotlin, any further invocations of the coroutine repeat the last step and cause it to print "d" again and again.

At the end of the day, there is no magic going on. All the perceived magic comes from the suspend keyword. Kotlin compiles the body of suspend functions into a state machine that contains the code and a return with a state machine flag at any point where suspension can occur (i.e., a call to another suspend function).

Java Platform Implementation Details

If you *really* want to dig deep, you can look at the generated byte code.

If you use IntelliJ IDEA, you can open a class file in the folder *build/classes/kotlin/ main* and use the feature *Tools ➤ Kotlin ➤ Decompile to Java*. This code won't be particularly readable, but you'll see exactly what the Kotlin compiler does to generate Java platform–compatible code from suspend functions. Listing 8-13 shows a full example of the compiled output of the createContinuation function in Listing 8-12.

Listing 8-13. A full example of the compiled output of the `createContinuation` function

```
Int label;

public final Object invokeSuspend(@NotNull Object $result) {
  label17: {
    Object var2 = IntrinsicsKt.getCOROUTINE_SUSPENDED();
    Continuation var10000;
    switch (this.label) {
      case 0:
        ResultKt.throwOnFailure($result);
        System.out.println("a");
        var10000 = (Continuation)this;
        this.label = 1;
        if (ContinuationTestKt.haltHere(var10000) == var2) {
          return var2;
        }
        break;
      case 1:
        ResultKt.throwOnFailure($result);
        break;
      case 2:
        ResultKt.throwOnFailure($result);
        break label17;
      default:
        throw new IllegalStateException("call to 'resume' before 'invoke'
        with coroutine");
    }

    System.out.println("b");
    System.out.println("c");
    var10000 = (Continuation)this;
    this.label = 2;
```

```java
    if (ContinuationTestKt.haltHere(var10000) == var2) {
      return var2;
    }
  }
  System.out.println("d");
  return Unit.INSTANCE;
}
```

This code is full of things you don't normally see in Java code, such as label blocks and breaks with labels (the `label17` stuff). But it serves as a good demonstration to understand how Kotlin manages to not block threads. It takes your linear Kotlin code in `createContinuation` and compiles it into a hard-coded state machine. The initial case 0 first prints `"a"`, steps the `label` state from 0 to 1, and then returns a continuation object, `var2`. The next time Kotlin invokes the continuation, the case 1 runs, which does nothing, and continues to the code below the case statement where you print `"b"` and `"c"`, and the `label` state is set to 2. On the next invocation, the case 2 runs, which just breaks the entire `label17` block, and continues to the code below it, which prints `"d"`. Kotlin doesn't change the state machine when this happens, which is why you repeatedly get `"d"` printed when you invoke the continuation multiple times after it's "finished", as seen at the end of Listing 8-12.

This code isn't exactly idiomatic Java code, but that doesn't matter. Idiomatic Java is for humans, not computers. You'll be reading and writing the Kotlin code, and this compiled output is only there to make it possible for Kotlin to automatically turn your synchronous-looking code to asynchronous code that the runtime can interrupt and resume (or continue) at pre-compiled points in the code.

I find that it really helps to understand the deepest levels of what's really going on in coroutines. Turning synchronous statements into a state machine that Kotlin can interrupt and resume is what enables high-performance asynchronous `kotlinx.coroutines`, as well as Arrow's ability to halt execution of code after certain states occur, without having to resort to exceptions.

By compiling your linear-looking Kotlin code to a state machine, you get to write nice-looking code, without having to block the thread and without having to resort to writing code like the one in Listing 8-13 yourself.

CHAPTER 9

Building Traditional Web Apps with HTML and CSS

In this chapter, you'll learn how to generate HTML on the server and how to set up your web app to serve CSS, images, and other static content.

You'll also set up authentication and a login form and enhance your existing `user_t` table to support production-grade password security and encryption.

If you're new to Kotlin, here are some language features that you'll see examples of in this chapter:

- The safe call operator

- Operator overloading

- Using domain-specific languages (DSLs)

- Details about the precedence rules of extension functions

- Object expressions

Also in this chapter, you will learn the following about building traditional web apps with HTML and CSS:

- Using the kotlinx.html (*https://github.com/Kotlin/kotlinx. html*) DSL to build HTML

- Making reusable layouts

- Logging in and authenticating users

- Encrypting and signing session cookies

- Hashing and securely storing user passwords

When you're done, you'll have a fully working HTML-based setup with all the necessary components for building a production-grade web app.

161

© August Lilleaas 2023
A. Lilleaas, *Pro Kotlin Web Apps from Scratch*, https://doi.org/10.1007/978-1-4842-9057-6_9

Patterns and Organization

There are many frameworks and libraries available for making traditional server-side web apps and many ways to organize and structure them.

I've used the a priori assumption that you want to generate static HTML on the server, without any additional functionality. For example, the JavaScript framework Next.js (*https://nextjs.org/*) is set up so that your React-based web app automatically renders server-side and is *hydrated*, meaning that the pre-generated server-side HTML is "updated" to become a full-fledged JavaScript single-page app (SPA). In this chapter, you'll just generate "dumb" HTML from a Kotlin-powered web app back end.

There are also frameworks like Vaadin (*https://vaadin.com/*), which is a full-stack solution bundled with UI components, a built-in CMS, and so on. This is a framework, not a library, so it's not a good fit for this book. And you won't be building any sophisticated user interfaces in this book either; you'll just learn how to set up the basics, so you won't be needing UI components.

As for structuring your code, I consider that to be outside of the scope of this book. The main goal is to teach you how to use libraries and to learn a lot of Kotlin along the way. The topic of code organization quickly becomes subjective and opinion-based, and I don't think I've ever worked with a real-world web app where the structure always makes sense and where every component of the codebase has a sensible home. In fact, I often have a namespace called something like `myapp.homeless` where I deliberately place things that are hard to find a good home for.

Generating HTML

In this section, you'll learn the essentials for generating HTML and how to do so from Kotlin and Ktor.

Using the `kotlinx.html` DSL

You'll use the `kotlinx.html` *DSL* (domain-specific language) to generate HTML. The Ktor HTML DSL plugin adds a small wrapping layer around `kotlinx.html` and makes it easy to use from Ktor web handlers.

A DSL is a language within a language. Kotlin has powerful features for building DSLs, and using the `kotlin.xml` DSL means that you can express all your HTML as plain Kotlin code. If you need loops, conditionals, variables, and other features, you write those as plain Kotlin. Having all the power of Kotlin available when you write HTML is a big win. Ktor also has support for various templating engines, like Mustache, FreeMarker, and others. But all of those have the disadvantage of needing a separate templating language for loops, conditionals, etc.

Additionally, `kotlinx.html` is easy to use outside of Ktor, which will come in handy in later chapters when you'll run your web handlers in various contexts.

Using the Ktor HTML DSL

The Ktor HTML DSL is available as a plugin to Ktor that you'll need to add to your project as a dependency in *build.gradle.kts*:

```
implementation("io.ktor:ktor-server-html-builder:2.1.2")
```

The Ktor HTML DSL includes extension functions on the call inside Ktor route handlers for responding with HTML content built using `kotlinx.html`.

The most basic one is `call.respondHtml`. Listing 9-1 demonstrates how to use this function, which allows simple inlining of HTML content inside your web handlers.

Listing 9-1. Using `call.respondHtml` in Ktor web handlers

```
get("/html_test") {
  call.respondHtml {
    head {
      title("Hello, World!")
    }
    body {
      h1 { +"Hello, World!" }
    }
  }
}
```

You can now open *http://localhost:4207/html_test* in your browser and behold the fantastic web page seen in Figure 9-1.

Figure 9-1. *HTML output in the browser*

That's all it took to get basic HTML output added to your web app! Later in this chapter, you'll learn how to use shared HTML layouts across multiple web handlers.

The Power of the DSL

kotlinx.html makes substantial use of extension functions to allow for a type-safe DSL for generating HTML. How is this implemented?

One of the most convenient features of the DSL is that it uses the type system to only allow valid HTML output. For example, the h1 function is only available inside body. You can't put h1 inside head. And you can't write h1 at the top level, as siblings of head and body. Ktor does have escape hatches to allow for arbitrary tags in arbitrary locations, so you're not restricted from doing whatever you want. But out of the box, the DSL helps you generate valid HTML output.

If you use IntelliJ IDEA, you've already seen a hint of how this works. Figure 9-2 shows the gray blocks at the start of each lambda, indicating the type of the implicit receiver inside the lambda.

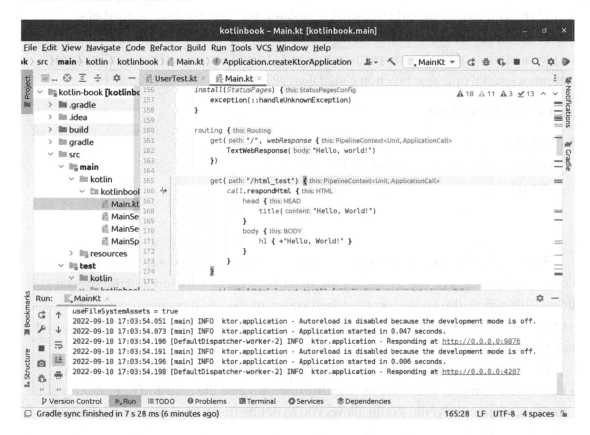

Figure 9-2. *IntelliJ IDEA shows gray boxes that indicate the receiver type inside lambdas*

The lambdas you pass to generateHtml, head, and body have the respective receiver of HTML, HEAD, and BODY. The DSL then defines the various functions, such as head and h1, as extension functions of the respective tag types. So the DSL internally defines h1 as fun BODY.h1(...) { ... }. (In fact, it's defined as an extension function on the more abstract type FlowOrHeadingContent, which BODY is a child type of.)

Operator Overloading

kotlinx.html leverages operator overloading in its DSL. You've already used one of the overloaded operators: using + to add text content to HTML tags.

In Kotlin, operator overloading allows custom definitions of otherwise built-in operators, such as the + sign. You won't be able to override what + means on things like numbers, but you can override what + means when called on your own types.

When you write your `kotlinx.html` templates, you can use `text` instead of +. So `h1 { text("Hello, World!") }` is the same as `h1 { +"Hello, World" }`. The implementation of `text` is where the actual code to add text lives. Then, kotlinx.html defines a special operator function called `unaryPlus` inside the `Tag` interface:

```
package kotlinx.html

interface Tag {
  operator fun String.unaryPlus(): Unit {
    text(this)
  }
}
```

By defining the extension function inside Tag, the function is only available in the context of instances of `Tag`. By adding the special `operator` keyword and the special `unaryPlus` name, the Kotlin compiler then knows that when it encounters `+"some string"` in the context of a `Tag`, it calls that function, and this is bound to the string you called + on.

The name *unary plus* refers to what's typically used on numbers in the form of `+i` and the sibling `-i`, which are the identity operator and the negation operator on numbers, respectively. But Kotlin allows you to define these operators so you can use them on any type.

Adding Custom Tags

If you need to insert an arbitrary tag, the DSL has two options.

You can use the `unsafe` function to write raw HTML output to your template. Anywhere in the DSL, add `unsafe { +"""<my-tag class="foo"></my-tag>""" }`, and your template output will include that raw HTML. As the name implies, `unsafe` does not escape the output, so using it opens your web app to HTML injection attacks.

Instead, you should create custom extension functions for new tags you want to add to the DSL. Listing 9-2 shows how you can write a custom tag named `<my-tag>` to the `kotlinx.html` DSL itself.

Listing 9-2. Adding custom tags to the `kotlinx.html` DSL

```
class MY_TAG(consumer: TagConsumer<*>): HTMLTag(
 "my-tag", consumer, emptyMap(),
  inlineTag = true,
  emptyTag = false
)

fun FlowOrHeadingContent.myTag(
  block: MY_TAG.() -> Unit = {}
) {
  MY_TAG(consumer).visit(block)
}
```

This custom tag in the DSL is completely safe and automatically handles escaping of HTML input correctly.

The MY_TAG class defines how `kotlinx.html` should write the output when it generates the actual HTML. The myTag function is an extension function on FlowOrHeadingContent, which makes it available in the body part of the template, as well as most of the child elements in body.

If you want to restrict or change the context you can call myTag on, change the receiver type of the extension function accordingly. For example, to only make myTag available inside head, use the receiver type HEAD instead of FlowOrHeadingContent.

CSS and Assets

Serving HTML content is a good start, but you're likely to need some CSS and other assets such as image files as well.

Serving Static Files

Ktor has built-in support for serving static files. Ktor can serve any static file, such as images, JavaScript, and video files, not just CSS files.

To add serving of static files to your web app, add a `static` route to your Ktor config. Listing 9-3 demonstrates how to add one.

Listing 9-3. Adding a `static` route to `createKtorApplication` for serving files inside

```
fun Application.createKtorApplication(
  dataSource: DataSource
) {
  // ...

  routing {
    static("/") {
      resources("public")
    }
```

Here, the static route is set up to handle the path /. That means all the files in the *public* folder on the Java runtime class path are available via your embedded Ktor web server. For example, if you have a file *public/app.css* on the class path, you can access it using *http://localhost:4207/app.css*.

The best place to put your assets in the file system is in *src/main/resources*. Your Gradle setup already adds all the files in that folder to the Java runtime class path. You can add as many subfolders in assets as you like. All the files in *src/main/resources/public* are recursively available to the corresponding path in your web app.

Try to create a CSS file now and include it in your HTML output in your web handler! Listing 9-4 shows how to update the HTML output from Listing 9-1 to include a stylesheet using the `kotlinx.html` DSL.

Listing 9-4. Linking to a CSS file in the `kotlinx.html` DSL

```
get("/html_test") {
  call.respondHtml {
    head {
      title("Hello, World!")
      styleLink("/app.css")
    }
    body {
      h1 { +"Hello, World!" }
    }
  }
}
```

The route is unchanged, except from the added styleLink call inside the head block.

This example demonstrates one of the benefits of using a DSL instead of plain HTML. The DSL adds convenient shortcuts, so you don't have to remember how to fully type out a valid <link> tag for stylesheets. (Is it href="/app.css" or src="/app.css"? Do you have to remember to set rel="stylesheet"? And so on.) Note that there is also a link DSL method available, if you need full control of the attributes of your CSS links or need to use the <link> tag for other purposes such as linking to an RSS feed or setting alternate rel="alternate" links with hrefLang for multilingual sites.

Restart your web app, and refresh your browser, and you should see your website like in Figure 9-3, with the CSS in app.css applied. In this case, the CSS file contains body { font-family: sans-serif; font-size: 50px; } to change the default browser font with a different one.

Figure 9-3. *HTML output with CSS applied*

Writing unrealistic CSS is an effective way to easily see if everything works and that your setup correctly applied the CSS file. A favorite trick of mine is to say `body {` `background-color; red; }`, which looks horrible in any browser on any platform.

Instant Reloading

One issue with this setup is that you must restart and recompile your web app every time you make changes to your CSS file.

That's because the Java runtime loads the files from the class path. And it's not actually the folder *src/main/resources* that's on the class path when your web app is running locally. As a part of the compile step, Gradle moves everything that's on the class path into the *build/* folder, where all the compiled output lives. Gradle doesn't compile the files in *src/main/resources*, but it does copy them to *build/resources/main*. It's those files that your web app is loading.

This is fine in a production environment and is in fact the preferred approach. But it's not really suited for a development environment.

To fix this, you'll do two things: add a config property for toggling class path loading vs. file system loading and set up Ktor so it loads from *src/main/resources* when configured to do so.

You've added config properties before, so I'll only summarize it here: In *app.conf*, add `useFileSystemAssets = false`. You want this to be off by default, so you don't accidentally break your production setup later. In *app-local.conf*, enable file system loading by setting `useFileSystemAssets = true`. Then, update the `WebappConfig` data class with a new property, `val useFileSystemAssets: Boolean`. Finally, update `createAppConfig` to set `useFileSystemAssets` to the value of `it.getBoolean("useFileS` `ystemAssets")`.

Next, you'll need to update the `static` route you added to Ktor in Listing 9-3. You also need to update `createKtorApplication` to receive your app config. Listing 9-5 shows how to extend it to load files from the file system when configured and otherwise load them from the class path like it does now.

Listing 9-5. Receive app config in `createKtorApplication`, and load assets directly from the file system when running your web app locally

```
fun Application.createKtorApplication(
  appConfig: WebappConfig,
  dataSource: DataSource
) {
  // ...

  routing {
    static("/") {
      if (appConfig.useFileSystemAssets) {
        files("src/main/resources/public")
      } else {
        resources("public")
      }
    }
  }
```

This way, Ktor will load your static files directly from your source code when you run your web app locally, instead of loading copies from the *build/* folder.

You could have named this config property something generic, like `isDevMode`, and used the concept of "dev mode" to determine what to do. But in my experience, more specific config properties are better than general and reusable ones. If you use the same config property for multiple different things, you lose the ability to have granular control of your web app in different environments. Additionally, you'd have to grep your entire code base for `isDevMode` to figure out what it does, whereas `useFileSystemAssets` is more descriptive.

Reusable Layouts

In most web apps, you're going to need a layout that's shared across multiple routes. A layout adds shared defaults, such as which stylesheet to load on all pages, which meta tags to set, a header and a footer, and so on.

Instead of copy-pasting the same HTML DSL code, you can create a reusable layout that you can programmatically reuse in multiple web handlers.

You'll also set it up so that it's completely optional to use the layout in case you have routes in your web app where you need full control of the output, without forcing a layout on it.

Adding a Layout

The Ktor HTML DSL has built-in support for layouts. The basic structure of a layout is to create a subclass of Template<HTML> and implement the required methods. Listing 9-6 shows an example of a basic, but still useful, template.

Listing 9-6. A basic Ktor HTML DSL template

```
class AppLayout(
  val pageTitle: String? = null
): Template<HTML> {
  val pageBody = Placeholder<BODY>()

  override fun HTML.apply() {
    val pageTitlePrefix = if (pageTitle == null) {
      ""
    } else {
      "${pageTitle} - "
    }

    head {
      title {
        +"${pageTitlePrefix}KotlinBook"
      }

      styleLink("/app.css")
    }

    body {
      insert(pageBody)
    }
  }
}
```

The template is just a normal Kotlin class. The class has a single constructor argument, pageTitle. It's just a normal class, so you can set it up to take as many constructor arguments as you need. You use pageTitle just like a normal property of a normal class, to insert a page title inside the head block. Plain Kotlin code sets it up to always contain the name of the app, "KotlinBook" and, if the pageTitle is set, prefix it so you get "My page title - KotlinBook". This shows another benefit of using the kotlinx.html DSL. You don't need a special templating language to add logic to your templates; it's all expressed as plain Kotlin code.

The class also sets up a pageBody property of the type Placeholder<BODY>. You can have as many of these placeholders as you like, as they too are plain properties of your template class, and you use them to insert kotlinx.html DSL code that you provide to the template when you invoke it. Since it's of the type BODY, you're allowed to call insert(pageBody) inside the body block, as the types all match up. And when you use the template, the type system knows that the placeholder can only use tags that are allowed by kotlinx.html inside BODY.

Using the Layout

To use this layout in a web handler, you can use call.respondHtmlTemplate. Listing 9-7 shows how to call your template correctly.

Listing 9-7. Loading a reusable template in a Ktor web handler

```
call.respondHtmlTemplate(AppLayout("Hello, world!")) {
  pageBody {
    h1 {
      +"Hello, World!"
    }
  }
}
```

The implicit this inside the lambda is the instance of your template. That's why you're allowed to call pageBody, as it's just a shortcut for this.pageBody. All the kotlinx. html DSL code inside the pageBody block is added to the corresponding location of your AppLayout template, just as you set it up in Listing 9-6.

Adding WebResponse for HTML

So far, you've worked with kotlinx.html using the Ktor APIs directly. But you also need to be able to write HTML when you use your webResponse and webResponseDb helpers.

Implementing HtmlWebResponse

webResponse and its namesakes are set up to handle any subclass of the WebResponse abstract class. To be able to handle kotlinx.html, you need to add a new subclass of WebResponse that holds the desired HTML output and add a mapping inside webResponse to write that HTML output to your Ktor web handlers (and, later in the book, other web frameworks and server environments). Listing 9-8 shows the first step, which is to implement this new data class.

Listing 9-8. An implementation of HTML responses in WebResponse

```
data class HtmlWebResponse(
  val body: Template<HTML>,
  override val statusCode: Int = 200,
  override val headers: Map<String, List<String>> = mapOf(),
) : WebResponse() {
  override fun copyResponse(
    statusCode: Int,
    headers: Map<String, List<String>>
  ) =
    copy(body, statusCode, headers)
}
```

There's not much going on here, as the purpose of WebResponse classes is to simply hold on to the data that represents your response.

The next step is to add mapping for this new type in your mapping code between Ktor and WebResponse. You'll need to update the webResponse function and add a separate case for the new HtmlWebResponse class. Listing 9-9 shows how to do that.

Listing 9-9. Implementing and mapping `HtmlWebResponse` to Ktor in `webResponse`

```
when (resp) {
  is TextWebResponse -> {
    ...
  }
  is JsonWebResponse -> {
    ...
  }
  is HtmlWebResponse -> {
    call.respondHtml(statusCode) {
      with(resp.body) { apply() }
    }
  }
}
```

You don't need to use `respondHtmlLayout` in this mapping, as you can still use layouts without any special mapping, as you'll see later in this chapter.

Extension Function Precedence

There's a little bit of Kotlin trickery needed to make the mapping between `HtmlWebResponse` and Ktor work, namely, the code `with(resp.body) { apply() }` in Listing 9-9.

The problem is shadowing, which means that two different things have the same name. `resp.body` is of the type `Template<HTML>`. That class has a method declared on it, named `apply`. But Kotlin *also* has a built-in function called `apply`, which is part of the scope function suite, with `let`, `also`, etc. So you need to ensure that you're calling the correct one.

If you wrote `resp.body.apply()`, you'd get a compile error. That's because the Kotlin compiler thinks you're attempting to call the built-in scope function `apply`. That scope function takes a lambda as a required argument, which you're not passing, which causes the compile error.

with is another built-in scope function, and it's used to solve this problem. with takes an object and calls the lambda with that object as the default receiver. In blocks with a default receiver, that receiver and its methods take precedence. So the apply inside the with block targets the apply method on Template<HTML>.

This is a little tricky, but the example in Listing 9-10 shows a small demonstration of this precedence rule in isolation, which might help you better understand what's going on.

Listing 9-10. Demonstrating extension function precedence

```
class MyThing {
  fun String.testMe() {
    println("MyThing testMe")
  }
}

fun String.testMe() {
  println("Top level testMe")
}

"Hello!".testMe()
// Top level testMe

with(MyThing()) { "Hello!".testMe() }
// MyThing testMe
```

If you want to read about this in full detail, the Kotlin specification includes complete definitions of all the behavior of the Kotlin compiler: *https://kotlinlang.org/spec/ kotlin-spec.html*.

Responding with **HtmlWebResponse**

To respond with HTML from a webResponse handler, all you need to do is to return a HtmlWebResponse instance in your web handler.

You don't have the call.respondHtmlTemplate helper available in webResponse, but you can use a layout fine without it, by calling apply on the template and using the already familiar template placeholders inside the apply block. Listing 9-11 demonstrates how to do this.

Listing 9-11. A `HtmlWebResponse` with a layout

```
get("/html_webresponse_test", webResponse {
  HtmlWebResponse(AppLayout("Hello, world!").apply {
    pageBody {
      h1 {
        +"Hello, readers!"
      }
    }
  })
})
```

Responding without a layout is a little tricker, because the `HtmlWebResponse` class expects a full instance of `Template<HTML>`. You can use Kotlin's *object expressions* to create on the fly implementations of classes, denoted by the object keyword. Listing 9-12 shows how to do this.

Listing 9-12. A `HtmlWebResponse` without a layout

```
get("/html_webresponse_test", webResponse {
  HtmlWebResponse(object : Template<HTML> {
    override fun HTML.apply() {
      head {
        title { + "Plain HTML here! "}
      }

      body {
        h1 { +"Very plan header" }
      }
    }
  })
})
```

This creates an inline template that's only used once, which practically becomes the equivalent of using no template for that web handler.

A Note on Abstractions

A small but important detail in this setup, which you might not have noticed, is how unintrusive the webResponse abstraction is. Earlier in this chapter, you wrote plain Ktor web handlers, using the Ktor call API, without any interference from the webResponse helper functions and data classes. By not being too smart about it, and by having to explicitly "opt in" to the webResponse API by calling methods on it, you don't have to find or invent escape hatches to avoid using your own abstraction in certain cases – you just don't use them, and that's all there is to it.

User Security

To enable users to log in, you'll build a system for authenticating your users with a username and a password and replace the current hard-coded system from Chapter 5, where the password is stored as plain text.

Password Hashing

Currently, you have a table user_t with a password_hash column. You also have a function createUser that writes to the user_t table and stores the provided password as plain text (by converting it to UTF-8 encoded bytes).

Storing passwords as plain text is a big no-no, and you only did that earlier for brevity and because you didn't use the password for anything. You should always one-way hash your passwords. You shouldn't even encrypt the passwords. Encrypting means you also can decrypt, and you should never need to decrypt passwords.

How do you log in users if you can't decrypt their passwords? That's solved with password hashing. Hashing is a one-way algorithm that will always produce the same output given the same input, but the output has no correlation with the provided input and can't be used to determine what the original input was. SHA256 and MD5 are examples of hashing algorithms. The procedure is as follows:

- When you create a user, one-way hash the password, and store that hash.

- When you want to authenticate a user, one-way hash the password input, and compare that with the hash in the database.

That way, you have absolutely no way of knowing what user passwords are, but you have everything you need when you'll verify password inputs later.

Using Bcrypt for Hashing

You'll need a password hashing algorithm, and in this book, you'll use bcrypt. I've used bcrypt in multiple projects, and it's an algorithm that's widely available, with libraries for all platforms and languages. Bcrypt also has built-in password salting, which in short means that if two users have the same password, they won't get the same hash, by adding an un-hashed random blob to the hashing process.

You'll need a bcrypt library, and the one I've used multiple times in production is one simply named "bcrypt" by Patrick Favre-Bulle (*https://github.com/patrickfav/ bcrypt*). Add it as a dependency to your *build.gradle.kts*:

```
implementation("at.favre.lib:bcrypt:0.9.0")
```

The first step is to write a failing test for storing and verifying user passwords. Listing 9-13 shows an example of what that test might look like.

Listing 9-13. Automated tests in **UserTests.kt** for storing and verifying passwords

```
@Test
fun testVerifyUserPassword() = testTx { dbSess ->
  val userId = createUser(
    dbSess,
    email = "a@b.com",
    name = "August Lilleaas",
    passwordText = "1234",
    tosAccepted = true
  )

  assertEquals(
    userId,
    authenticateUser(dbSess, "a@b.com", "1234")
  )
  assertEquals(
    null,
    authenticateUser(dbSess, "a@b.com", "incorrect")
  )
```

```kotlin
    assertEquals(
      null,
      authenticateUser(dbSess, "does@not.exist", "1234")
    )
}

@Test
fun testUserPasswordSalting() = testTx { dbSess ->
  val userAId = createUser(
    dbSess,
    email = "a@b.com",
    name = "A",
    passwordText = "1234",
    tosAccepted = true
  )

  val userBId = createUser(
    dbSess,
    email = "x@b.com",
    name = "X",
    passwordText = "1234",
    tosAccepted = true
  )

  val userAHash = dbSess.single(
    queryOf("SELECT * FROM user_t WHERE id = ?", userAId),
    ::mapFromRow
  )!![ "password_hash"] as ByteArray
  val userBHash = dbSess.single(
    queryOf("SELECT * FROM user_t WHERE id = ?", userBId),
    ::mapFromRow
  )!![ "password_hash"] as ByteArray

  assertFalse(Arrays.equals(userAHash, userBHash))
}
```

The first test, `testVerifyUserPassword`, checks that you can get the user ID for a user by providing the correct email and password combination. It also checks that if you pass the incorrect password or a user that doesn't exist, `authenticateUser` returns `null`.

The second test, `testUserPasswordSalting`, creates two users with the same password and queries the database to check that the raw stored data has different contents in the `password_hash` column. This test verifies two important things: that you've hashed and salted the password and not stored it as plain text and that salting was set up correctly, so that it's impossible to determine if two users have the same password by looking at the raw data.

The next step is to implement the new `authenticateUser` function and implement the hashing in `createUser`. Listing 9-14 shows the first step, which is to implement `authenticateUser` and create the necessary instances of bcrypt objects for both verifying and hashing.

Listing 9-14. Implementation of `authenticateUser`

```
val bcryptHasher = BCrypt.withDefaults()
val bcryptVerifier = BCrypt.verifyer()

fun authenticateUser(
  dbSession: Session,
  email: String,
  passwordText: String
): Long? {
  return dbSession.single(
    queryOf("SELECT * FROM user_t WHERE email = ?", email),
    ::mapFromRow
  )?.let {
    val pwHash = it["password_hash"] as ByteArray

    if (bcryptVerifier.verify(
        passwordText.toByteArray(Charsets.UTF_8),
        pwHash
      ).verified)
    {
      return it["id"] as Long
    } else {
```

```
        return null
    }
  }
}
```

This function fetches the user row based on the provided email. If no such user exists in the database, the optionally chained `let` extension function causes the whole function to return `null`. Then, you use the bcrypt library to verify that the hash stored in the database is the same as the one provided in `passwordText`. If it is, you get the ID of the matching user. If not, you get `null`.

You also need to update `createUser` so it hashes the password with bcrypt before storing it in the database. Replace the current `passwordText.toByteArray(Charsets. UTF_8)` with the code in Listing 9-15.

Listing 9-15. The code to hash a password string with bcrypt

```
bcryptHasher.hash(
  10,
  passwordText.toByteArray(Charsets.UTF_8)
)
```

The first argument, the number 10, is the *difficulty factor* in bcrypt. This number decides how much computing power you'll need to perform the hashing. Too low, and the password is easy to crack. Too high, and your servers will spend multiple seconds verifying the password, at 100% CPU capacity. I've used 10 for many years, and that's worked fine for me. But ask your local cryptography and security expert before you commit to a number, and don't take my word for it.

Run your tests, and everything should pass. You now have real passwords for your users that are stored securely!

Updating Your Migrations

Your web app has a repeatable migration that upserts a user row, in *src/main/resources/ db/migration/R__insert_user.sql*. This migration writes a hard-coded password text that bcrypt won't be able to decrypt. So you need to update the migration to insert a real password, to be able to authenticate the user you create in the migration.

I could have included a full 120-character encrypted version of the password 1234 here that you could have manually typed in from the book and into your migration file. But you wouldn't be able to type all those characters correctly the first handful of times you tried. Instead, you'll write some code to generate that string, so you can paste it into the repeatable migration instead.

The column `password_hash` is a BYTEA column, so it expects raw bytes. The easiest way to put this in a SQL statement that works for SQLite is to use a HEX-encoded string and escape it with `x''`. For example, `x'2e744c21'` is how you would encode a 4-byte hex-encoded sequence. Listing 9-16 shows how to generate a HEX string for any password, leaning on the `bcryptHasher` from Listing 9-14.

Listing 9-16. A utility function for generating hex-encoded bcrypt encrypted passwords

```
hex(
  bcryptHasher.hash(
    12,
    "1234".toByteArray(Charsets.UTF_8)
  )
)
```

This statement will yield a string in the correct format that you can copy/paste into the repeatable migration using the format `x'<hex string here>'`.

Adding a Login Form

For HTML-based web apps, it's common to log in using a `<form>` tag that posts the username and password to the back end, which in turn sets a cookie or shows an error, based on whether it accepted the credentials. Ktor has all the facilities you need to make that work.

Wiring Up Your Web App

You need a few things in place to prepare your web app for authenticating users via login forms.

The first is to install the two plugins needed for handling user authentication to your *build.gradle.kts*:

```
implementation("io.ktor:ktor-server-auth:2.1.2")
implementation("io.ktor:ktor-server-sessions:2.1.2")
```

These plugins handle the session storage that your web app uses to access information about the currently logged-in user and the ability to compartmentalize routes in your web app to only be accessible to logged-in users.

Next, you need to update your config files. You'll add three different properties: useSecureCookie (Boolean) will toggle whether your session cookie will only work over HTTPS. cookieEncryptionKey and cookieSigningKey (String) will set up the session cookie so that it's encrypted, which blocks hackers from forging a fake cookie. Listing 9-17 shows what you need to add to your config files.

Listing 9-17. The default values of the various config files for the new config properties

```
// app.conf
useSecureCookie = true
cookieEncryptionKey = ""
cookieSigningKey = ""

// app-local.conf
useSecureCookie = false
cookieEncryptionKey = "<ADD LATER>"
cookieSigningKey = "<ADD LATER>"
```

Also remember to add these properties to your WebappConfig data class, by adding properties to the data class itself with the same name as the properties you added to your config file, and update createAppConfig to load in these values.

By default, your web app is set up to use secure cookies, which means that cookies will only be accessible over HTTPS and not HTTP. However, your local development environment runs your app over HTTP, so you need to disable secure cookies there.

You'll need actual random keys for cookieEncryptionKey and cookieSigningKey. To generate these keys, you can use the following utility function:

```
fun getRandomBytesHex(length: Int) =
  ByteArray(length)
    .also { SecureRandom().nextBytes(it) }
    .let(::hex)
```

You can call this function by temporarily adding calls to it in your main() function and print or log the output to the console. Run this function with getRandomBytes(16) for the cookieEncryptionKey and getRandomBytes(32) for the cookieSigningKey. Paste the output of those calls into *app-local.conf*.

It's important for these values to be consistent every time you restart your web app, which is why they're stored in the config file. If these keys change, all currently logged-in users with cookies stored in their browsers will have to log in again, as your web app won't be able to decrypt and verify the cookies with changed keys.

Just like your database password, you should keep the actual values you use in your production environment secret and not check them into version control. So, in production, your config file is set up to load these values from environment variables.

Different Types of Sessions

The session is the place that stores information about the currently logged-in user. Having access to this information is vital to make web app authentication work. You'll use the session as parameters to database queries, to check if the incoming request has a logged-in user attached to it in the first place and so on.

You have two main options for session storage: cookie-based storage and server-side storage.

Technically speaking, you'll always use a cookie. When users log in, you'll set a cookie that you'll use to verify that the user is indeed logged in. The cookie will contain the ID of the logged-in user. You'll also cryptographically sign the cookie, so that attackers can't just forge it by setting its contents to arbitrary values.

You can use this cookie to store additional state that you need about the currently logged-in user. But cookies have a hard limit on size, 4 kilobytes, enforced by all browsers. If you try to set a cookie that exceeds this limit, the browser will ignore it, causing bugs and unexpected behavior.

To remedy this, you can set up server-side session storage. There are many session storage types available. You should always avoid storing it in RAM, as that will break the moment you have more than one server running at the same time.

You could store session data in a distributed cache or in the database. But all production-grade web apps I've ever worked with have used cookie-based session storage, with no server-side session storage at all. If you need to store extra info about the currently logged-in user somewhere, I recommend storing it in whatever mechanisms you have available for caching arbitrary values elsewhere in your web app or setting up a cache if you don't have one. It's not necessary to have a specific cache only for storing info about a logged-in user. For example, if you have a distributed cache like Memcached (*https://memcached.org/*) or Redis (*https://redis.io/*) set up, you can store info about the current session there and retrieve it just like you would retrieve any other piece of cached information.

Adding a New Ktor Extension Function

To separate your authentication setup from the rest of your routes, you'll create a new extension function on `Application`, instead of putting it in your existing `createKtorApplication`.

For example, later in this chapter, you'll set up authentication using Spring Security (*https://spring.io/projects/spring-security*). By separating your main web app from your authentication configuration, you'll be able to have both setups running concurrently.

Above or below your existing function `createKtorApplication`, you'll create a new function, called `setUpKtorCookieSecurity`. Listing 9-18 shows what that function should look like.

Listing 9-18. The empty skeleton function `setUpKtorCookieSecurity`, where your security config will reside

```
fun Application.setUpKtorCookieSecurity(
  appConfig: WebappConfig,
  dataSource: DataSource
) {

}
```

Later in this chapter, you'll fill this function with your authentication setup.

To make your Ktor web app use this security setup, remember to invoke it in your call to embeddedServer where you already have your existing call to createKtorApplication. Listing 9-19 shows how to call it properly.

Listing 9-19. Adding a call to your new security setup function in embeddedServer

```
embeddedServer(Netty, port = config.httpPort) {
  setUpKtorCookieSecurity(config, dataSource)
  createKtorApplication(config, dataSource)
}.start(wait = true)
```

Configuring Session Cookies

The next step is to set up Ktor with cookie-based sessions. You already have the dependencies and configuration properties needed to make this work.

The Sessions plugin is at the core of the setup. You'll set up this plugin just like you've already set up the StatusPages plugin, except you'll add it to your new setUpKtorCookieSecurity function. Listing 9-20 shows how to do this.

Listing 9-20. Adding setup for cookie-based sessions to setUpKtorCookieSecurity

```
data class UserSession(val userId: Long): Principal

fun Application.setUpKtorCookieSecurity (
  appConfig: WebappConfig,
  dataSource: DataSource
) {
  install(Sessions) {
    cookie<UserSession>("user-session") {
      transform(
        SessionTransportTransformerEncrypt(
          hex(appConfig.cookieEncryptionKey),
          hex(appConfig.cookieSigningKey)
        )
      )
```

187

```
        cookie.maxAge = Duration.parse("30d")
        cookie.httpOnly = true
        cookie.path = "/"
        cookie.secure = appConfig.useSecureCookie
        cookie.extensions["SameSite"] = "lax"
      }
   }
}
```

This code configures several important aspects of cookie-based session storage.

The UserSession data class holds the data that the session cookie will contain. You can put as much data as you want here – but don't go too far. Remember, the browser limits the cookie output to 4 kilobytes.

The transform function sets up the encryption of the actual cookie. Without this step, the cookie would store the session information as plain text. This means that anyone could set the session cookie to anything, meaning an attacker could set the user ID of the cookie to any ID they want, effectively giving anyone the ability to log in to your web app as any user they could guess the ID for. With the transform, however, the cookie is both signed and encrypted. The signature means that any change to its contents would break the signature. Encrypted means that any secrets you store in the cookie are not visible to hackers – Ktor encrypts the actual contents of the cookie using the key you supplied.

The various cookie flags you set are also important.

You're free to set maxAge to whatever you want. The effect of maxAge is that the cookie will expire after the given amount of time, causing your users to have to log in again.

The path must also be set to /, so that the cookie applies to all pages of your web app. If you don't set it, the cookie will only apply to the path you're on when your web app sets the cookie.

secure means that the cookie will only work on HTTPS, so that the cookie is safe from man-in-the-middle attacks. You use the config flag you created in Listing 9-17 so that the cookie is secure by default, but not when developing locally, where you run your web app over HTTP, not HTTPS.

Finally, SameSite is set to lax to protect your cookie from cross-origin attacks. The browser will only send the cookie for requests that originate from your own web app. If an attacker tries to post a form from another web page to your web app, the browser will not transmit the cookie with the request.

Logging In

With authentication and session storage set up, you're ready to add the login form itself.

Your login form will be on a separate route, /login. It won't be looking pretty and stylish, but it will work. I'll leave the prettifying up to you. Listing 9-21 shows the code for the login page.

Listing 9-21. The route handler for the login form

```
get("/login", webResponse {
  HtmlWebResponse(AppLayout("Log in").apply {
    pageBody {
      form(method = FormMethod.post, action = "/login") {
        p {
          label { +"E-mail" }
          input(type = InputType.text, name = "username")
        }

        p {
          label { +"Password" }
          input(type = InputType.password, name = "password")
        }

        button(type = ButtonType.submit) { +"Log in" }
      }
    }
  })
})
```

This login form is a straightforward HTML form that will post the username and the password to another route. They'll both have the path /login, but a different verb. GET /login will display the login form, and POST /login will perform the actual login and set of the session.

The next step is to implement the POST /login request to perform the login when a user submits the form. Listing 9-22 shows the code for the login handler.

Listing 9-22. The route handler inside `setUpKtorCookieSecurity` for handling the submitted login form

```
post("/login") {
  sessionOf(dataSource).use { dbSess ->
    val params = call.receiveParameters()
    val userId = authenticateUser(
      dbSess,
      params["username"]!!,
      params["password"]!!
    )

    if (userId == null) {
      call.respondRedirect("/login")
    } else {
      call.sessions.set(UserSession(userId = userId))
      call.respondRedirect("/secret")
    }
  }
}
```

Remember to add this routing handler to `setUpKtorCookieSecurtity` and not `createKtorApplication`.

I prefer to store only the ID of the user in the session cookie. You could also store the email there. But if the user changes their email, you'll display the old, cached email in the session cookie, until the user logs out and in again.

Note that you're not wrapping this route handler in `webResponse` or any of its variants. You haven't implemented a `WebResponse` data class for performing redirects. And you don't really need to. It's easy enough to just start a Kotliquery session by hand from any Ktor handler and use the Ktor API to do the redirect itself. The handling of session-related code is very Ktor specific anyway, so there's no real use case for disassociating it from Ktor.

For reading the submitted form data, you'll use `call.receiveParameters()`. This causes Ktor to load and parse the request body and makes the form data available to you as a `Map` structure. You already have an `authenticateUser` function, so you call that function with the provided parameters. The type system does not know which parameters it receives when your web app runs, so the types of the username and password parameters are String?. You're casting it to String by using the double exclamation mark (!!) non-null assertion operator. If they are null, your code will throw an exception. That's fine in this case, as browsers will always pass them as strings as the user submits the form on GET /login. So you'll only get an exception if someone manually tries to call POST /login with invalid parameters.

If you find a user that matches the username and password from the form, you'll set the session cookie using call.sessions and redirect to the page where you want your users to see after they log in. This causes Ktor to set a Set-Cookie header, with the contents of your cookie encrypted and signed and with the flags you configured in Listing 9-20.

If you don't find a user, you redirect the user back to the GET /login page (redirects are always GET requests), and the user can try to log in again.

Protecting Routes with Authentication

When a user successfully logs in, your code redirects them to /secret. Next, you'll implement that route and set it up so that it's only accessible for users who have logged in.

The first step is to set up the Authentication plugin. You'll set it up just like you've set up Sessions and StatusPages before. Listing 9-23 shows what you need to invoke to set it up correctly.

Listing 9-23. Adding setup for authentication to setUpKtorCookieSecurity

```
install(Authentication) {
  session<UserSession>("auth-session") {
    validate { session ->
      session
    }
    challenge {
      call.respondRedirect("/login")
    }
  }
}
```

The `validate` block adds an opportunity to invalidate sessions. For now, you don't need to do any invalidation here. This is a good place to check that the user still exists in your database, that you haven't disabled the user by flagging it in your database, and other checks. Ktor performs the validation on every request to your web app that requires authentication. (You'll add authentication to routes later in this chapter.)

Ktor calls the `challenge` block when an unauthenticated user tries to access a protected route. When that happens, you'll redirect to the `/login` page. You're free to do whatever you want here with the Ktor `call` API, though, such as rendering an error message.

To make specific routes available to logged-in users only, you'll wrap them in the `authenticate` interceptor that you get from the Ktor authentication plugin. Listing 9-24 shows how to protect specific routes.

Listing 9-24. Wrapping a route in `setUpKtorCookieSecurity` to only be accessible after users have logged in

```
authenticate("auth-session") {
  get("/secret", webResponseDb(dataSource) { dbSess ->
    val userSession = call.principal<UserSession>()!!
    val user = getUser(dbSess, userSession.userId)!!

    HtmlWebResponse(
      AppLayout("Welcome, ${user.email}").apply {
        pageBody {
          h1 {
            +"Hello there, ${user.email}"
          }

          p { +"You're logged in." }
          p {
            a(href = "/logout") { +"Log out" }
          }
        }
      }
    )
  })
}
```

The function getUser is from Listing 7-9, back in Chapter 7 about writing tests.

The name "auth-session" is from Listing 9-23, where you configured the session and named it "auth-session". Ktor supports multiple session regimes operating concurrently in your web app, identified by their names.

All the routes that you wrap in authenticate("auth-session") will redirect to the /login page if the user has not logged in, as per the setup of the "auth-session" in Listing 9-23.

The protected route /secret uses call.principal<UserSession>()!! to retrieve the session that represents the currently logged-in user. This function returns the data that you stored in the session cookie earlier. Ktor automatically decodes and encodes to and from the UserSession data class.

The Kotlin type system does not know that the session is always present in an authenticated route, though. The principal function is available on all call instances, even routes that aren't in the authenticate interceptor. But since you know it will always be there for authenticated routes, it's fine to use the double exclamation marks to cast it to a non-null type.

The session cookie contains the user ID, via the UserSession data class. So you'll use that ID to fetch the actual user from the database. You use the user row from the database to display the email of the logged-in user. Figure 9-4 shows how this page looks in a browser.

Hello there, august@crud.business

You're logged in.

Log out

Figure 9-4. *Your web app when a user has logged in*

To see this for yourself, open *http://localhost:4207/secret* in your browser. That should redirect you to the login page, where you can log in with the credentials for the user you created in your repeatable migration. After login, you're redirected back to / secret again.

Logging Out

The /secret route has a link to a route you haven't implemented yet, /logout. You'll implement this route next, so that users can log out of your web app.

A route for logging out should not do much other than performing the logout and redirecting the user to a page that's accessible for users who haven't logged in. In this example, you'll redirect the user back to the /login page. Listing 9-25 shows how to implement that route.

Listing 9-25. Adding a route in `setUpKtorCookieSecurity` for logging out a user

```
authenticate("auth-session") {
  get("/logout") {
    call.sessions.clear<UserSession>()
    call.respondRedirect("/login")
  }

  // ...
```

As you can see from the code, you've wrapped the logout page in the `authenticate` interceptor. That's not important for security, but it doesn't really make sense to have the logout page available for users who haven't logged in.

The handler itself clears the session cookie and redirects back to the login page. Note that it's not actually possible to unset a cookie. The only way to set a cookie is to use the `Set-Cookie` header and set it to something. So Ktor and the session plugin set the cookie to `""` (an empty string). That causes subsequent requests that hit the `authenticate` interceptor to treat the request as non-authenticated.

CHAPTER 10

Building API-Based Back Ends

In the modern world of web apps, it's common to have back ends that are completely API based and have either a mobile app or a JavaScript-based web front end that interacts with them. In this chapter, you'll learn how to set up an API for those scenarios.

If you're new to Kotlin, here are some language features that you'll see examples of in this chapter:

- Parsing and producing JSON with third-party libraries

Also in this chapter, you will learn the following about building API-based back ends:

- Different types of authentication

- How to securely set cookies for browsers

- Building APIs for single-page web apps and native apps

Handling API Calls

An API call is just a normal route, like any other route. All the routes you've made so far that use `JsonWebResponse` are API routes, as they return machine-readable data.

In this section, you'll learn some details about best practices for making an API.

Parsing Input

Most web apps receive inputs in some way or another, so you'll need to know how to read data that external parties post to your web handlers.

© August Lilleaas 2023
A. Lilleaas, *Pro Kotlin Web Apps from Scratch*, https://doi.org/10.1007/978-1-4842-9057-6_10

You've already read form-encoded data in Chapter 9, where you received form parameters for the username and password for the form-based login in your HTML-based web app setup. To do that, you used `call.receiveParameters()`, which parses the HTTP request body with the form data encoding browsers use for HTML forms.

To read JSON, all you must do is to read the HTTP request body as a plain string and parse it using the Gson library (*https://github.com/google/gson*) you've already installed in Chapter 4 for writing JSON output via `JsonWebResponse`. The only extra step you need to take for reading JSON compared with writing it is to specify the class that Gson should serialize your data to – `Map` or `List`. Listing 10-1 shows an example of how to read JSON in your web handlers.

Listing 10-1. Parsing JSON in your web handlers

```
post("/test_json", webResponse {
  val input = Gson().fromJson(
    call.receiveText(), Map::class.java
  )

  JsonWebResponse(mapOf(
    "input" to input
  ))
})
```

All this web handler does is to parse the received JSON and return a response that re-encodes the parsed JSON back to JSON.

The Ktor function `call.receiveText()` will handle encoding automatically and parse the bytes submitted over HTTP to a string using either the encoding specified in the HTTP headers of that request or the system-default encoding if the request didn't specify one.

Validating and Extracting Input

To make the input you receive from your web handlers useful, you need to extract the content of the data you've received and ensure that it has the correct format for the business logic in your web app.

You don't just want to validate that the types are correct. Programming language data types are too general to be useful. For example, you should validate that an email address that someone posts to your API is something that looks like an email address. Just checking that it's of the type String is not sufficient.

The library I prefer to use for data validation is Arrow. In Chapter 8, you installed Arrow (*https://arrow-kt.io/*), to demonstrate the difference between kotlin. coroutines and kotlinx.coroutines. And the example used was data validation. So let's build on the small examples demonstrated there and use that to build actual data validation in a web handler.

Arrow has the benefit of giving you full flexibility of the shape of the data that you're validating. Arrow lets you start with a map and end with either a validation error or an initialized data class, whereas most other Kotlin data validation libraries are tightly coupled with data classes, forcing you to instantiate a data class first and then validate it later.

In Listing 8-10, you created a ValidationError data class, two functions to perform validations (validateEmail and validatePassword), as well as a data class (MyUser) to hold the final validated value. Listing 10-2 shows how to wire those functions up for data validation inside a web handler.

Listing 10-2. Validating JSON input with Arrow

```
post("/test_json", webResponse {
  either<ValidationError,MyUser> {
    val input = Gson().fromJson(
      call.receiveText(), Map::class.java
    )
    MyUser(
      email = validateEmail(input["email"]).bind(),
      password = validatePassword(input["password"]).bind()
    )
  }.fold(
    { err ->
      JsonWebResponse(
        mapOf("error" to err.error),
        statusCode = 422
      )
    },
```

```
    { user ->
      // .. do something with `user`
      JsonWebResponse(mapOf("success" to true))
    }
  )
})
```

The use of Arrow in this code makes it look straightforward and natural, but at the same time, Arrow's use of `kotlin.coroutines` makes it quite clever. `Either` and `bind` are both *left biased*, so as soon as a bound statement returns the left side of the `Either` (i.e., a `ValidationError`), the execution of the code inside the `either` block stops at that point, and that left side is the "winner." If all the bound `Either` statements return the right side, that value is simply returned as the result of those statements, and the right side with `MyUser` is the "winner."

`fold` is a function on `Either` that calls either a left or a right lambda, depending on what the result of the `Either` was. `fold` is also a function that's tagged with `inline`. If you're used to callbacks in a language like JavaScript or even Java, the code might look like it just calls one of the two lambdas passed to fold, without returning anything. But because fold is inline, you can think of the contents of the lambdas as if you wrote them at the top level, outside of the fold function, and therefore the return values from the lambdas in `fold` are what's returned from the entire statement.

So, in short, this code either returns the error `JsonWebResponse` or the successful `JsonWebResponse`, based on whether any of the validations inside the either block returned a `ValidationError`.

Avoid Automatic Serialization

When building web apps, you should always be explicit about serialization and avoid automatic serialization from dynamic data formats like XML and JSON to type-safe data classes.

Kotlin has plenty of libraries for converting dynamic data formats like XML and JSON to typed data classes automatically. Ending up with type-safe data classes is a good thing. But automatically converting dynamic data to a type-safe data class is problematic.

An example of automatic data serialization is `kotlinx.serialization` (*https://github.com/Kotlin/kotlinx.serialization*). There's no problem with the library itself; it's a well-made library that does exactly what it's supposed to. The essence of kotlinx.serialization is that you make data classes and annotate them with kotlinx.serialization.Serializable. These data classes can transform to and from various data formats. Listing 10-3 shows how you can serialize to and from JSON, via a type-safe data class.

Listing 10-3. Demonstrating kotlinx.serialization basics

```kotlin
@Serializable
data class MyThing(val myVal: String, val foo: Int)

val obj = Json.decodeFromString<MyThing>(
  """{"myVal":"testing", "foo": 123}"""
)

obj.myVal
// "testing"

Json.encodeToString(obj)
// Returns {"myVal":"testing", "foo": 123}
```

Using kotlinx.serialization saves you from a lot of manual typing, as all you need to do is to combine a data class with a JSON string and have Kotlin do the rest of the work.

However, the major downside is that this tightly couples your public API to your internal code base. If you change the name MyThing.myVal in your own code, you also break callers to your own API.

Another downside is that your API entities are forced to follow Kotlin naming conventions. In JSON, it's common to use underscore_case and not camelCase for property names. But since you're doing a 1:1 serialization between dynamic data and typed Kotlin data classes, they must be the same.

Note that this is heavily in the camp of opinionated best practice, and there are plenty of smart and productive developers who will disagree with this proposition. But I consistently make this distinction in all my production-grade web apps, to maintain flexibility and agility in my own code while at the same time allowing stability and backward compatibility for external callers of the API.

Internal vs. External APIs

What you've learned in this section is mostly applicable for internal APIs. By that, I mean APIs that you consume with your own code or with code that's written by people whom you'll work closely with.

If you're writing a public-facing API, such as an API that's a part of a SaaS product, you should make sure that your API has stellar error messages and behaves perfectly with correct HTTP status codes, no matter what you throw at it. The current code will just throw a 5xx error (server error) if you post invalid JSON to it, for example, whereas technically the correct status code would be in the 4xx series (client error).

The techniques in this chapter are not sufficient for that level of detail. There are two reasons I'm not teaching you how to do it "properly" for large-scale public APIs.

The first is that it's costly. When you and people you work with are the only consumers of your API, you'll get far with a README file that explains the basics and an API that yields useful error messages most of the time, but will occasionally throw a 500 error if someone posts sufficiently bad data to your API.

The second is that I've never actually made a public-facing API. I have lots of ideas on how to do it correctly. But since I don't have any real-world experience doing it, I don't think I'm the right person to teach you how to do it.

Single-Page Apps

A use case for APIs often seen in the wild is to target browsers and JavaScript-based *single-page apps* (SPAs).

Hosting Alongside API

One way to set up a single-page app is to host both the API and the front end from the same web app.

At the core of the SPA is an `index.html` file that loads your JavaScript code and other vital assets. In most modern single-page apps, your JavaScript is set up to use the `pushState` browser API as a part of its routing from various parts of your SPA. For example, the often-used routing library React Router for the React JavaScript framework operates in this manner. What this means is that when you first open the URL / (the root page), the back end serves the index.html file, which in turn loads your JavaScript, and the SPA router renders the correct content. Then, you click a button in your SPA, and JavaScript ends up invoking pushState so that the URL changes from / to /something_ else, and your JavaScript renders some different content appropriate for that URL.

The problem with this is when you share a link to that page or the user tries to refresh, the current URL in the browser is /something_else, and that's the route that your Ktor routing will try to load. So, if all you did was set up / to serve index.html, you'd now get a 404 page because your Ktor back end does not have a mapping for / something_else.

One solution would be to manually add all known routes in your SPA and copy them to your Ktor routing. That's not really a feasible option, though, as you'd end up with lots of manual and error-prone copy-pasting.

Another option is to use the special singlePageApplication route type in Ktor. singlePageApplication works just like static, except that it also sets up your routes so that any route that Ktor does not handle will render your index.html file. With this setup, refreshing the page directly on /something_else works, because you don't have a route handler in your Ktor web app for that path, which in turn causes the singlePageApplication route to trigger and load the index.html, causing your JavaScript to run and handle the rendering of the correct page. Listing 10-4 shows how to set it up.

Listing 10-4. Setting up singlePageApplication inside createKtorApplication to host a SPA from your web app

```
singlePageApplication {
  if (appConfig.useFileSystemAssets) {
    filesPath = "src/main/resources/public"
  } else {
    useResources = true
    filesPath = "public"
  }
  defaultPage = "index.html"
}
```

You should make sure to remove your existing static("/") route before you add the singlePageApplication("/") route. The old static("/") route conflicts with singlePageApplication("/"), which does everything your old static("/") route did anyway.

The config properties in `singlePageApplication` are the same as those you use in static. When running locally, you point to the files in the file system, whereas when running in production, you point to the assets that your Gradle build compiles into the Java class path of the compiled output.

The `defaultPage` points to the index.html file that bootstraps your SPA. This file should live in `src/main/resources/public/index.html`. Typically, this file only contains a bare-bones HTML file that loads the JavaScript that you use to load your SPA. The reason it's a HTML file, and not `kotlinx.html` DSL code, is that you'll likely use some kind of SPA build tool such as Webpack to build your SPA, which often generates its own HTML bootstrapping code that you must use. Additionally, the file should be completely static and not change contents based on which route you're looking at. So having it as a static file works fine.

Keep in mind that to avoid conflicts between web pages and your API handlers, all your API routes with `/api/....` So, instead of logging in with a request to `POST /login`, you should change that to `POST /api/login`. Then, make sure that your single-page app does not have any pages that start with `/api`. That way, you'll never have conflicting routes between your Ktor back end and your JavaScript router.

Hosting Separately with CORS

Another way to set up a single-page app is to host the JavaScript code and HTML bootstrapping on a separate domain name from the API and use XHR/fetch with CORS for cross-domain access between your single-page app and your API.

The actual static HTML and JavaScript files have the same structure as when you host them alongside your API with the `singlePageApplication` route. The difference is that you host them externally. So you can host your API on `api.myapp.com` and your SPA on `www.myapp.com`. You can then choose a hosting platform for your SPA that's more suited for serving raw static files, such as a CDN like AWS CloudFront, Cloudflare, Azure Static Web Apps, or anything you want.

CORS (short for Cross-Origin Resource Sharing) is an API that all modern browsers support, which allows your JavaScript code to call APIs on domain names other than its own. Traditionally, browsers have limited to HTTP calls to the domain that you're currently on, and you would get an error if you attempted to call a different domain (e.g., a cross-origin request). So, if you follow the preceding example, you'd get an error message if you tried to use JavaScript to call `api.myapp.com` when the browser is showing `www.myapp.com`.

When JavaScript performs a request to a different domain name, it first sends an OPTIONS request to that server. (OPTIONS is another HTTP verb, like GET, POST, PUT, etc.). If that OPTIONS request responds with the correct CORS headers, the browser will continue and perform the actual request that you initiated. If not, you'll get an error message.

You need to set up your Ktor API to handle these CORS requests. You could manually intercept the OPTIONS requests and respond with the correct headers. But the easier way to do it is to install the CORS plugin that does it for you.

The first step is to add the plugin as a dependency to your *build.gradle.kts*:

```
implementation("io.ktor:ktor-server-cors-jvm:2.1.2")
```

To make CORS work, you need to change a few things. In setUpKtorCookieSecurity, change the SameSite attribute of your session cookie from "lax" to "none". You'll run your web app across different origins now, so for the browser to correctly transfer your session cookie, you'll need to disable SameSite.

Next, you'll set up the CORS plugin itself. Add it to your createKtorApplication, alongside your StatusPages plugin. Listing 10-5 shows how to set it up correctly.

Listing 10-5. Adding CORS setup to your Ktor app

```
install(CORS) {
  allowMethod(HttpMethod.Put)
  allowMethod(HttpMethod.Delete)
  allowHost("localhost:4207")
  allowHost("www.myapp.com", schemes = listOf("https"))
  allowCredentials = true
}
```

The HTTP methods GET and POST are enabled by default. Most of my real-world web apps also use at least PUT and DELETE, so you should allow those as well. You also need to enable specific host names. CORS supports wildcard origins, but not when you want to include credentials (i.e., cookies). Finally, you need to enable credentials in the first place, by setting allowCredentials to true.

You also need to have a way to host your web app HTML locally. That's why you're adding localhost:4207 to the list of allowed origins, which means that you can use the singlePageApplication plugin in development and configure it to only load in the local environment and not in production. Alternatively, you can use something like create-react-app or set up Webpack yourself, to host an index.html file and build your JavaScript. If you use an external server like Webpack, update the port number to point to the port of your Webpack server. (The intricate details of building a SPA are outside of the scope of this chapter, so I'm deliberately skipping a lot of details on how to set it up.)

Authenticating Users

With this set up and ready to go, you can perform a request with your JavaScript to log in, and it will work fine even if your JavaScript runs on a different origin than your API.

You can use the existing POST /login handler from Chapter 9 to log in from your single-page app. That web handler expects form-encoded data, posted by a normal HTML <form>. But you can generate that same type of request from JavaScript as well. Listing 10-6 shows an example of how to do that.

Listing 10-6. Calling your API using JavaScript from a different origin

```
fetch("/login", {
  credentials: "include",
  method: "POST",
  headers: {
    "Content-Type": "application/x-www-form-urlencoded"
  },
  body: new URLSearchParams({
    username: ...,
    password: ...
  })
})
```

It's important to remember to set credentials: "include" when you call fetch. If you don't, it won't receive and send any cookies alongside your request.

Since the cookie is HTTP only, it's impossible to access it from JavaScript. That means that if you for some reason become the victim of a script injection attack, there's no way for the attacker to extract session keys, which is a big win for security.

If you're making a pure API without any HTML, you could also change POST /login to receive and parse JSON instead of data that's like what you'd get in a HTML <form> tag. If you do that, you should also change your API to return a 200 OK instead of a redirect upon successful login.

Native Apps

Non-web native apps, such as mobile apps and native desktop apps, can also call your API. This category also includes web-based wrappers, where a native app wraps web technologies, such as Electron. Even if those apps use web technologies, they don't have to succumb to the security sandbox of browsers and can perform network calls just like plain native apps.

Using Cookies for Authentication

The only thing you need to consider in native apps, compared with web-based SPAs, is authentication. There are two main ways to set up your API for authenticating users in non-browser-based apps. The first is to use cookies for authentication, just like you do for a HTML-based web app or a SPA like you did earlier in this chapter.

Most HTTP clients available to native apps will automatically handle cookies or can be set up to handle them. That means that the HTTP client will behave just like a browser and store any cookies that are set using the Set-Cookie header and send them back to the server in the requests you perform. This is an easy and convenient way to have the same API setup for both web-based apps and native apps.

Make sure that you don't enable CORS and don't use auth tokens for SPAs. For native apps, having exposed auth tokens does not matter. But for web apps, where cross-origin attacks are a common attack vector, it's important to hide the authentication credentials behind a cookie that is not accessible from the JavaScript runtime.

Using JWTs for Authentication

If you're making an API from scratch that's only meant for use by native clients, you can still use cookies. But it's more common to use token-based authentication for those cases. Particularly, JSON Web Tokens (JWTs) are the established way to set that up.

A JWT is a blob of data formatted to follow the open JWT standard (*https://jwt.io/*), which contains securely signed JSON-encoded authentication information. In addition to the cryptographic signature, a JWT includes metadata about which encryption algorithm the token uses and a block of JSON that contains arbitrary information about the logged-in user. The JSON data typically contains the property "sub" (short for subject), which contains the unique ID for the user the token represents. Typical properties are also "name" and "email", but what exactly you want your JWT to contain is up to you.

When you authenticate your user, you respond with data that contains the auth token itself. Then, in subsequent requests, you send this auth token back to the server using the Authorization header.

Ktor has built-in support for JWT authorization, so that's what you'll use to set it up in your web app. The first thing you need to do is to add the required dependency to *build.gradle.kts*:

```
implementation("io.ktor:ktor-server-auth-jwt-jvm:2.1.2")
```

The next step is to set up your JWT authentication. You'll do that in a new Ktor Application extension function, like your existing functions createKtorApplication and setUpKtorCookieSecurity. Listing 10-7 shows how to set that up.

Listing 10-7. Setting up JWT authentication

```
fun Application.setUpKtorJwtSecurity(
  appConfig: WebappConfig,
  dataSource: DataSource
) {
  val jwtAudience = "myApp"
  val jwtIssuer = "http://0.0.0.0:4207"

  authentication {
    jwt("jwt-auth") {
      realm = "myApp"
      verifier(JWT
        .require(Algorithm.HMAC256(appConfig.cookieSigningKey))
        .withAudience(jwtAudience)
        .withIssuer(jwtIssuer)
        .build())
      validate { credential ->
        if (credential.payload.audience.contains(jwtAudience))
          JWTPrincipal(credential.payload)
        else
          null
      }
    }
  }
}
```

To simplify the setup, you're reusing the config property cookieSigningKey for the JWT signing key. You can add a separate config property for the JWT only if you want.

The authentication process itself does not use the issuer and audience properties. They're only there for verification purposes, which can be useful if your API can accept JWTs from various sources or if you want to issue JWTs that you can use in different authentication scopes.

The next step is to add a web handler for performing the actual logging in and creation of new JWTs. Listing 10-8 shows how to set that up.

Listing 10-8. Performing a login inside the setUpKtorJwtSecurity configuration

```
routing {
  post("/login", webResponseDb(dataSource) { dbSess ->
    val input = Gson().fromJson(
      call.receiveText(), Map::class.java
    )
    val userId = authenticateUser(
      dbSess,
      input["username"] as String,
      input["password"] as String
    )

    if (userId == null) {
      JsonWebResponse(
        mapOf("error" to "Invalid username and/or password"),
        statusCode = 403
      )
    } else {
      val token = JWT.create()
        .withAudience(jwtAudience)
        .withIssuer(jwtIssuer)
        .withClaim("userId", userId)
        .withExpiresAt(
          Date.from(LocalDateTime
            .now()
            .plusDays(30)
```

```
            .toInstant(ZoneOffset.UTC)
        )
    )
    .sign(Algorithm.HMAC256(appConfig.cookieSigningKey))

    JsonWebResponse(mapOf("token" to token))
  }
})
}
```

This code is like the `<form>`-based login code from `setUpKtorCookieSecurity` in that it receives the username and password as parameters and either returns an error or valid authentication credentials, depending on the input parameters.

If the username and password are a match, you create a new JWT that's signed with the same signing key as your authorization setup from Listing 10-7 and add the ID of the signed-in user as a part of the token payload. Since you're using token-based authentication, you don't have to set a cookie or do anything special. All you need to do is to return the token as a part of the data in the HTTP response, in this case as a JSON-encoded map.

To secure routes behind authentication, the procedure is the same as with cookie-based auth. Listing 10-9 shows how to set that up.

Listing 10-9. Securing routes inside the `routing` block with JWT authentication

```
authenticate("jwt-auth") {
  get("/secret", webResponseDb(dataSource) { dbSess ->
    val userSession = call.principal<JWTPrincipal>()!!
    val userId = userSession.getClaim("userId", Long::class)!!
    val user = getUser(dbSess, userId)!!

    JsonWebResponse(mapOf("hello" to user.email))
  })
}
```

Instead of using the custom principal data class you set up for cookie-based auth, you use the built-in `JWTPrincipal` class that represents JWTs. This principal is set up to parse the correct headers automatically and decode the token.

The JWT contains the `userId` claim you specified when you created the token on `POST /login`.

This code has lots of potential for null pointer exceptions in it. There are three `!!` operators, which cause your code to throw a `NullPointerException` if the value is `null`. I prefer to keep the type system as clean as possible and be explicit about the types I require in my business logic and whether they're nullable. But for code at the edges of the system, where all sorts of weird things can happen based on user input, I don't mind using the `!!` operator to fail early and sanitize input. It's a cheap form of input validation, which generates bad error messages, but it is really easy to add and is much better than passing nullable types all over your code.

Performing Authentication

To demonstrate how you'll authenticate against this API, you'll use cURL in a terminal to perform API calls.

First, make sure your API is ready to go with JWT-based authentication. In `embeddedServer`, remove the existing call to `setUpKtorCookieSecurity`, and replace it with your new function from this chapter, `setUpKtorJwtSecurity`, and run your main function to start up your web app.

You'll get the JSON you generated in your code in Listing 10-8 in return. First, try to call `GET /secret` without an auth token, to see what happens:

```
$ curl -I http://localhost:4207/secret

HTTP/1.1 405 Method Not Allowed
```

To perform authentication, you'll call `POST /login` with the username and password from the user in your repeatable migration:

```
$ curl -X POST \
    -d '{"username":"august@crud.business","password":"1234"}' \
    http://localhost:4207/login

{"token":"<token here>"}
```

Next, perform a request to GET /secret and pass in the auth token you got, and you should get a successful result in return:

```
$ curl -H "Authorization: Bearer <token here>" \
    http://localhost:4207/secret
```

```
{"hello":"august@crud.business"}
```

If you did everything correctly, you got the email of the user that the JWT represents.

Note the format of the Authorization header. It starts with the text "Bearer", followed by the actual token. This is a part of the HTTP specification, as Authorization headers should first state the authentication method (in this case, a JWT bearer) and then the actual authorization parameters (the JWT itself). You won't be able to authenticate successfully without the "Bearer " prefix.

CHAPTER 11

Deploying to Traditional Server Based Environments

The most common way to deploy production-grade web apps today is in a traditional server-based environment. This chapter covers how to package your web app so you can deploy it in several types of environments, be it a single-node dedicated server or a distributed multi-server Kubernetes cluster.

Packaging as Self-Contained JAR Files

For any type of deployment setup, you'll need to package your web app as a self-contained *Java archive* (JAR) file.

What's a JAR File

A JAR file is a file in the Zip package format that contains your code, as well as some metadata that points to the class that contains your `main` function.

When you compile your web app, Gradle writes the compiled output to *build/classes/kotlin/main* and copies your resources to *build/resources/main*, as seen in Figure 11-1. The essence of a JAR file is to place the contents of those folders into a single Zip file – and that's about it.

© August Lilleaas 2023
A. Lilleaas, *Pro Kotlin Web Apps from Scratch*, https://doi.org/10.1007/978-1-4842-9057-6_11

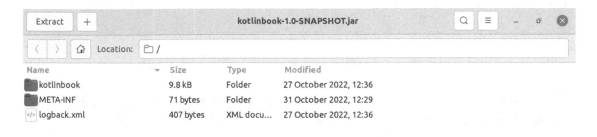

Figure 11-1. *The contents of a .jar file, opened as a normal Zip file by Archive Utility on Ubuntu Linux*

Additionally, the JAR file will contain the file *META-INF/MANIFEST.MF*, which is a text file that contains some metadata about the build and the line Main-Class, which points to the specific class that the Java runtime should load and invoke the `main` function on.

Self-Contained JAR Files

A self-contained JAR file is just like a normal JAR file, but that also includes your third-party dependencies, all in a single file.

To be able to run your web app, you need the third-party dependencies available. Third-party dependencies are also packaged as JAR files. When you run your web app locally, Gradle downloads and manages these JAR files and makes them available on the class path of the Java process that runs your code.

When you build a JAR file for your server environment, you can set up Gradle to add all the third-party dependencies into the JAR file itself. That way, you end up with a self-contained JAR file that contains all your own code, as well as all the code for your third-party dependencies.

The Java community commonly uses the names *fat jars* and *uberjars* to refer to self-contained JAR files that include third-party dependencies.

Packaging with Gradle

You'll use Gradle to build self-contained JAR files. Gradle doesn't have built-in support for building self-contained JAR files, or fat jars. So you'll need to add the Shadow Gradle plugin (*https://github.com/johnrengelman/shadow*) to your *build.gradle.kts*:

```
plugins {
  id("com.github.johnrengelman.shadow") version "7.1.2"
}
```

Note that you're not just adding a dependency this time. In fact, you're not adding a dependency at all, and you should leave the dependencies block unchanged. You're installing a plugin and configuring a task for it.

You already have a plugins block in *build.gradle.kts* that installs the Kotlin plugin itself, so you can add the Shadow plugin to the existing plugins block instead of duplicating the plugins block statement. It will work either way, though.

The Shadow plugin needs to know which class it should execute the main function on, so that it can write the correct main class name to *META-INF/MANIFEST.MF* in the generated JAR file. You don't have to add any additional configuration for this, though, as Shadow piggybacks on the plain JAR file that Gradle already knows how to build and that JAR file gets the main class name from the application plugin that you've already configured back in Chapter 1.

Building the JAR File

With the Shadow plugin installed, and Gradle configured, you can now execute the Gradle task shadowJar to build the actual fat jar file.

You can either run ./gradlew shadowJar in a terminal, or you can use the sidebar in IntelliJ to find the Gradle task there. It's in the category "shadow," as shown in Figure 11-2.

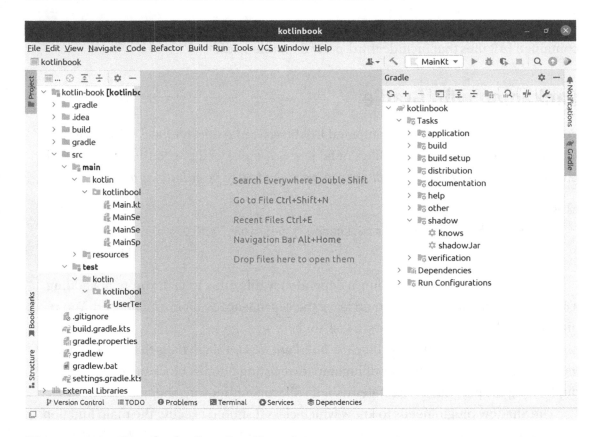

Figure 11-2. *The shadowJar Gradle task*

When the `shadowJar` task has finished, your fat jar file is available in *build/libs/kotlinbook-1.0-SNAPSHOT-all.jar*. This file contains all your own code, as well as all the third-party dependencies you've specified in *build.gradle.kts*.

Executing the JAR File

Later, you'll set up the JAR file so that your production server environment is able to execute it. But first, you'll test that it works correctly by executing it locally, in your own development environment.

The essence of running a JAR file is to run the command `java -jar myfile.jar`. Try that now, but replace the name of the JAR file with the path to your actual JAR file that you built using the `shadowJar` Gradle task:

```
java -jar build/libs/kotlinbook-1.0-SNAPSHOT-all.jar
```

Lo and behold! Your web app is up and running!

It's running in the "local" environment. That's because your main function sets up the environment to run your web app in with the statement val env = System. getenv("KOTLINBOOK_ENV") ?: "local". And the JAR file you've built contains all the config files from *src/main/resources*. So your web app starts up out of the gate, in this new running environment.

You can change the environment your web app runs in by setting KOTLINBOOK_ENV. If you're on Windows, set it with $Env:KOTLINBOOK_ENV = production. On Linux or macOS, set it with export KOTLINBOOK_ENV production. Try running your web app again using java -jar and see what happens.

It crashed! That's because of the way you've structured your config files:

```
Exception in thread "main" com.typesafe.config.ConfigException$Unresolved
Substitution: app-production.conf @ jar:file:/home/augustl/IdeaProjects/
kotlin-book/build/libs/kotlinbook-1.0-SNAPSHOT-all.jar!/app-production.
conf: 2: Could not resolve substitution to a value: ${KOTLINBOOK_COOKIE_
ENCRYPTION_KEY}
```

For the local environment, you've hard-coded default values for all the config properties in your system. But the secrets for your production environment should be secret, as explained in Chapter 3. So, in production mode, your web app expects that several environment variables are set. Typesafe Config will fail early, so it crashes immediately when it tries to load *app-production.conf* but is unable to find a value for the environment variables that you've specified that it should load its config values from.

Packaging for Production

You now have your code packaged as a JAR file that you can execute independently with all your code and third-party dependencies included. Next, you'll learn how to package this JAR file so that you can easily run it in production.

Building Docker Images

The established way to package any software that's going to run on a server is to build Docker images that package your web app JAR file, along with all the runtime dependencies.

The benefit of containers like Docker (*/www.docker.com/*) is that they include absolutely everything, from the operating system you use to the exact version of the Java runtime and to the exact `java` command that's used to start up your web app. Additionally, pretty much all the production environments that exist support Docker images in some form. So packaging your web app in Docker images should work no matter which production environment you'll use.

At the core of Docker images is the *Dockerfile*. This is a specification file that tells Docker how to build your container image and how to start running the software that you've packaged. Listing 11-1 shows how to write a *Dockerfile* for your web app.

Listing 11-1. A **Dockerfile** for your web app

```
FROM amazoncorretto:17.0.4

RUN mkdir /app
COPY build/libs/kotlinbook-1.0-SNAPSHOT-all.jar /app/
CMD exec java -jar /app/kotlinbook-1.0-SNAPSHOT-all.jar
```

That's all there is to it. The first line says which Docker image you want to inherit from. `amazoncoretto:17.0.4` is an image that the Amazon teams provide, which includes a full Linux distribution, and comes preinstalled with Java 17 Corretto, the same version of Java you've used to run the code you've written in this book. You can see all the Amazon Corretto Java versions available on the Docker Hub page for the `amazoncoretto` image at *https://hub.docker.com/_/amazoncorretto*.

There are many other Docker base images available that you can use instead, for different versions and builds of Java. For example, the Zulu Java distributions by Azure and Microsoft are available at *https://hub.docker.com/r/azul/zulu-openjdk*. Open JDK's Alpine Linux–based images (*https://hub.docker.com/_/openjdk*) used to be popular choices, but you should avoid them as Open JDK has deprecated their own images and won't release any updates. There are other vendor-neutral alternatives available now, such as the Eclipse Temurin builds (*https://hub.docker.com/_/ eclipse-temurin*).

You set up the Docker image to create a folder */app* and to copy the fat jar that you build with `shadowJar` from your machine and into the Docker image container. Then, you use `CMD` to specify exactly how to load your web app. You can use the `CMD` to specify additional flags to the Java command too, such as flags to configure the memory limits, which garbage collector to use, JMX setup, and so on.

To build the Docker image, run `docker build`:

```
docker build -f Dockerfile -t kotlinbook:latest .
```

This builds a Docker image into the local Docker repository. `-f` specifies the path to the *Dockerfile*. `-t` specifies tags. You can have as many tags as you like. By convention, `myimagename:latest` is how you point to the latest version of an image called `myimagename`, so you should always include that tag. Finally, `.` points to the working directory, which is how `docker build` knows where to find the files you tell it to COPY.

Note that as your application grows, and your Docker build commands start taking too long, you can split up the Docker image into layers. For example, you could have your external dependencies in one layer and your own code in another. That way, your production environment doesn't have to re-download your third-party dependencies every time you deploy the latest version, as that layer is unchanged and already cached on the production servers. This is not something I've needed to do in a real-world web app yet, but it's worth mentioning regardless. You can investigate using a tool like Jib from Google (*https://github.com/GoogleContainerTools/jib*) instead of the Shadow plugin if you need to create layered Docker images.

Running Docker Images Locally

When you've built a Docker image, you can easily run it on your own machine.

To run the Docker image you just built, use the following command:

```
docker run -p 9000:4207 --name kotlinbook kotlinbook:latest
```

The `-p` flag specifies port mapping. Here, you say that you want the port 9000 on your machine to bind to the port 4207 inside the Docker image. Then, you name the running Docker image `kotlinbook`. And the Docker image you want to run is `kotlinbook:latest`, which refers to the tag you used when you built the Docker image using `docker build` earlier.

When you run this command, you'll see all the console output of the Java `-jar` command that the Docker image executes. And if you open your browser on *http://localhost:9000*, you'll see your web app up and running!

Just like when you ran it directly on your machine using `java -jar`, your web app starts up in the default mode, which is in the local environment, which causes it to load your development default configuration values in *app-local.conf*.

You can also pass the additional -d flag to docker run to make Docker run the image in the background, instead of taking up the entire terminal and displaying all the log output.

If you want to rebuild and rerun your Docker image, you'll have to remove the named kotlinbook image first by running the following command:

```
docker rm -f kotlinbook
```

If you try to run docker run again without first removing the kotlinbook image, you'll get an error message saying that an image named kotlinbook already exists.

Deploying to Production

When you have a Docker image that you can run, the next step is to use that Docker image and run it in production.

Explaining how to set up a fully working production environment is outside of the scope of this book. Instead, I'll give you a general overview of the pieces you need that are common to all production environments.

The most common way to run Docker images in production on your own servers is to use Docker Swarm (*https://dockerswarm.rocks/*), Kubernetes (*https://kubernetes.io/*), or Apache Mesos (*https://mesos.apache.org/*). All these solutions can run multiple instances in parallel, with load balancers in front that direct traffic dynamically to your multiple instances, automatically kill unhealthy instances, and so on.

You need to set a collection of environment variables for your production setup. You'll need to set KOTLINBOOK_ENV to production so that your web app loads the environment variable–based *app-production.conf* setup. You can set KOTLINBOOK_HTTP_PORT, if you want to use a different HTTP port than the default 4207 from *app.conf*. Then, you'll need to update *app-production.conf* so that it points to environment variables for all your config properties, instead of pointing to the default null values in *app.conf*. For example, dbUrl should point to an environment variable like KOTLINBOOK_DB_URL, dbPassword should point to KOTLINBOOK_DB_PASSWORD, and so on.

You also need some way of setting environment variables and managing secrets. If you use Kubernetes, you can use Helm and Helm Secrets (*https://github.com/jkroepke/helm-secrets*) to encrypt secrets at rest and manage environment variables in your Kubernetes cluster.

You'll also need a Docker image registry. For example, if you use managed Kubernetes on Azure, you'll get access to a managed registry at *myapp.azurecr.io*. When you build Docker images that you'll deploy in Kubernetes, you'll run `docker push kotlinbook:latest`, where the name `kotlinbook:latest` refers to a tag that you assigned when you ran `docker build`. You'll then configure your Kubernetes cluster to pull images from the Azure container registry at *myapp.azurecr.io* and always deploy the tag `kotlinbook:latest` when you run `kubectl rollout restart` to recreate your running pods.

If you don't need a multi-node cluster setup, you can also use Docker to run a single instance of an image on a single virtual or physical server. If you SSH into your server and start up your Docker image using the command `docker run -restart=always -d kotlinbook`, Docker will automatically start your Docker image when your server reboots. This also restarts if the `java -jar` process you start with the `CMD` in your *Dockerfile* crashes.

CHAPTER 12

Building and Deploying to Serverless Environments

In this chapter, you'll learn how to take your existing handlers that you currently run in Ktor and invoke them in a serverless environment, without Ktor.

In this chapter, you'll learn the following about building and deploying to a serverless environment:

- Setting Java runtime flags to optimize startup time

- Intricate details about the Java runtime class loading and performance characteristics

- How AWS Lambda executes your code

- Important cost-saving tips in serverless environments

An important disclaimer about this whole chapter is that I have extensive experience with serverless architectures using AWS and Node.js. And I have extensive experience with running Java platform web apps in production. But I've never actually deployed a Java-based web app to a serverless environment. So keep that in mind, and use this chapter as a guide to get started and not distilled advice from a seasoned Java + serverless expert.

© August Lilleaas 2023
A. Lilleaas, *Pro Kotlin Web Apps from Scratch*, https://doi.org/10.1007/978-1-4842-9057-6_12

Detaching Your Code

When you run your code in a serverless environment, you won't be using Ktor at all. How will that work, seeing how the preceding chapters in this book are all about setting up various aspects of Ktor to make your web app do what it's supposed to?

Separating Handlers from Ktor

So far in this book you've written most of your web handlers with the Ktor-specific route definition and the actual implementation of that web handler in the same block of code:

```
get("/foo", webResponse {
  // Do something ...
  JsonWebResponse(mapOf("success" to true))
})
```

There's one notable exception, though. In Chapter 8, you wrote handleCoroutineTest as a standalone function that you call from a Ktor handler:

```
get("/coroutine_test", webResponseDb(dataSource) { dbSess ->
  handleCoroutineTest(dbSess)
})

suspend fun handleCoroutineTest(
    dbSess: Session
) = coroutineScope {
  // ...
  TextWebResponse("...")
}
```

In a real-world web app, you'll separate most of your web handlers into separate functions.

This book has purposefully glossed over code organization, and in addition to not separating the route definition from the handler implementation, you've written everything inside one huge and unorganized Main.kt file. That's fine for a book, where the main goal is to avoid the friction and confusion induced by trying to textually explain which file should contain what. But when you write your own web apps, you should split your code between multiple files.

Basic Structure

The structure I usually follow is that my `Main.kt` does all the bootstrapping, loading of config files, and starting of servers, just like in this book. It also contains all the web handler route declarations in a single file, but not the *implementation* of those routes. So it typically looks something like this:

```
fun main() {
  val config = createConfig(...)
  val dataSource = createAndMigrateDataSource(config)
  val stuff = createStuff(config)

  embeddedServer(Netty, port = config.httpPort) {
    createKtorApplication()
  }
}

fun Application.createKtorApplication(
  dataSource: DataSource
) {
  routing {
    get("/foo", webResponse(::handleGetFoo))
    get("/bars", webResponseDb(dataSource, ::handleGetBars))
    get("/bars/{id}", webResponseDb(dataSource) { dbSess ->
      handleGetBar(dbSess, call.parameters["id"])
    })
    post("/bars", webResponseTx(dataSource) { txSess ->
      handleCreateBar(
        txSess,
        Gson().fromJson(call.receiveText(), Map::class.java)
      )
    })

    // ...
  }
}
```

The various handler functions have no knowledge of Ktor and only work on a combination of plain data such as a `Map` from JSON parsing and a `String` corresponding to the ID path parameter from Ktor.

Having all the routes in a single file makes it easier to read the code. The process of debugging a web app is often that you see a request that's made to some URL and the first thing you need to figure out is which code that runs when a given URL is invoked against a web app.

For this reason, I also tend to avoid using what I call "path prefix wrappers", no matter if I use Ktor or another routing library (or programming language) entirely. For example, Ktor allows you to wrap routes with a path prefix like this:

```
routing {
  get("/foo", webResponse(::handleGetFoo))

  route("/api") {
    get("/version", webResponse(::handleGetApiVersion))
    post("/order", webResponseTx(dataSource) { txSess ->
      handleCreateOrder(txSess, call.receiveText())
    })
  }
}
```

This works fine and isn't a problem if you have a small collection of routes. But as your web app grows, it's a time saver to be able to search for `"/api/order"` in your project and find the code that corresponds to that path instantly. So I prefer the boilerplate of stating the full path of all my web handlers:

```
routing {
  get("/foo", webResponse(::handleGetFoo))

  get("/api/version", webResponse(::handleGetApiVersion))
  post("/api/order", webResponseTx(dataSource) { txSess ->
    handleCreateOrder(txSess, call.receiveText())
  })
}
```

Here, all the paths that your web app supports are present in the code base, making your code more explicit and readable, at the cost of having to manually repeat nested path segments.

Detached Web Handlers

The reason I'm going over this in a chapter about deploying to serverless is that separating your handlers into plain functions is what enables you to easily run your web handlers in a serverless environment.

When you write your web handlers in functional style, as plain Kotlin functions that receive input as arguments and return a `WebResponse`, you have the flexibility of running your business logic in any environment, not just Ktor.

In the preceding examples, the functions `handleCreateOrder` and `handleGetFoo` are all plain Kotlin functions that operate on data, return data, and have no knowledge of Ktor.

The only place that knows about Ktor is your `Main.kt` file and your routes. That makes sense, as you're using Ktor heavily in that file anyway. `Main.kt` serves as a mapping layer between the routing library you've chosen and your business logic, which has no knowledge of the environment it runs in.

Run Web Handlers on AWS Lambda

To run your web handlers in a serverless environment, you'll use AWS Lambda. Most of the steps here are logically identical to those of other cloud providers, like Google Cloud Platform and Azure. The main difference is just the wiring together and the naming of various components of the system. So don't take this as an endorsement of AWS Lambda over other cloud providers; it's mostly just a random pick based on which cloud provider I have the most experience with.

Making AWS Lambda Web Handlers

Currently, you call your web handlers from Ktor route definitions. To run them in AWS Lambda, you need to wrap your web handlers in something that AWS Lambda understands how to execute.

The only thing you'll do in this chapter is to invoke your web handlers on AWS Lambda. Typically, you'll use AWS API Gateway to do routing and authentication, and you set up individual API Gateway routes to call the correct lambda where the actual handler code runs. Setting that up is outside the scope of this book, though.

The first step is to add the required dependencies to *build.gradle.kts*:

```
implementation("com.amazonaws:aws-lambda-java-core:1.2.1")
```

This library contains the necessary wrapping code to write Kotlin code that AWS Lambda can invoke. The essence of AWS Lambda and the Java platform is that you package your code as a JAR file the same way you package for a traditional server-based environment. Then, your JAR file contains special classes that represent individual lambda handlers. These classes inherit from `com.amazonaws.services.lambda.runtime.RequestHandler`, which gives them a signature that AWS Lambda knows how to invoke and process the return value of.

To separate your existing code from the AWS Lambda environment, you'll create a new file, *MainServerless.kt*. In this file, you'll include all your AWS Lambda handlers, as well as the code needed to bootstrap your code to run in the AWS Lambda environment. Listing 12-1 shows how to do that.

Listing 12-1. Setting up **MainServerless.kt** with basic AWS Lambda handlers

```
import com.amazonaws.services.lambda.runtime.Context
import com.amazonaws.services.lambda.runtime.RequestHandler

class GetTestHelloWorld :
  RequestHandler<Any?, String>
{
  override fun handleRequest(
    input: Any?,
    context: Context
  ): String {
    return Gson().toJson(mapOf(
      "statusCode" to 200,
      "headers" to mapOf("contentType" to "text/plain"),
```

```
      "body" to "Hello, World!"
    ))
  }
}
```

Your AWS Lambda handler class implements the `RequestHandler` interface and returns a `String` with JSON content. AWS Lambda itself does not do any validation of its output. The JSON format you use in `GetTestHelloWorld` is the format that AWS API Gateway expects when it invokes lambdas to handle web requests. So, if you set up API Gateway to invoke your lambdas, you'll get errors from API Gateway if you forget to include a `"statusCode"` or return non-JSON output. But later, when you'll invoke your lambda handlers manually to test them, there's no requirement on the output format of your lambda handlers.

Deploying to AWS Lambda

To run your `GetTestHelloWorld` handler function on AWS Lambda, you need to package it and upload it to your AWS environment.

The packaging itself is identical to the setup from Chapter 11, when you deployed your web app to a traditional server-based environment. So the first step is to run the `shadowJar` Gradle task to build a self-contained fat jar of your code.

Next, you'll need to upload the JAR file to AWS Lambda. For this step, I'll assume that you already have an AWS account set up, as this book is primarily about the concept of making your code work in a serverless environment and not about AWS specifically.

In the AWS console at *https://console.aws.amazon.com*, log in, and open to the Lambda console, as seen in Figure 12-1.

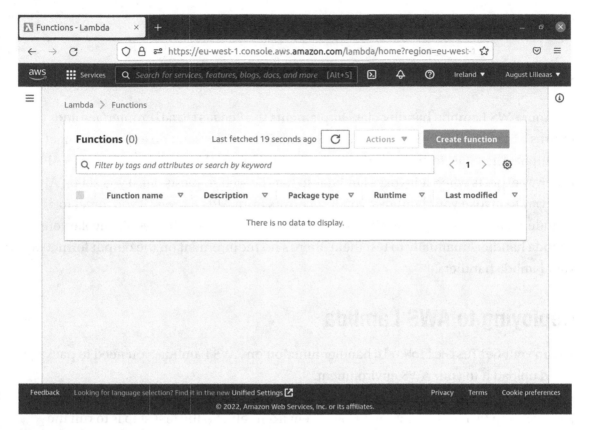

Figure 12-1. *The AWS Lambda console*

Click the big orange button labeled "Create function." That takes you to the page seen in Figure 12-2.

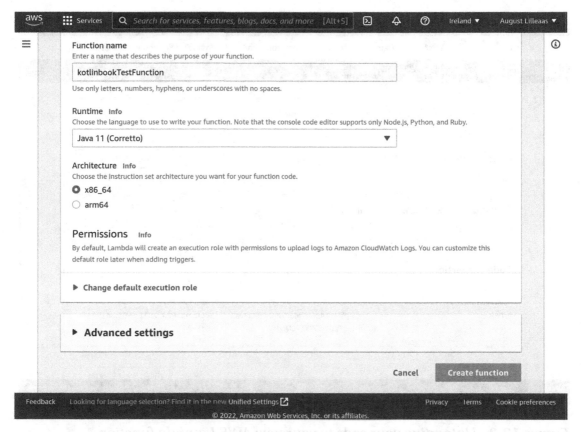

Figure 12-2. *Creating a new function in the AWS Lambda console*

Leave the option "Author from scratch" selected, name your function
kotlinbookTestFunction, choose "Java 11 (Corretto)" as the runtime, and click the
"Create function" button at the bottom of the screen.

When AWS has finished creating your function, you need to upload your code. You'll
upload the entire fat jar that you assembled with the shadowJar Gradle task earlier. Click
the white button labeled "Upload from," and click the option labeled ".zip or .jar file," as
seen in Figure 12-3.

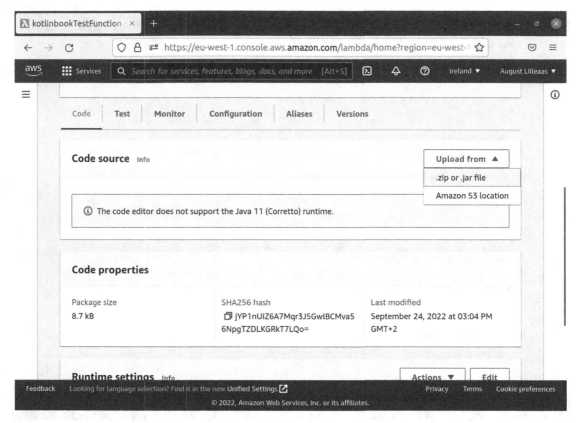

Figure 12-3. *Uploading your code to your new AWS Lambda function*

In the popup that appears, click the white button labeled "Upload," choose your fat jar file in the file finder window that appears, and click the orange button labeled "Save," as seen in Figure 12-4.

Note that the location of the fat jar file that you should upload to AWS Lambda is in the folder *build/libs/kotlinbook-1.0-SNAPSHOT-all.jar* alongside your source code and Gradle configuration in your web app project.

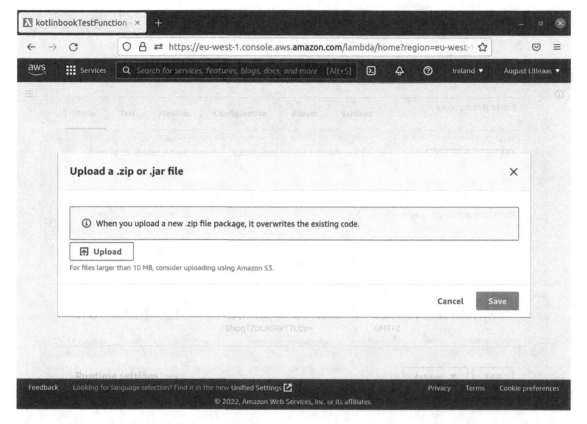

Figure 12-4. *Choosing a file and performing the upload in AWS Lambda*

When your browser has finished uploading that file to AWS Lambda, you're returned to the same screen as you saw in Figure 12-3. Remain on that screen and scroll down a bit. You'll see a section named "Runtime settings." Click the white "Edit" button, as seen in Figure 12-5.

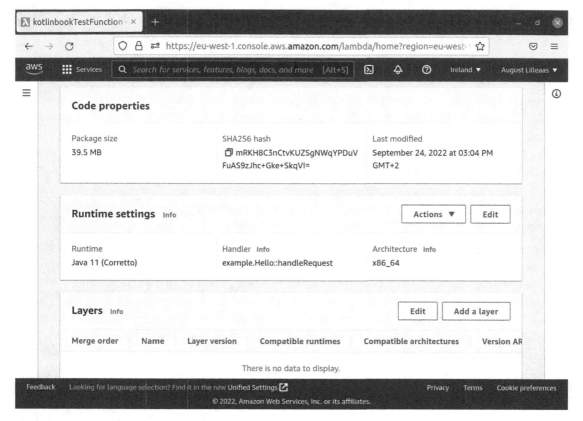

Figure 12-5. *Editing the runtime settings of your AWS Lambda function*

In the popup that appears, you need to change the name of the class that AWS
Lambda will invoke. It's currently set to example.Hello, which is not a class that
exists in your web app. You need to change it to the name of your actual handler
class, kotlinbook.GetTestHelloWorld, as seen in Figure 12-6. The function name
handleRequest should stay the same, as that's what you've named that function in the
code that you just uploaded. Click the big orange button labeled "Save" to continue.

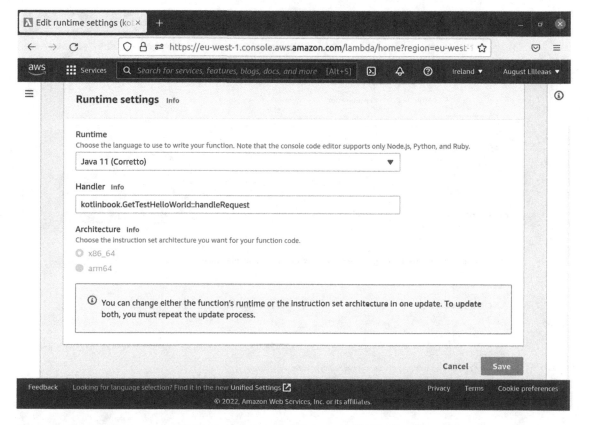

Figure 12-6. *Pointing AWS Lambda to the correct handler class in your code*

You're not ready to invoke your function, to see if everything works correctly! Scroll up to the tabs, where "Code" is the tab that's currently activated, and choose the "Test" tab. On that page, click the big orange button labeled "Test." In the following, you can change the parameters passed to your lambda as well. But your test handler does not do anything with the input AWS Lambda passes to it, so you don't have to change anything there. Figure 12-7 shows what this looks like.

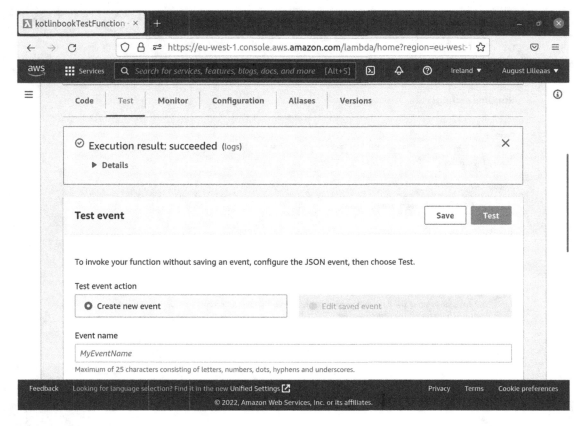

Figure 12-7. *You've successfully tested your function!*

If you click "Details" in the green box in Figure 12-7, you'll see more information about the execution of your AWS Lambda handler, as seen in Figure 12-8.

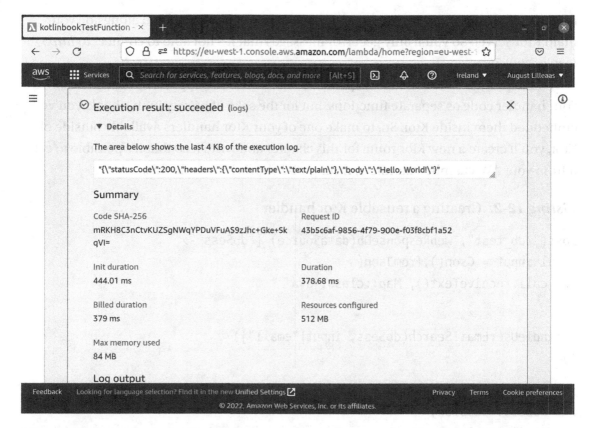

Figure 12-8. *Detailed info about the execution of your AWS Lambda handler*

There's the output from your code! As previously mentioned, AWS Lambda itself does not interpret the output in any way; it just forwards it to the caller, which in this case was the AWS Lambda testing console. It's up to the caller to interpret it, and if you set up API Gateway to call your lambdas, it will use this JSON output to determine how to respond to incoming HTTP requests.

Calling Your Existing Handlers

Next, you'll run one of your actual handlers that you've used in Ktor so far.

Currently, you only have one handler that's extracted from Ktor, `handleCoroutineTest`. Unfortunately, you can't call that function from your AWS Lambda handlers. It's not because coroutines won't work in a serverless environment. It's easy to make them work. Just wrap your invocation in `runBlocking`, and you're good to go. The only reason you can't call `handleCoroutineTest` from AWS Lambda is that it talks to a server that runs locally on your machine, embedded alongside your main Ktor server. So you'll only get error messages that it's not able to connect to *http://localhost:9876*.

As mentioned earlier in this chapter, in a real-world web app, you would write all your handler code as separate functions, but for the sake of brevity in this book, you've embedded them inside Ktor. So, to make one of your Ktor handlers available outside of Ktor, you'll create a new Ktor route for this chapter and write it so that it's possible to call it from your AWS Lambda handlers. Listing 12-2 shows how to do this.

Listing 12-2. Creating a reusable Ktor handler

```
post("/db_test", webResponseDb(dataSource) { dbSess ->
  val input = Gson().fromJson(
    call.receiveText(), Map::class.java
  )

  handleUserEmailSearch(dbSess, input["email"])
})

fun handleUserEmailSearch(
    dbSess: Session,
    email: Any?
): WebResponse {
  return JsonWebResponse(dbSess.single(
    queryOf(
      "SELECT count(*) c FROM user_t WHERE email LIKE ?",
      "%${email}%"
    ),
    ::mapFromRow)
  )
}
```

Here, you've created a Ktor handler that parses the JSON input on the Ktor side of things and passes a database session and the username property from the parsed JSON into a stand-alone function.

Next, you'll invoke this stand-alone function, handleUserEmailSearch, from AWS Lambda. The first thing you'll need is a way to map your WebResponse data to AWS Lambda. Listing 12-3 shows how to do that.

Listing 12-3. Mapping WebResponse to AWS Lambda

```
fun getAwsLambdaResponse(
  contentType: String,
  rawWebResponse: WebResponse,
  body: String
): String {
  return rawWebResponse.header("content-type", contentType)
    .let { webResponse ->
      Gson().toJson(mapOf(
        "statusCode" to webResponse.statusCode,
        "headers" to webResponse.headers,
        "body" to body
      ))
    }
}

fun serverlessWebResponse(
  handler: suspend () -> WebResponse
): String {
  return runBlocking {
    val webResponse = handler()

    when (webResponse) {
      is TextWebResponse -> {
        getAwsLambdaResponse(
          "text/plain; charset=UTF-8",
          webResponse,
          webResponse.body
        )
      }
      is JsonWebResponse -> {
        getAwsLambdaResponse(
          "application/json; charset=UTF-8",
          webResponse,
          Gson().toJson(webResponse.body)
        )
```

```
      }
      is HtmlWebResponse -> {
        getAwsLambdaResponse(
          "text/html; charset=UTF-8",
          webResponse,
          buildString {
            appendHTML().html {
              with(webResponse.body) { apply() }
            }
          }
        )
      }
    }
  }
}

fun serverlessWebResponseDb(
    dataSource: DataSource,
    handler: suspend (dbSess: Session) -> WebResponse)
= serverlessWebResponse {
  sessionOf(
    dataSource,
    returnGeneratedKey = true
  ).use { dbSess ->
    handler(dbSess)
  }
}
```

The function serverlessWebResponse is slightly overengineered for your current demands. It supports coroutines in your handler functions. The function you just wrote, handleUserEmailSearch, does not use coroutines. But since it's likely that your real-world handlers will include coroutines, the mapping code supports them, so make it as useful as possible in real-world scenarios.

serverlessWebResponse takes a WebResponse and converts it into AWS API Gateway–compatible JSON. TextWebResponse and JsonWebResponse are straightforward. The most complicated conversion is for HtmlWebResponse, as it must take kotlinx.html DSL code and convert it into a `String`. Thankfully, `kotlinx.html` has some convenient helper functions that make the job easy. `buildString` in Listing 12-3 comes from the Kotlin standard library and is a convenience API around the Java platform `StringBuilder` API for taking chunks of strings and bytes and converting them into a single big `String`. `appendHTML` is from `kotlinx.html` and expects an `Appender`, which a `StringBuilder` is, and appends its HTML to it in chunks. That way, kotlinx.html doesn't have to create the entire HTML string first and then return it to the caller. Finally, you're using the same trick we've used before to invoke `apply()` on the `webResponse.body` object using with, to avoid calling the built-in scope function `apply`.

Note that you could have implemented `getAwsLambdaResponse` as a single-expression function, that is, a function with an = after the name, which doesn't have to specify the return type and so on. But the value you return is the result of `Gson().toString()`, which is a Java class that returns a platform type `String!`. So, to avoid passing around platform types in your code, you explicitly state that it's a String to make Kotlin able to better work its logic for automatically detecting potential null pointer exceptions at compile time.

To create the actual AWS Lambda handler function, you'll also need a database connection. Listing 12-4 shows how to set both up correctly.

Listing 12-4. The implementation of an AWS Lambda handler inside **MainServerless.kt**, as well as database initialization code

```
private val dataSource = HikariDataSource()
  .apply {
    jdbcUrl = "jdbc:h2:mem:test;MODE=PostgreSQL;DATABASE_TO_
    LOWER=TRUE;DEFAULT_NULL_ORDERING=HIGH"
  }.also {
    migrateDataSource(it)
  }

class UserEmailSearch :
  RequestHandler<Map<String, String>, String>
{
  override fun handleRequest(
    input: Map<String, String>,
    context: Context
  ): String {
```

```
    return serverlessWebResponseDb(dataSource) { dbSess ->
      handleUserEmailSearch(dbSess, input["email"])
    }
  }
}
```

Your database initialization code just sets up H2 directly and migrates that H2 database using your Flyway (*https://flywaydb.org/*) migrations. You could use your config file system to configure H2 if you wanted to, but in the world of serverless and AWS Lambda, it's more common to use environment variables that are specific to that handler, instead of using config files that are baked in alongside your code. So, to make the code more realistic, you've skipped WebappConfig entirely.

The RequestHandler type of this lambda is slightly different, as it takes a Map<String, String> instead of Any?. The actual input you'll get will always be of the type Map<String, String>, so using Any? before in your GetTestHelloWorld handler in Listing 12-1 was just a shortcut to save you some typing, as you didn't actually use the input parameters there.

Rebuild your code with the Gradle shadowJar task, upload the new JAR file to the AWS Lambda console as described in Figure 12-3, and change the name of the handler class from kotlinbook.GetTestHelloWorld::handleRequest to kotlinbook. UserEmailSearch::handleRequest as shown in Figure 12-5. Before you run your code by hitting the orange button labeled "Test" under the "Test" tab shown in Figure 12-7, remember to update the parameters. Set the key "email" to a value that matches the user that you insert in your repeatable migration, as seen in Figure 12-9.

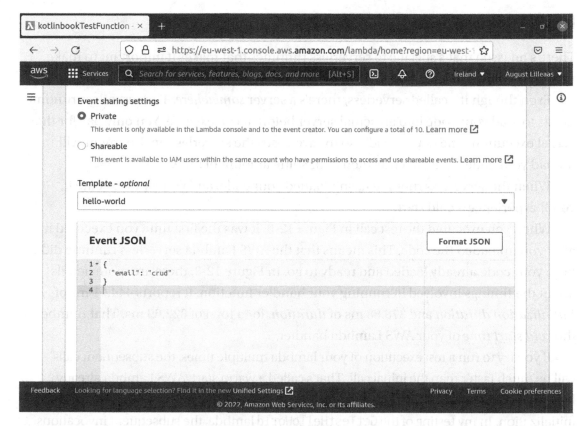

Figure 12-9. *Specifying input parameters when running your AWS Lambda function*

If everything worked correctly, you should get a green box exactly like the one you got in Figure 12-7 when you ran your AWS Lambda function the first time, and if you expand the "Details" section of the green box, you'll should see the JSON output with the result of your database query.

Improving Performance

There are many things you can do to improve the performance of your AWS Lambda handlers, which will help with both cost-saving and reducing latency and execution times of your web app.

Performance and Cold Starts

There's an issue that's specific to serverless runtimes that makes it important to make your handling code initialize as fast as possible: cold starts.

Even though it's called serverless, there's a server *somewhere*. The serverless runtime needs to load your code into an actual server before it can execute. You only pay for the actual execution time of your code, so to save costs, the serverless environment will unload your code if it hasn't executed it for some amount of time.

When the serverless runtime hasn't loaded your code, and you try to execute it, you'll experience a cold start.

When you executed the test call in Figure 12-8, it was the first time you executed it after you uploaded the code. This means that the AWS Lambda serverless runtime didn't have your code already loaded and ready to go. In Figure 12-8, there are more details about the timings involved in running your handler function. It reports 444.01 ms of *initialization duration* and 378.68 ms of *duration*, for a total of 822.69 ms. That number is the *cold start time* of your AWS Lambda handler.

If you try to run a test execution of your lambda multiple times, the subsequent calls will be much faster than the initial call. That's called a warm start. AWS Lambda already has your code loaded into its serverless runtime, and it doesn't need to spend any time on initialization. In my testing of the GetTestHelloWorld lambda, the subsequent invocations only took about 2–3 ms. That makes sense – invoking a function on a Java process that's up and running is fast and has little to no overhead compared with other runtime environments.

Initialization Time vs. Execution Time

To further optimize performance, you'll investigate the separation of initialization time and execution time in AWS Lambda.

Initialization time refers to cold starts only, specifically the time from when AWS Lambda starts loading your code and until the code has finished loading and AWS Lambda invokes your handler function (handleRequest).

During this special initialization time, AWS Lambda beefs up the runtime by giving it the maximum amount of RAM and CPU, so that your code loads as fast as possible and gets the lowest possible cold start time. When the initialization phase is complete, AWS Lambda speeds down the runtime to match what you configured it to use. You pay for RAM-seconds, so the more RAM you allocated to your AWS Lambda handler, the more expensive it is to run it.

On top of that, you don't pay for initialization time. You only pay for the execution time of the first and subsequent invocations of your handler function.

Because of this, you should take advantage of the high performance and free initialization phase and do as much work as possible statically, in the part of your code that runs before your handler executes.

Lazy Loading

There's a red flag in the timings you received when you executed `GetTestHelloWorld`. For the cold start invocation, the initialization time was 444.01 ms, and the execution time was 378.68 ms. On subsequent invocations, there was no initialization time, as the serverless runtime already had your code loaded, but the execution time was only 2–3 ms.

Why is the execution time so different on the cold start compared with subsequent warm start invocations?

This is hard evidence that there's initialization happening in your handler function. The first time you execute your handler function, there's something that the serverless runtime for some reason hasn't fully loaded.

The reason for this is that the Java runtime lazily initializes all classes. And that's a good thing. Your JAR file contains all of Ktor as well as the entirety of the dependencies that you've specified in *build.gradle.kts*. The Java runtime only parses and loads the compiled class files when they're used by running code. Without this feature, you would soon hit the 10-second hard limit on initialization time on AWS Lambda, as loading and parsing all that code is a lot of work, which the Java runtime skips because of the lazy loading.

But this has the side effect of causing the serverless runtime to load all the dependencies of your lambda classes during execution, not initialization! All the code in H2, HikariCP, *Main.kt*, and so on loads during the execution phase, as that's the first time running code that references those classes.

This also applies to your top-level `private val dataSource` declaration in `UserEmailSearch`. It might look like this code runs statically when you look at your Kotlin code. But because of implementation details in the way the Kotlin compiler writes Java class files, it doesn't. Under the hood, Kotlin compiles the top-level declarations in *MainServerless.kt* to a Java class named `MainServerlessKt`. That class has a `static` initialization block that contains the code to initialize the `dataSource` property. But the first time your code refers to that class is inside the `handleRequest` function. Kotlin compiles `dataSource` to `MainServerlessKt.getDataSource()`. When the Java runtime encounters that call, it registers that it hasn't loaded `MainServerlessKt` yet. So it loads that class, causing the corresponding static block to run. But that's too late – you're in the execution phase by that time, not in the initialization phase.

Initializing Correctly

To fix this, you need to somehow invoke code in `MainServerlessKt` during the initialization phase, so that the Java runtime loads that class during initialization and not during the first cold start execution.

Before optimizing, I got an initialization time of 354.8 ms and an execution time of 5678.15 ms. Subsequent invocations only took around 3–4 ms. This is really bad and indicates that almost nothing happens during the initialization phase and that this code needs a lot of initialization time to work, as it spends almost 6 seconds initializing itself on the first call.

The long initialization time makes sense. `GetTestHelloWorld` does almost no work, so it doesn't take as long to initialize. But `UserEmailSearch` loads Gson, your `WebResponse` handling code, HikariCP, Flyway, and the entirety of H2, which is a whole embedded database engine.

The easiest way to do fix this is to add a companion object with an initialization block to your `UserEmailSearch` handler class. The Kotlin compiler compiles that `init` block to a `static` initialization block in the underlying `UserEmailSearch` Java class. This static initialization block will run during the initialization phase of your AWS Lambda handler runtime, because `UserEmailSearch` is the class you specify that AWS Lambda should execute to run your code. Listing 12-5 shows how to update your handler with static initialization.

Listing 12-5. Adding static initialization of `dataSource` to your `UserEmailSearch` handler

```
class UserEmailSearch :
  RequestHandler<Map<String, String>, String>
{
  companion object {
    init {
```

```
    runBlocking {
      serverlessWebResponseDb(dataSource) { dbSess ->
        dbSess.single(queryOf("SELECT 1"), ::mapFromRow)
        JsonWebResponse("")
      }
    }
  }
}

override fun handleRequest(
  input: Map<String, String>,
  context: Context
): String {
  return serverlessWebResponseDb(dataSource) { dbSess ->
    handleUserEmailSearch(dbSess, input["email"])
  }
}
}
}
```

The init block does as much as possible to match what the actual handler code does. This is to ensure that the Java runtime loads as many of the classes you use during execution as possible. It initializes the Kotlin coroutine classes with runBlocking, it initializes the whole WebResponse handling code, and it runs an actual dummy query against H2, causing all database-related code to load as well.

With this small tweak, I now got an initialization time of 1298.85 ms, up from 354.8 ms, but an execution time of just 22.12 ms, down from 5678.15 ms. That's a big win! You're now down to a total of 1320.77 ms on a cold start, compared with 6032.95 ms from before. So, instead of AWS Lambda billing you for 5679 ms of execution handler time that included loading of all the code running in that lambda, you're now only billed for 23 ms of execution time for your handler code.

If you compare the execution time of the first call, 22.12 ms, with subsequent warm invocations, you can see that there's still a difference. Subsequent warm calls still only take 3–4 ms to complete. So there's still at least some initialization going on during the initial execution. But 23 ms is a low enough number that it's not worth going down the rabbit hole of figuring out what could lower that number even further.

Migrations and H2

Note that one of the things that causes your initialization time to be almost 1300 ms, is that you're loading in all H2, a full database engine, and you're also running your Flyway migrations, on every cold start.

This is an unrealistic scenario for a real-world web app. In the world of serverless, it's common to not even use a connection pool library like HikariCP, because a serverless function should never have to manage multiple simultaneous connections. In fact, if you use a serverless database such as AWS Aurora (`https://aws.amazon.com/rds/aurora/`), you can run queries against it using HTTP requests, so that you don't have to manage any connections at all and instead run low-latency fire-and-forget queries.

Additionally, if you use an external SQL database from your serverless handlers, you wouldn't run the migrations on every cold start. You wouldn't even include the migrations in the JAR file you build for your serverless execution environment. Instead, you would either run the database migrations in your build pipeline or create a dedicated serverless function that runs your migrations that your build pipeline invokes when it deploys a new version of your code.

Java Runtime Flags

To further optimize performance, you can investigate the world of setting Java runtime compiler flags.

For example, you can set the environment variable `JAVA_TOOL_OPTIONS` to `-XX:+TieredCompilation -XX:TieredStopAtLevel=1`, which disables *tiered compilation*. Tiered compilation is a feature where the Java runtime analyzes your code as it's running. The runtime optimizes your code on the fly, based on the result of the analysis. This is a part of the just-in-time (JIT) compiler in the Java platform, where the Java runtime dynamically compiles Java bytecode into native machine code.

Tiered compilation makes sense for traditional server-based processes that run for hours or days without shutting down but might not make sense in an environment where fast start times are important. When I tested this using the lambda you wrote in this chapter, initialization duration went form around 450 ms to consistently only spending about 330 ms. But this book is not about optimizing the Java runtime performance, so I won't go into further detail on that front.

GraalVM, Kotlin/JS, and Kotlin Native

Another way to improve cold start performance of Java platform AWS Lambda handlers is to compile your Java platform code using GraalVM or to use the JS and Native output alternatives for the Kotlin compiler.

GraalVM (*/www.graalvm.org/*) is an alternative Java compiler that compiles Java bytecode (and, by extension, Kotlin) down to native executables. That means that you don't incur any runtime costs and your code can start executing immediately without having to wait for the Java runtime to load. A trade-off to be aware of with GraalVM is that your compile times will increase, which makes sense seeing how GraalVM moves a lot of the work of the Java runtime to its own compile time.

Kotlin can also compile to JavaScript and native code directly, out of the box. JavaScript with Node.js as a runtime is highly suitable for a serverless environment, as Node.js is hyper-optimized for fast startup times, which will cause much faster cold starts.

There are two reasons I'm not showing you how to do that in this book.

The first is that I've simply never done it myself. I could probably have written a somewhat usable section about GraalVM after some Googling and research, but I want this book to be as much as possible about things I've actually done myself in real-world scenarios. This chapter is already balancing on the edge in that regard, as I mentioned in the introduction. And compiling and running Java platform code in GraalVM is way outside of my real-world experience. The same goes for Kotlin/JS and Kotlin Native. I have no experience in using either of those compilation output targets for Kotlin, so it would be disingenuous for me to teach you how to do it.

The second, when doing some basic research on GraalVM for this book, is I managed to get `GetTestHelloWorld` to run, but `UserEmailSearch` crashed immediately upon execution. Something about how HikariCP and H2 interacted meant that HikariCP was not able to load the classes for H2 and it crashed with a `ClassNotFound` exception.

If I were to set up a real-world web app using Kotlin on AWS Lambda, I would be careful in introducing GraalVM. You can get it to work, but then you add a dependency to your web app that is not compatible with GraalVM for some reason, and your entire setup blows up.

Kotlin/JS sounds like a more viable alternative. But Kotlin/JS can't, for obvious reasons, invoke Java dependencies. All the code you've written that's plain Kotlin supports Kotlin/JS. But you would have to switch out Gson, HikariCP, Flyway, and H2 with something else. A surprising amount of Kotlin will compile to JavaScript. For example, Java-like constructs such as `Appendable` and string builders are also available in Kotlin/JS, so your code for converting `HtmlWebResponse` to a `String` will work. But I'm not going to go into further detail on this. An expert in Kotlin/JS might have great advice on getting Kotlin code to run in the Node.js runtime on AWS Lambda. But my expertise, and the focus of this book, is on the Java platform side of Kotlin.

CHAPTER 13

Setup, Teardown, and Dependency Injection with Spring Context

In this chapter, you'll learn how to use Spring Context for managing resources in your web app and wire components together using dependency injection.

If you're new to Kotlin, here are some language features that you'll see examples of in this chapter:

- Null safety with `lateinit`

- Using lambdas in place of object literals

Also in this chapter, you will learn the following about using Spring Context:

- Programmatically creating and configuring Spring Context – no XML!

- Setting up lazy beans

- Initializing Spring Context to fail early

- Gracefully cleaning up all your resources on shutdown

In this chapter, you'll learn how to write up the resources in your web app using dependency injection instead of explicit initialization, using Spring Context, the popular and ubiquitous Java dependency injection library.

© August Lilleaas 2023
A. Lilleaas, *Pro Kotlin Web Apps from Scratch*, https://doi.org/10.1007/978-1-4842-9057-6_13

Why Spring and Dependency Injection?

There are several Kotlin-specific dependency injection libraries available that you could also consider using, such as Koin (*https://insert-koin.io/*). But in this chapter, you'll learn how to use the Java library Spring Context directly.

Spring Context is a part of the Spring Framework (*https://spring.io/projects/spring-framework*), where it's a core component of both old-school Spring MVC apps and more modern Spring Boot apps. It's not common to use Spring Context as a library, but I've done it many times in real-world production-grade web apps, exactly because of the familiarity for the other more framework-minded developers on the team. In fact, Spring Context is so core to the Spring Framework that if you google Spring Context, all you'll get are links to the documentation of the Spring Framework itself.

Spring Context's main interface is the `ApplicationContext` class and is what you'll use to manually configure Spring beans and is also the place where Spring places all its auto-configured beans in Spring Boot (*https://spring.io/projects/spring-boot*).

If your app has lots of stateful moving pieces, such as queue consumers or in-memory `ThreadPoolExecutor`-based data processing, etc., it's nice to make Spring Context do the work of setting up and tearing down all your resources automatically, in the correct order. In fact, in the Clojure language community, where frameworks are rare to nonexistent, it's popular to use Mount (*https://github.com/tolitius/mount*) or Component (*https://github.com/stuartsierra/component*) for this exact purpose.

The main reason for choosing Spring Context in this book is to bridge the gap between the traditional world of the Spring Framework and the library-based approach used here. The Spring Framework is a huge system but is fundamentally composed of well-designed libraries with clear boundaries of separation. Spring Context is one such library, and it's easy to use it in a library-like fashion that's a good fit for this book, where there's no implicit magic and nothing happens unless you invoke methods or functions to make things happen.

Having Spring Context at the core of a library-based web app will make the setup and feel of the code familiar to people who have experience with the Spring Framework. In fact, you can use this approach to embed whole legacy Spring Framework applications in a library-based Kotlin app. I've done this in real-world projects. A client I worked with had severe Java allergy, and nobody wanted to touch an old Spring Framework code base. To help solve this issue, I removed all the Spring Web–specific parts of the Java code (which were only a handful of lines in an otherwise enormous code base), created a Clojure app (the same would apply for Kotlin), wired up Spring Context from Clojure (an `AnnotationConfigApplicationContext` in that case, to support annotations), and loaded the entire Java app and embedded it in the library-based Clojure app. That way, the app could be rewritten piece by piece, by removing parts of the Java code and rewriting it in Clojure, without having to do a full wholesale rewrite of the entire Java code base. And having the main entry point of the app be familiar Clojure code, the Java allergy faded quickly.

Setting Up Spring Context

The first thing you'll need is Spring Context itself. Add it as a dependency to *build. gradle.kts*:

```
implementation("org.springframework:spring-context:5.3.23")
```

You'll use Spring Context to initialize your web app. To avoid conflicts with your existing code, you'll create a new main file, *MainSpringContext.kt*, to separate your Spring initialization from your existing initialization in *Main.kt*. Spring Context will initialize the components and resources of your web app in the correct order, based on the dependency graph Spring Context detects between them. So you won't need any of the "manual" initialization code already present in *Main.kt*.

At the core of Spring Context is the application context object. This is often a resource that's created via XML config files. But here, you'll set it up programmatically. Listing 13-1 shows how to get the basics up and running.

Listing 13-1. Creating and initializing Spring Context

```
fun createApplicationContext(appConfig: WebappConfig) =
  StaticApplicationContext().apply {
    beanFactory.registerSingleton("appConfig", appConfig)

    refresh()
    registerShutdownHook()
  }
```

This small snippet demonstrates some important concepts in Spring Context.

First, there's the concept of *beans*. A bean is Spring's name of an instance of an object in the world of dependency injection. You define the `"appConfig"` bean as a "singleton bean," which is Spring lingo for a bean where you provide the instance of the bean, instead of telling Spring how to create that instance. You already have a convenient function for creating an instance of your app config, so there's no need to wrap that in Spring Context.

You also call two important methods on the context. `refresh()` causes all the beans you define to be instantiated right away, instead of being lazily instantiated later. Later, you'll initialize resources in the context, and it's nice to have a setup that fails on startup, instead of starting up fine and only failing when you start calling your web app, potentially seconds or minutes later.

`registerShutdownHook()` will set up the Spring Context object so that when the Java runtime receives a shutdown command, Spring Context will try to shut down gracefully. It will also shut down components in the opposite order of startup, so that components that require other components don't fail because one of their dependencies has shut down before the parent component shut down.

Adding Your Data Source

The next step is to initialize your web app resources in Spring Context. You'll start with initializing the data source.

When you set up your data source with Spring Context, you need to solve two problems: create the actual data source itself and make sure that it migrates before other beans in your Spring Context call it.

Creating the data source itself is straightforward and just a manner of specifying the class and its properties, as shown in Listing 13-2.

Listing 13-2. Creating a data source inside `createApplicationContext`

```
registerBean(
  "unmigratedDataSource",
  HikariDataSource::class.java,
  BeanDefinitionCustomizer { bd ->
    bd.propertyValues.apply {
      add("jdbcUrl", appConfig.dbUrl)
      add("username", appConfig.dbUser)
      add("password", appConfig.dbPassword)
    }
  }
)
```

Here, you've registered a bean the traditional way. It's not a singleton, so you tell Spring Context how to create an instance of a class you provide and various attributes of the instance that's created. In this case, you say that the properties `jdbcUrl`, `username`, and `password` are to be set to the corresponding values in your `WebappConfig`.

If you ask Spring Context for an instance of `"unmigratedDataSource"`, you'll get just what the name suggests – a raw HikariCP data source that you can use to query your database. But it won't run any pending Flyway (*https://flywaydb.org/*) database migrations before you start executing queries. Listing 13-3 shows how to set up an additional bean that also runs your migrations.

Listing 13-3. A `FactoryBean` class that runs your migrations and a bean declaration for it

```kotlin
class MigratedDataSourceFactoryBean : FactoryBean<DataSource> {
  lateinit var unmigratedDataSource: DataSource

  override fun getObject() =
    unmigratedDataSource.also(::migrateDataSource)

  override fun getObjectType() =
    DataSource::class.java

  override fun isSingleton() =
    true
}

// Inside createApplicationContext:
registerBean(
  "dataSource",
  MigratedDataSourceFactoryBean::class.java,
  BeanDefinitionCustomizer { bd ->
    bd.propertyValues.apply {
      add(
        "unmigratedDataSource",
        RuntimeBeanReference("unmigratedDataSource")
      )
    }
  }
)
```

There are several important things happening here.

The first is the class `MigratedDataSourceFactoryBean` itself. The reason you create this class is so that you have a place to invoke your code for running your Flyway database migrations. The implementation of this class declares everything Spring Context needs to be able to create instances of your bean. `getObject()` is set up to perform the actual invocation of `migrateDataSource`. `getObjectType()` tells Spring which class your bean creates an instance of. `isSingleton()` is set to `true`, so that Spring never creates more than one instance of this bean and instead reuses the same data source across your entire web app.

When you register your `"dataSource"` bean, you use the `MigratedDataSourceFactoryBean` class and pass on a `RuntimeBeanReference` to the `"unmigratedDataSource"` property. A runtime bean reference is what allows Spring Context to lazily create instances of your beans and lets Spring Context have full control of the order of initialization of the objects it controls. If you somehow were able to get a full instance of your `"umigratedDataSource"` object when you registered the bean declaration for `"dataSource"`, Spring Context would have to create and fully initialize an instance of that object. The runtime bean reference is just a named reference, which lets Spring Context create the actual object later, as it sees fit.

lateinit in Kotlin

The most interesting thing about Listing 13-3 is the keyword `lateinit`.

One big problem with the way Spring Context initializes your objects is that it uses properties instead of constructor arguments. When you manually configure bean instantiation, it's technically possible to pass bean references as constructor arguments. But that requires extra work and breaks as soon as you try to use something like `@Autowired`, which is an annotation you add to properties of beans.

The consequence of that is that all the properties that Spring Context sets must be nullable and mutable. If you declare properties as `val String myProp`, Kotlin won't compile that class unless the compiler can guarantee that `myProp` is set by the constructor of that class, which means Kotlin can enforce its null-safety guarantees. So you'll have to declare all properties as `var String? myProp = null` instead, so that the property starts out as `null` and is set to a `String` later when Spring Context runs through your object graph and initializes everything.

This means that every time you access `myProp`, you must check if it's `null` or use the non-null assertion operator (`!!`) to forcefully cast it to a non-null type.

This is the problem that `lateinit` solves.

For code that for technical reasons must start out as `null` when a class is instantiated, but that you know will be set to a non-null value before you are able to use an instance of that class, you can declare a property as a `lateinit var`. This lets you override the compile-time checks of Kotlin and tell the type system, "I promise this will be a non-null value by the time I use it."

In Listing 13-3, you declare a reference to the unmigrated data source as `lateinit var unmigratedDataSource: DataSource`. By the time Spring Context calls `getObject()` on your `MigratedDataSourceFactoryBean`, Spring Context will have set `unmigratedDataSource` to the proper value from your bean declarations. In other words, internally in the Spring Context state machines, it will never invoke methods on a bean until it has initialized all that bean's dependencies. So, from a practical perspective, there's no way `unmigratedDataSource` will ever be `null` when your code runs, and so it's safe to use `lateinit` on properties that Spring Context initializes as part of the bean wiring process.

Additionally, if you try to access a `lateinit var` that hasn't been set yet, Kotlin will immediately throw a `kotlin.UninitializedPropertyAccessException`. So you won't get a `null` in return, and you won't accidentally pass nulls along to other parts of your system.

This is an example of pragmatism of the Kotlin type system and is one of my favorite features in the whole Kotlin language. Kotlin is very explicit about handling values that can be `null`, but it still allows you to be a responsible programmer and lean on Kotlin's null-safety guarantees even in scenarios where it's technically possible that a value can be `null`.

Starting Your Web App

Your Spring Context initialization in `createApplicationContext` is now good to go, so the next step is to use it to start your actual web app.

The initialization is like what you already have in *Main.kt*. Listing 13-4 shows how to start up your web app using your Spring Context.

Listing 13-4. A main() function in **MainSpringContext.kt**

```kotlin
fun main() {
  log.debug("Starting application...")
  val env = System.getenv("KOTLINBOOK_ENV") ?: "local"

  log.debug("Application runs in the environment ${env}")
  val config = createAppConfig(env)

  log.debug("Creating app context")
  val ctx = createApplicationContext(config)

  log.debug("Getting data source")
  val dataSource =
    ctx.getBean("dataSource", DataSource::class.java)

  embeddedServer(Netty, port = config.httpPort) {
    createKtorApplication(config, dataSource)
  }.start(wait = true)
}
```

You still create your WebappConfig manually. You could set up createApplicationConfig so that it creates its own WebappConfig, but it's convenient to be able to have full control of which exact database URL and so on that your Spring Context will use.

createKtorApplication needs the plain data source to work, so you extract the "dataSource" bean from your Spring Context ctx object. Because you configured the "dataSource" bean to also run your migrations, you don't have to explicitly run your migrations, as Spring Context has already run them.

Extended Usage

What about extended usage of Spring Context? For example, all your web handlers now operate exactly as before, by taking the parameters they use in as arguments, in plain functional style.

You could write a web handler as a bean like this:

```
beanFactory.registerSingleton(
  "springContextTestHandler",
  webResponse {
    TextWebResponse("Hello from Spring!")
  }
)
```

Then, you could add a route mapping for that handler like this:

```
get(
  "/spring_context_test",
  ctx.getBean("springContextTestHandler") as
    PipelineInterceptor<Unit, ApplicationCall>
)
```

The problem with this solution is that you haven't really added any extra value, other than wrapping lambdas in Spring Context instead of inserting the lambda directly. There's no way to inject dependencies into a lambda.

You could go down the route of making factory holder beans and other noun-ridden constructs, but I tend to stay away from that sort of thing. Dependency injection adds value for initialization and teardown of resources, but for the implementation of web route handler functions, the only value dependency injection adds is that it adds some extra ceremony to the simple task of passing arguments to functions.

CHAPTER 14

Enterprise Authentication Using Spring Security

In this chapter, you'll learn how to bridge the gap between the old and the new and add Spring Security (*https://spring.io/projects/spring-security*) to your Ktor-based web app.

If your organization is already widely using Spring Security, you might already have lots of infrastructure in place that would take heroic efforts of breaking Conway's law to change. Instead, you can add Spring Security to your modern Kotlin web app and leverage your organization's existing plugins and expertise.

Note that Spring Security is not meant to compose. Spring Security wraps your entire web app, and if you already have something else set up for authentication, such as the cookie-based authentication from Chapter 9 or a third-party system such as Keycloak (*www.keycloak.org/*), they will conflict and step on each other's toes.

Preparing Your Web App

To make it possible to use Spring Security in your web app, there are some steps you need to take first. In short, your web app needs to be based on the servlet spec. Then, you'll add Spring Security as a servlet filter, the main way of using Spring Security.

Setting Up Embedded Jetty

So far, you've used the Ktor embedded server and Netty to run your web app. To get full control of the setup and to add support for servlets, you need to switch that around. Instead of using embeddedServer form Ktor, you'll start an embedded Jetty server from scratch, configure it to use the servlet spec, and attach your Ktor web app as a servlet.

© August Lilleaas 2023
A. Lilleaas, *Pro Kotlin Web Apps from Scratch*, https://doi.org/10.1007/978-1-4842-9057-6_14

First, you need to add the necessary dependencies to your *build.gradle.kts*:

```
implementation("io.ktor:ktor-server-servlet:2.1.2")
implementation("org.eclipse.jetty:jetty-server:9.4.49.v20220914")
implementation("org.eclipse.jetty:jetty-servlet:9.4.49.v20220914")
```

You'll use Jetty for the actual server and `ktor-server-servlet` for mapping your existing Ktor app to the Jetty servlet setup.

The latest version of Jetty is 11. The reason you're using the latest version of v9 is that the later version of Jetty uses the new `jakarta.*` namespaces for the standard library APIs on the Java platform. Because of licensing and patent issues, the Java community is moving away from the `javax.*` named packages. But for now, you'll have to stick with the `javax` ones, and versions compatible with them, as the latest version of Spring Security still uses the `javax` namespaces. When Spring 6 is released, you can upgrade all these versions, as Spring 5 uses `javax.*`, whereas Spring 6 uses the new `jakarta.*` namespaces.

This new setup is completely disconnected from your existing setup, so you'll write all this code in a new file. Instead of adding more stuff to your existing *Main.kt*, you'll create a new *MainSpringSecurity.kt* where all the new servlet and Jetty-based code will live. Listing 14-1 shows the full *main()* function you'll need to get Jetty up and running, configured in servlet mode.

Listing 14-1. Start and configure Jetty for servlet hosting

```
import org.eclipse.jetty.server.HttpConnectionFactory
import org.eclipse.jetty.server.Server
import org.eclipse.jetty.server.ServerConnector
import org.eclipse.jetty.servlet.ListenerHolder
import org.eclipse.jetty.servlet.ServletContextHandler

private val log = LoggerFactory.getLogger(
  "kotlinbook.MainSpringSecurity"
)

fun main() {
  val appConfig = createAppConfig(
    System.getenv("KOTLINBOOK_ENV") ?: "local"
  )
```

```kotlin
val server = Server()

val connector = ServerConnector(
  server,
  HttpConnectionFactory()
)
connector.port = appConfig.httpPort
server.addConnector(connector)

server.handler = ServletContextHandler(
  ServletContextHandler.SESSIONS
).apply {
  contextPath = "/"
  resourceBase = System.getProperty("java.io.tmpdir")
  servletContext.setAttribute("appConfig", appConfig)
  servletHandler.addListener(
    ListenerHolder(BootstrapWebApp::class.java)
  )
}

server.start()
server.join()
}
```

Jetty is a full-featured Java platform server, which implements lots of APIs, and is extremely flexible. Unlike embeddedServer in Ktor, Jetty doesn't have much of any defaults either, so you must explicitly specify everything to get it up and running.

The main part of this setup is the Jetty server's handler property, which is set to a ServletContextHandler. The ServletContextHandler.SESSIONS flag you pass to it enables servlet sessions, which you'll need to make Spring Security work. The handler needs a context path, which is the base path where your web app will be available. It also needs a resource directory to work, which points to the system default temporary directory so that the operating system automatically cleans up whatever files Jetty creates. The servlet context, which is available to all individual servlets and filters, gets access to the application config, which will come in useful later. Finally, a listener is set up, which is a class that the Jetty server executes when Jetty has finished starting up. This class is where you'll configure and initialize the actual servlet you'll use for your web app and Spring Security itself.

If you type in this code now, you'll get a compile error for `BootstrapWebApp`. That class doesn't exist yet, so you'll write that one next.

Initializing the Servlet

Now that Jetty is set up in servlet mode, you need to initialize your servlet. Servlet initialization is an ancient Jedi guru art on the Java platform. The initialization code you'll write for your servlet stack will have no knowledge of Jetty, and any environment that supports servlets can execute it – even old-school server containers like Apache Tomcat (*https://tomcat.apache.org/*) and IBM WebSphere (*www.ibm.com/products/websphere-application-server*).

You've already typed in the name of the initializer class in Listing 14-1, `BootstrapWebApp`. Listing 14-2 shows how to create and set up this class properly.

Listing 14-2. A basic shell for servlet initialization

```
import javax.servlet.annotation.WebListener
import javax.servlet.ServletContextEvent
import javax.servlet.ServletContextListener

@WebListener
class BootstrapWebApp : ServletContextListener {
  override fun contextInitialized(sce: ServletContextEvent) {
    val ctx = sce.servletContext
  }

  override fun contextDestroyed(sce: ServletContextEvent) {

  }
}
```

This initializer doesn't do any work yet. You'll add more stuff here later in this chapter. For now, try to run your main class, and check that everything compiles correctly. If you've done everything right, your servlet-based Jetty server should start up fine and listen to the correct port based on your config files. Note that you should stop your existing main function if it's already running in the background, as the Jetty server will try to use the same port since it's using the same config files and the same config loading code.

Tip The `WebListener` annotation on `BootstrapWebApp` is not necessary, and everything will work fine if you remove it. However, adding it means that you can build and run your web app on an old-school container-type Java server, and it will pick up the `WebListener` annotation and mount your servlet, without running your `main()` function!

Everything you need to set up will happen in the `contextInitialized` function of your `BootstrapWebApp` class.

You'll add more things to `contextInitialized` later. For now, all you need is to extract the config and get hold of a data source. Listing 14-3 shows how to do this.

Listing 14-3. Accessing config and data source inside `contextInitialized`

```
override fun contextInitialized(sce: ServletContextEvent) {
  val ctx = sce.servletContext

  log.debug("Extracting config")
  val appConfig = ctx.getAttribute(
    "appConfig"
  ) as WebappConfig

  log.debug("Setting up data source")
  val dataSource = createAndMigrateDataSource(appConfig)
```

The `"appConfig"` attribute comes from Listing 14-1, where you created the servlet context and assigned the `"appConfig"` attribute to your instance of `WebappConfig`. That means you can access it from the servlet context, inside `contextInitialized`. The type of `getAttribute` is the platform type `Object!`, so you need to cast it to a `WebappConfig`. Then, you create a data source just like you've done it in your main Ktor setup and inside your tests.

Adding Ktor to Your Servlet

Now that you have a servlet with all the basics like your config and a data source available, the next step is to connect your Ktor web app to the servlet.

Because of the way the Ktor servlet package is structured, some manual work is needed. There's a built-in servlet that mounts a Ktor web app, io.ktor.server. servlet.ServletApplicationEngine, and that's the one you're going to use. But that servlet class is not that flexible, and it will by default try to create its own instance of a Ktor application, based on loading some default config files and wiring it up internally. You need to be able to programmatically pass your instance of a Ktor app that you create with createKtorApplication from Chapter 2. Listing 14-4 shows how to set it all up.

Listing 14-4. Setting up Ktor as a servlet inside contextInitialized

```
log.debug("Setting up Ktor servlet environment")
val appEngineEnvironment = applicationEngineEnvironment {
  module {
    createKtorApplication(appConfig, dataSource)
  }
}

val appEnginePipeline = defaultEnginePipeline(
  appEngineEnvironment
)

BaseApplicationResponse.setupSendPipeline(
  appEnginePipeline.sendPipeline
)

appEngineEnvironment.monitor.subscribe(
  ApplicationStarting
) {
  it.receivePipeline.merge(appEnginePipeline.receivePipeline)
  it.sendPipeline.merge(appEnginePipeline.sendPipeline)
  it.receivePipeline.installDefaultTransformations()
  it.sendPipeline.installDefaultTransformations()
}

ctx.setAttribute(
  ServletApplicationEngine
    .ApplicationEngineEnvironmentAttributeKey,
  appEngineEnvironment
)
```

```
log.debug("Setting up Ktor servlet")
ctx.addServlet(
  "ktorServlet",
  ServletApplicationEngine::class.java
).apply {
  addMapping("/")
}
```

Most of this initialization code is based heavily on the existing initialization code in Ktor's built-in `ServletApplicationEngine`, where Ktor tries to create its own instance of a Ktor application. The `appEngineEnvironment` and `appEnginePipeline` are internal objects that the `ServletApplicationEngine` needs. There's also some required wiring for the `ApplicationStarting` event, and the `ServletApplicationEngine` servlet also expects to be able to fetch the `appEngineEnvironment` instance on a particular named attribute on the servlet context.

Hopefully, a future release of the servlet package in Ktor makes it easier to pass your own instance of a Ktor application programmatically. For now, though, you'll need the preceding wiring code to make everything work.

When you have everything set up, you use the standard servlet API to add a servlet and add a mapping.

You're now set up with a servlet-based version of your Ktor web app! Try to start the app, and you should see all your web handlers responding properly, just like when you run your old `main` function that starts up Ktor using `embeddedServer` and Netty.

Using Spring Security

You now have the basics up and running, with your Ktor app running as a servlet on Jetty. The next step is to add Spring Security to your servlet stack.

Setting Up the Servlet Filter

The first thing you need to do is to add the required dependencies to *build.gradle.kts*:

```
implementation("org.springframework.security:spring-security-web:5.7.3")
implementation("org.springframework.security:spring-security-config:5.7.3")
```

Next, you'll need to wire up Spring Security in your servlet environment. To do that, you need three things: a role hierarchy, a Spring Security web application context, and a Spring Security filter that's mapped to your servlet. Listing 14-5 shows how to set all this up.

Listing 14-5. Setting up Spring Security inside `contextInitialized`

```
log.debug("Setting up Spring Security")
val roleHierarchy = """
  ROLE_ADMIN > ROLE_USER
"""
val wac = object : AbstractRefreshableWebApplicationContext() {
  override fun loadBeanDefinitions(
    beanFactory: DefaultListableBeanFactory
  ) {
    beanFactory.registerSingleton(
      "dataSource",
      dataSource
    )
    beanFactory.registerSingleton(
      "rememberMeKey",
      "asdf"
    )
    beanFactory.registerSingleton(
      "roleHierarchy",
      RoleHierarchyImpl().apply {
        setHierarchy(roleHierarchy)
      }
    )

    AnnotatedBeanDefinitionReader(beanFactory)
      .register(WebappSecurityConfig::class.java)
  }
}
```

```
wac.servletContext = ctx
ctx.addFilter(
  "springSecurityFilterChain",
  DelegatingFilterProxy("springSecurityFilterChain", wac)
).apply {
  addMappingForServletNames(null, false, "ktorServlet")
}
```

You can set up Spring Security without a role hierarchy, but it's likely that you're going to need multiple roles, so you might as well set it up right away.

The web application context is a dependency injection engine where you programmatically register singleton beans, meaning hard-coded instances of objects that will be dependency injected into your Spring Security config, for use later, when you configure authentication and filtering in Spring Security.

The `"rememberMeKey"` is a secret that Spring Security uses to create a session cookie. Instead of hard-coding to `"asdf"`, you should store this as a config property. By now, you've created several config properties, so you already know how to add more. Go ahead and update your config files, your config data class, and your config loader code to store the `"rememberMeKey"` there instead!

Configuring Spring Security

The next step is to implement the `WebappSecurityConfig` class that you've added as a bean to the Spring Security web app context in Listing 14-5.

Note that a detailed tutorial for how to configure and set up all the intricate details of Spring Security is outside of the scope of this book. For that, I refer you to the numerous online articles and other books on this subject. The goal of this book is just to show you how to get started.

The class name is not important for Spring Security, and you can name the config class anything you want. The reason it's picked up as a Spring Security config class is because of the annotations you'll add to it. Listing 14-6 shows an empty skeleton implementation of this class.

Listing 14-6. An empty Spring Security config class

```kotlin
import org.springframework.context.annotation.Configuration
import org.springframework.security.config.annotation.web.configuration.
EnableWebSecurity
import org.springframework.beans.factory.annotation.Autowired
import org.springframework.context.annotation.Bean
import org.springframework.security.core.userdetails.UserDetailsService
import org.springframework.security.core.userdetails.User
import org.springframework.security.config.annotation.web.builders.HttpSecurity
import org.springframework.security.web.SecurityFilterChain

@Configuration
@EnableWebSecurity
open class WebappSecurityConfig {
  @Autowired
  lateinit var dataSource: DataSource

  @Autowired
  lateinit var roleHierarchy: RoleHierarchy

  @Autowired
  lateinit var rememberMeKey: String

  @Autowired
  lateinit var userDetailsService: UserDetailsService

  @Bean
  open fun userDetailsService() =
    UserDetailsService { userName ->
      User(userName, "{noop}", listOf())
    }

  @Bean
  open fun filterChain(
    http: HttpSecurity
  ): SecurityFilterChain {
    return http.build()
  }
}
```

The annotations `@Configuration` and `@EnableWebSecurity` are what cause Spring Security and the `DelegatingFilterProxy` from Listing 14-5 to trigger the enabling and configuration of Spring Security in your servlet chain.

The `@Autowired` annotation means that Spring Security will assign the object instances (beans) from the web application context in Listing 14-5 to those properties, based on the property name and its type.

Later, you'll extend the `filterChain` to contain the actual configuration of the user and filtering part of Spring Security.

The `UserDetailsService` is a required part of the Spring Security setup. For now, all you'll use it for is to create a dummy user with a blank password (Spring Security interprets that `"{noop}"` string to not try to do anything fancy related to password decoding) with an empty list of roles.

Authenticating Users

To authenticate users, you'll need to configure the Spring Security filter chain with an authentication provider.

An authentication provider is where Spring Security asks you to handle login credentials, check if that user exists, and verify that you've received the correct credentials (password).

The authentication is set up inside the currently empty `filterChain` function that you created in Listing 14-6. Listing 14-7 shows how to set it up.

Listing 14-7. Adding an authentication provider for authenticating users to the `filterChain` method on `WebappSecurityConfig`

```
http.authenticationProvider(object : AuthenticationProvider {
  override fun authenticate(
    auth: Authentication
  ): Authentication? {
    val username = auth.principal as String
    val password = auth.credentials as String

    val userId = sessionOf(dataSource).use { dbSess ->
      authenticateUser(dbSess, username, password)
    }
```

```
  if (userId != null) {
    return UsernamePasswordAuthenticationToken(
      username,
      password,
      listOf(SimpleGrantedAuthority("ROLE_USER"))
    )
  }

  if (username == "quentin" && password == "test") {
    return UsernamePasswordAuthenticationToken(
      username,
      password,
      listOf(SimpleGrantedAuthority("ROLE_ADMIN"))
    )
  }

  return null
 }

 override fun supports(authentication: Class<*>) =
   authentication ==
     UsernamePasswordAuthenticationToken::class.java
})
```

This code uses the authenticateUser function from Chapter 9 to authenticate users against your existing setup. Spring Security provides the username and password via the principal and the credentials properties and expects your authenticate function to return null if you didn't find a user for those credential, or an instance of org.springframework.security.core.Authentication if you found a valid user.

For the sake of demonstration, the code also includes a hard-coded example of an admin user, which has the username "quentin" and the password "test". This is not something you should add to a real-world web app, for obvious reasons. But it provides an example of what you can do with Spring Security and how to create users with separate roles.

Filtering Requests

Currently, your Spring Security filter doesn't filter any requests. To do this, you need to set up a filter chain.

A filter chain is the set of rules that Spring Security uses to determine if a request needs authentication at all and, if there's an authenticated user available, if it has the correct access level.

The filter chain is set up using a programmatic builder DSL that is available on the `HttpSecurity` instance HTTP inside `filterChain` of your Spring Security config class. Listing 14-8 shows an example of some of the things you can do with it.

Listing 14-8. Filtering requests using the builder DSL inside of `filterChain`

```
http
  .authorizeRequests()
  .expressionHandler(
    DefaultWebSecurityExpressionHandler().apply {
      setRoleHierarchy(roleHierarchy)
    }
  )
  .antMatchers("/login").permitAll()
  .antMatchers("/coroutine_test").permitAll()
  .antMatchers("/admin/**").hasRole("ADMIN")
  .antMatchers("/**").hasRole("USER")
  .anyRequest().authenticated()
  .and().formLogin()
  .and()
    .rememberMe()
    .key(rememberMeKey)
    .rememberMeServices(
      TokenBasedRememberMeServices(
        rememberMeKey,
        userDetailsService
      ).apply {
        setCookieName("REMEMBER_ME_KOTLINBOOK")
      }
    )
```

```
.and()
  .logout()
  .logoutRequestMatcher(
    AntPathRequestMatcher("/logout")
  )
```

There are many ways to set up the filtering, and you need to change the specific config to alter your specific needs. This serves as an example of some of the possibilities and is a good starting point for most web apps.

The login page is set up to not require authentication, to avoid infinite redirect loops. All pages that start with *admin* require the admin role for that user. Otherwise, the filter requires authentications for all pages. The default `formLogin()` is set up as well, which uses the Spring Security default login GUI. It comes with a styled login form and some default error messages and is a nice way to get started and demonstrate a working setup without having to implement a login form yourself. Then, `logout` is set up so that when the user visits the path */logout*, Spring Security logs out the user and clears out the session.

To reiterate, this book is not a comprehensive tutorial on Spring Security. The purpose is to get Spring Security set up and ready to go, working alongside your library-based web app that you've written from scratch.

Accessing the Logged-In User

When you load web handlers that require logging in, it's also useful to be able to extract information about the currently logged-in user, so that you can display the name of the user on the web page and use the ID of the user in the database as inputs to various queries.

There are two main ways of accessing the currently logged-in user in Spring Security.

The first is to use the thread-local variable accessible form, `SecurityContextHolder.getContext().authentication`. This is globally available if you access this from a web handler thread. This is a convenient way to access the currently logged-in user, but it's a little bit problematic in the world of Kotlin. For example, if you aren't careful, your code is suddenly running in a different thread because you access it in a coroutine. And if you try to set up your servlet and servlet filter to be async, the `SecurityContextHolder` will also stop working, as async servlets are not limited to a single thread per request.

The second is to access the user principal on the servlet request itself. This is not relying on thread-local variables and is more functional and data driven in nature. Each request that your servlet stack is processing gets an instance of a servlet request, and you can pass this around wherever you like.

There's one problem with using the `javaSecurityPrincipal`, though. As I'm writing this chapter, Ktor 2.2.0 is not yet released. And there's a bug in earlier versions of Ktor where `javaSecurityPrincipal` does not work and always returns `null`. So, for now, you'll have to use non-async servlets and access the session using the thread-local `SecurityContextHolder.getContext().authentication`.

I advise you to check the Ktor issue tracker, at *https://youtrack.jetbrains.com/ issue/KTOR-4784*, and see if the issue has been resolved and released. The issue was reported by yours truly on August 22, 2022 (which also happens to be the birthday of yours truly), and fixed by the Ktor team just two days later, August 24. Yay, Ktor team!

PART III

Tools of the Trade

CHAPTER 15

Choosing the Right Library

In this chapter, I'll share some of my thoughts about libraries, how to compare libraries with frameworks, and some tools for choosing the right library. Usually, there's more than one library available that you can choose from for doing the same task. So it's useful to know how to pick the right one.

What's a Library?

Our industry has no widely agreed-upon definition of the difference between a library and a framework. The distinction I use is

A library is something you call. A framework is something that calls you.

Another practical distinction is that in a library, nothing happens that you didn't ask for. The trade-off is that you need to wire up things yourself and write some bootstrapping code to get everything up and running.

In contrast, in a framework, a lot of things happen automatically, to save you some work and make your life easier. The trade-off is that when something breaks or if the framework isn't calling your code automatically when it should be, it can be difficult to figure out why or even to figure out that something is wrong in the first place.

One of the main real-world problems I have when I use frameworks is that when things go wrong, you're confronted with mountains of framework code that you weren't aware of before and that you suddenly must understand to be able to move forward. Framework code that stops automatically calling your own code can require lots of work to understand what happened and why.

There is a gray area here, though. In Chapter 9, you configured Ktor to handle session cookies and authorization. You don't see that code anywhere. All you did was to wrap your routes in `authenticate("auth-session")` and hope for the best. There's a lot of

© August Lilleaas 2023
A. Lilleaas, *Pro Kotlin Web Apps from Scratch*, https://doi.org/10.1007/978-1-4842-9057-6_15

mapping and action going on under the hood of Ktor to make that work, and if that stops working, you wouldn't necessarily know why.

The benefit of Ktor and libraries is that you do call a function (`authenticate`) and you refer to the config by name (`"auth-session"`). So it's not *that* implicit and magical. Ktor won't do anything automatically with authentication; you must tell it to.

You're not necessarily immune from magic that stops working when you use libraries. But you drastically reduce the chance of that happening, eliminating a whole category of bugs from your web app.

Popularity Is Largely Irrelevant

Some people see the popularity of a library as an important metric. Popularity isn't a *completely* irrelevant metric. If you find two libraries that do the same thing, you should probably choose the more popular one.

However, using popularity as the main metric when choosing a library can get in the way of thinking for yourself. The most important thing when choosing a library is to use all the good taste and judgment you've accumulated over time, evaluate the options, and make an informed choice. If the answer is simply "use Spring Security because everyone is using Spring" or "use React because everyone is using React," then you're not really thinking.

The assumption baked into using popularity as a metric is that the people who choose popular libraries (or frameworks) do that because it's always the best choice and because everyone who chose that library chose it after deep thinking and evaluation. Usually, it's more of a zeitgeist that picks which libraries are popular. And often, the most popular libraries are the ones that people choose when they *don't* think deeply about what's right for their project.

Keep in mind, though, that there is one type of popularity that's important: the availability of libraries. If you use a programming language that's very unpopular, you'll have to write a lot of code from scratch, without the help of libraries.

In Paul Graham's 2001 essay Beating the Averages (*www.paulgraham.com/avg.html*), Graham argues that Lisp is such an excellent choice of programming language that they got ahead of their competition just because of the sheer power of the Lisp language itself. This is true, of course (I am a Lisp weenie at the core, after all), but only to some extent. If someone invents the best language in the universe tomorrow that's super-efficient and has a sound and complete type system that never gets in your way but solves the halting problem and makes it impossible to write bugs, you still might not speed ahead of your competition that uses Java or PHP. The sheer amount of third-party libraries available on those platforms allows you to beat users of Perfect Language 9000 almost every time.

Documentation and Stability Are Important

An objective measure you can use to evaluate a library is the quality of its documentation and the stability of its APIs.

Ktor is a good example of a library that scores off the charts on these metrics. The amount of documentation available at *https://ktor.io/docs/welcome.html* is almost unparalleled. Every little detail of the library is documented, with lots of examples and explanations to go with all the modules that Ktor is composed of. Ktor is also very stable. All experimental features are explicitly tagged with annotations, and you have to use other annotations to opt in to use them, so that you don't accidentally auto-complete in some part of Ktor that might change in the future. Once the Ktor team releases something publicly and removes the unstable tabs, they will do everything they can to never break APIs.

In fact, all the libraries chosen in this book have these properties. Flyway, HikariCP, Kotliquery, Typesafe Config, Gson, bcrypt, and Spring Security are all libraries with great documentation and almost complete stability of public APIs.

If anything, I prioritize stability over documentation. Kotliquery is a small library, without thousands of GitHub stars, and the documentation is a little sparse. But the API surface is small enough that extensive documentation isn't that important, and it's a well-designed library that has kept working and that I've safely bumped as new versions have been released, without any issues.

Avoid Following the "X Way"

When you read about libraries and frameworks, you'll see things like "the Ktor way" or "the Spring way" or "the Rails way." I tend to avoid those kinds of patterns and do it my way. (I'm also a team player, so by *my way* I mean *my team's way*.)

That's not to say that I ignore best practices completely. I try to accumulate as much knowledge as I can on the numerous ways people in the industry structure code and abstractions to make it maintainable and readable.

However, no "X way" can cover all cases, and wholesale following a prescribed pattern is not a good substitute for thinking. Just like you need to use all your acquired judgment and good taste when you choose which libraries to add to your project, you need that same skillset for writing most of your code. You should always strive to make active decisions about what to do and question why you're doing what you're doing. There's no pattern that always works or pattern that never works or a methodology for writing software that should never be evaluated and thought deeply about with a critical mind.

Additionally, if all the programmers on a project are used to working on functional-style Clojure apps and write SQL by hand, it's not necessarily a good idea to do everything "the Rails way" and use an ORM for everything. Even though the ORM ActiveRecord is a main selling point of Rails, it will get in the way of the experience of the developers on the team and not necessarily add any value.

Don't Shy Away from Platform Libraries

When a new language is created, there's a tendency in that language's community to write everything from scratch, to make it "language native." There are zillions of libraries available for doing most things, but new languages can't always leverage those libraries.

However, languages like Clojure and Kotlin embrace the platform. And you don't need to wrap everything in a Kotlin-specific library to be able to use it.

Many libraries only exist as Java libraries. For example, the library for interacting with the Stripe payment APIs is only available in Java. There's no Kotlin version of that library. And you don't really need one. It's super easy to invoke Java code from Kotlin. You've done lots of that in this book. For example, in Chapter 14, you've interacted with the most Java-esque code of all Java code, the Spring Security APIs. Kotlin is beautifully designed to take advantage of everything Java has to offer.

In my experience, some programmers reach desperately for a language-native library. *Maybe there's a ubiquitous library for doing bcrypt on the Java platform. But there is a Kotlin library available, written from scratch in pure Kotlin, so let's use that! Maybe it only has three stars on GitHub and isn't really maintained, but anything goes as long as it's 100% Kotlin.*

I advise against doing this. In Clojure and Kotlin alike, I use Flyway for database migrations. It is familiar to existing Java platform developers, it has a small and flexible API surface, it lets me write migration scripts as plain SQL just as I want, and I can depend on an actively maintained library with a huge community instead of some Clojure- or Kotlin-only migration library that has a much higher chance of being abandoned in the future.

Additionally, the language-native libraries might not have close to the same number of features that the more widely used Java libraries have. For example, Flyway handles migrating old versions of Oracle. Your new-kid-on-the-block fancy language-native library is unlikely to support those kinds of edge cases. (Yes, I just called Oracle an edge case. Sue me!)

Boundaries and Layers

One of the things I really like about Ktor is that it has support for a vast selection of mechanisms that are useful for web apps out of the box. For example, Ktor has supplied cookie-based authentication, JWT authentication, a DSL for writing HTML in Kotlin, a servlet for mapping Jetty and Ktor to Spring Security, and so on. A library with a wide selection of building blocks that work well together can save you from a lot of work. And that's why I chose Ktor for the main workhorse in this book.

However, I steer vehemently away from libraries that doo to much without giving me escape hatches and composability. Ktor lets me control how it operates and lets me pick and choose from a large menu of features, without having to wrestle with it. Ktor doesn't set up anything by default; I must explicitly opt in to everything I want it to do.

Flyway, the library you've used for database migrations, is the same way. It has some defaults, such as what the naming prefix is for a repeatable migration vs. a versioned migration, where on the class path to load the migration files, and so on. But you can easily override all those defaults. And, most importantly, Flyway doesn't do anything until you call `migrate()` on the Flyway object that you create.

Both Ktor and Flyway also have programmatic APIs. Ktor has a config file mode, where it loads a config file from the class path and sets up itself based on the contents of that config file. Instead of calling `embeddedServer` with the properties it should use for running, you can invoke `io.ktor.server.netty.EngineMain.main()` directly. Then, you can update the Ktor config file (either *application.conf* or *application.yaml* on the class path) to specify the name of the class where your Ktor initialization code lives. This way of using libraries is something I tend to avoid. Programmatic APIs keep me in control of everything, and the library does not dictate how I wire up my collection of libraries.

Frameworks are usually the complete opposite in this regard. Spring Boot follows a convention-over-configuration policy, and merely the presence of a library in your Gradle dependencies is enough to cause Spring Boot to pick that up and assume things about your setup. If you're allergic to code and explicitness, this is great, but that's pretty much the opposite of what I want when I write web apps.

CHAPTER 16

An Assortment of Kotlin Tricks

You've learned lots of neat Kotlin tricks along the way, as you've implemented a production-grade web app in the previous chapters. In this chapter, you'll learn some more neat Kotlin tricks that I didn't get to cover.

Many of these tricks are more useful to library authors than web app builders. In fact, most libraries will likely use most of the concepts mentioned in this chapter. But it's still nice to be aware of these concepts. You might end up debugging library code, and it's nice to know what you're looking at. And you never know! Perhaps you'll find some use for the Kotlin tricks in this chapter when you write utilities and helper functions for your own web apps.

Delegation (by lazy)

Lazy delegation allows you to defer expensive computations of values and properties, but still access them as if they were just normal properties like any other property.

In the web app you've built in this book, there aren't any expensive resources that are initialized too eagerly that would benefit from lazy initialization. It's not really common for web app back ends to have stateful components, as state typically lives in databases and queues. So, to demonstrate lazy initialization, you'll look at an imagined example.

One use case for lazy delegation are methods that compute expensive resources and that don't change over time. Instead of

```
class Foo(val myInput: String) {
  fun getExpensiveThing() =
    useLotsOfCpu(myInput)
}
```

© August Lilleaas 2023
A. Lilleaas, *Pro Kotlin Web Apps from Scratch*, https://doi.org/10.1007/978-1-4842-9057-6_16

you could write that as lazy delegation instead:

```
class Foo(val myInput: String) {
  val expensiveThing: String by lazy {
    useLotsOfCpu(myInput)
  }
}
```

The benefit of delegating with by lazy is that the lambda will only execute once, the first time you invoke it, whereas the method will execute the CPU-exhaustive code every time.

You also have control of how Kotlin manages parallel calls from multiple threads to your lazy property. You can choose between three thread-safety modes:

- NONE: No synchronization between threads. If multiple threads try to access the property simultaneously while it's not yet initialized, the behavior is undefined.

- PUBLICATION: Allows multiple computations to run in parallel, but it uses the result of the first call that successfully completes. Further invocations after this do not cause the computation to execute.

- SYNCHRONIZED: Protects the computation with locks to ensure that it only runs a single time. Simultaneous calls wait for the first one to complete.

The default mode is SYNCHRONIZED.

Delegation is a deep subject in Kotlin, and you can do many things with it, not just lazy initialization. For example, instead of subclassing, you can delegate a class to an instance of an object, effectively inheriting a class from an instance. You can read more about it in the official Kotlin documentation here: *https://kotlinlang.org/docs/ delegated-properties.html.*

Inline Functions

You can make functions in Kotlin that have zero overhead by making *inline functions*.

Inline functions also have the benefit of not altering the calling context in any way. A good example of this is the transaction function in Kotliquery, the SQL library you've used in this book. In fact, the pull request yours truly submitted to Kotliquery, mentioned in Chapter 6 (*https://github.com/seratch/kotliquery/pull/57*), made the `transaction` function inline. Listing 16-1 shows the rough outlines of the implementation of that function.

Listing 16-1. The outline of the implementation of the `transaction` function from Kotliquery

```
fun <A> Session.transaction(
  block: (TransactionalSession) -> A
): A {
  try {
    connection.begin()
    return block(TransactionalSession(connection)).also {
      connection.commit()
    }
  } catch (e: Exception) {
    connection.rollback()
    throw e
  }
}
```

This code works fine, but one problem with it is that code inside the transaction block breaks the coroutine context. Kotlin does not know statically how a function uses lambda you pass to it. So Kotlin can't assume that a function calls a lambda inline with the context it's declared in. The following code breaks:

```
runBlocking {
  dbSess.transaction { txSess ->
    delay(1)
    txSess.run(...)
  }
}
```

The fix for this issue is to mark the function as inline. Kotlin then knows that the function calls the lambda inline as well. It is possible to write inline functions that don't call lambdas inline, but you need to explicitly mark lambdas with `noinline` or `crossinline` if that's the case.

By adding the `inline` keyword (`inline fun <A> Session.transaction(...)` to the `transaction` function in Kotliquery, the code will run fine, as the Kotlin compiler treats the code in the lambda passed to transaction just the same it treats code outside of that lambda.

The built-in scope functions, like `apply`, `with`, `also`, etc. , are inline functions. That's why they also work in any context and do not incur any compile-time or runtime penalties for expressivity or performance.

Reified Generics

Reified generics (or reified type parameters) solve a common pitfall on the Java platform: generic types are compile-time only. Often referred to as *type erasure*, there is no trace left in the compiled bytecode of the generic type. So, if you have a `List<String>`, all the bytecode and Java runtime know is that it's a `List`. The type checking for it being strings happens in compiler passes before it generates the final output.

Kotlin is not able to magically work around Java platform limitations. But Kotlin does have a solution. The key is inline functions, and you can only use reified generics in inline functions.

The compiler removes (*inlines*) inline functions from the compiled output. The Kotlin compiler copies the body of the function into every location in your code where you call it. This means that it can replace the generic type with the actual type that you pass when calling the function. So a reified generic type to an inline function is just a shortcut for copying that code manually to all those places you call it from and replacing the generic with the actual type used at the call site.

For example, let's say you want to write a helper function that takes a JSON string and serializes it to the correct type. Listing 16-2 shows how you could attempt to do that.

Listing 16-2. Attempt to write a helper function for JSON serialization

```
fun <T> serializeJson(json: String): T =
  Gson().fromJson(json, T::class.java)
```

This code does not compile, though. That's because of type erasure. When this code runs, the type of T is lost. So there's no way for `serializeJson` to know what the type of T is.

However, if you write it as an inline function with a reified generic, the compiler has everything it knows to make it work. Listing 16-3 shows how that works.

Listing 16-3. Using reified generics to write a helper function for JSON serialization

```
inline fun <reified T> serializeJson(json: String): T =
  Gson().fromJson(json, T::class.java)
```

The code is the same, except for the `inline` and `reified` keywords. Because the compiler inlines the function, it knows what the type of the generic is, as Kotlin resolves the types of an inline function during compilation and not in the runtime.

Contracts

Have you ever wondered how Kotlin is able to do this?

```
val foo: MyFoo? = createFoo()
assertNotNull(foo)
foo.doSomething()
```

If you look carefully at this code, there's something weird going on. The type of foo is `MyFoo?`, which means it can be `null`. But you're still able to call `foo.doSomething()` without checking that foo is null. Calling a method on a nullable type is supposed to cause a compile error for null safety! What is this sorcery?

This is because `assertNotNull` implements a *contract*.

This is what `assertNotNull` looks like without a contract:

```
fun <T : Any> assertNotNull(
  actual: T?,
  message: String? = null
): T {
  asserter.assertNotNull(message, actual)
  return actual!!
}
```

This works fine and returns a non-null type. If the value is `null`, you'll get a `NullPointerException` from the non-null assertion operator (`!!`). But that does not solve the mystery. We don't use the return value from assertNotNull, so it does not matter to our program that assertNotNull throws an exception if you pass null to it and return a non-null type.

The actual implementation of assertNotNull looks like this:

```kotlin
fun <T : Any> assertNotNull(
  actual: T?,
  message: String? = null
): T {
  contract { returns() implies (actual != null) }
  asserter.assertNotNull(message, actual)
  return actual!!
}
```

Notice the added contract line. Contracts are ways of telling the type system about things it cannot infer on its own, but are nevertheless true statements. Technically speaking, it's possible to make a contract that doesn't hold true in the implementation. But when used correctly, contracts are powerful additions to the type system that enable third-party libraries, such as the assertion library in kotlin.test, to extend the built-in type checks.

The specific contract used here says that if the function returns a value (i.e., it does not throw an exception), it implies that the argument actual is non-null. Then, the Kotlin type system can smart cast the type MyFoo? to MyFoo. You've already seen smart casting by checking for null in if statements, and contracts allows third-party functions to do the same.

Note that contracts are an experimental API. This means that it's subject to change in the future, and you must explicitly opt in to use them, using @OptIn(ExperimentalSt dlibApi::class). The opting in is there so that you don't accidentally use unstable APIs that might break in future Kotlin releases and keeps your code future-proof.

And So Much More

The Kotlin language is full of tricks and constructs to make your life better. So why is this chapter so short?

I've worked hard to include as many Kotlin tricks as possible embedded in the rest of the book. This chapter only contains things that I believe are important, or at least interesting, for web app developers that I didn't get to cover as a part of a chapter about building actual web app functionality.

In Chapter 3, you learned about data classes, scope functions, nullability and null safety, and the Elvis operator. In Chapter 4, you learned about sealed classes, function types, destructuring, and extension functions. In Chapter 5, you learned about function references and the use scope function on closeable objects. In Chapter 6, you learned about smart casting of nullable types, companion objects, and generics in plain Kotlin functions. In Chapter 7, you learned about the unsafe cast operator and inline functions. In Chapter 8, you learned pretty much all there is to know about the usage and internals of coroutines. In Chapter 9, you learned about the safe call operator, operator overloading, DSLs, object expressions, and some vital details of precedence rules of extension functions and default receivers. In Chapter 13, you learned about null safety with lateinit and using lambdas in place of object literals.

All these tricks are good candidates for this chapter. But I've already covered them, so there's no need to repeat them all here.

If you want to dig deep into everything Kotlin has to offer, check out Tim Lavers' book *Learn to Program with Kotlin* (Apress, 2021), the official Kotlin documentation (*https://kotlinlang.org/docs/home.html*), and the many courses, resources, and books that you can find on the Internet at large.

There are many facets to the Kotlin language, and there are more language features to mention that I haven't mentioned in this book. But when you're learning to build pro Kotlin web apps from scratch, the focus should be on the language features that are useful for delivering real-world value. And that's what I believe this book has achieved.

APPENDIX A

Using Jooby Instead of Ktor

In this appendix, you'll learn how to use Jooby instead of Ktor. It doesn't cover everything you've done with Ktor in this book, but it covers enough to get you started.

Jooby (`https://jooby.io/`) is a Java library that's well suited in the context of this book, as it's a focused library that only does what you explicitly tell it to. It has a small Kotlin API, called Kooby, that adds some extra Kotlin-specific features that make it easy to work with from Kotlin.

The reason you're using Jooby, instead of something like Spring Boot, is that Jooby fits the library definition of this book. Architecturally, Jooby and Kotlin are similar in that they both have a function to start a server, you can programmatically declare your routes and web handlers in a main function, and so on. Spring Boot, on the other hand, is a framework full of implicit magic (for better or worse) and is not a good fit for this book.

Starting a Server

Jooby works like Ktor in that you explicitly start a server at the port you tell it to.

You'll need to add the following dependencies to your *build.gradle.kts*:

```
implementation("io.jooby:jooby:2.16.1")
implementation("io.jooby:jooby-netty:2.16.1")
```

The next step is to start up a Jooby server. Listing A-1 shows how to wire up the basics.

© August Lilleaas 2023
A. Lilleaas, *Pro Kotlin Web Apps from Scratch*, https://doi.org/10.1007/978-1-4842-9057-6

Listing A-1. Starting a Jooby server

```
fun main() {
  val env = System.getenv("KOTLINBOOK_ENV") ?: "local"
  val config = createAppConfig(env)
  val dataSource = createAndMigrateDataSource(config)

  runApp(arrayOf()) {
    serverOptions {
      port = config.httpPort
      server = "netty"
    }

    coroutine {
      get("/") {
        "Hello, World!"
      }
    }
  }
}
```

runApp() is the equivalent of embeddedServer() in Ktor. There's no version of runApp() that just takes a lambda, so you need to pass an empty array.

Jooby is written in Java, but the Kotlin layer in Kooby adds a coroutine block that you can wrap your routes in so that they all run in a coroutine context, just like in Ktor. You don't need coroutines for a simple "Hello, World", but you'll need them later.

Mapping WebResponse

Your existing handlers are lambdas or functions that return an instance of WebResponse. You've written a mapping layer between WebResponse and Ktor, and now you'll need to do the same for WebResponse and Jooby. Listing A-2 shows how to do that.

Listing A-2. Mapping WebResponse to Jooby

```
fun joobyWebResponse(
  handler: suspend HandlerContext.() -> WebResponse
): suspend HandlerContext.() -> Any {
```

```
return {
  val resp = this.handler()

  ctx.setResponseCode(resp.statusCode)

  for ((name, values) in resp.headers())
    for (value in values)
      ctx.setResponseHeader(name, value)

  when (resp) {
    is TextWebResponse -> {
      ctx.responseType = MediaType.text
      resp.body
    }

    is JsonWebResponse -> {
      ctx.responseType = MediaType.json
      Gson().toJson(resp.body)
    }

    is HtmlWebResponse -> {
      ctx.responseType = MediaType.html
      buildString {
        appendHTML().html {
          with(resp.body) { apply() }
        }
      }
    }
  }
}
}
```

This code is almost identical to the Ktor mapping code. The difference is in the type of the lambda that you return and the specific API you use to map to Jooby. For example, in Ktor, pass in the status code to Ktor's various response calls, whereas in Jooby, you call `ctx.setResponseCode()`. Additionally, Jooby handlers expect you to return a non-null object of the type Any, which represents the response body of your route handler.

You'll also need a variant that prepares a Kotliquery session. Listing A-3 shows how to implement that.

Listing A-3. Setting up a Kotliquery session for Jooby handlers

```
fun joobyWebResponseDb(
  dataSource: DataSource,
  handler: suspend HandlerContext.(
    dbSess: Session
  ) -> WebResponse
) = joobyWebResponse {
  sessionOf(
    dataSource,
    returnGeneratedKey = true
  ).use { dbSess ->
    handler(dbSess)
  }
}
```

This function is also almost identical to the Ktor equivalent and makes use of the existing joobyWebResponse to wrap the request handler in a Kotliquery session that it closes when the request completes or if an exception is thrown through the use scope function.

Serving Assets

Like Ktor, Jooby has a built-in routing setup for dealing with static files.

To set up static file serving, add a mapping for the assets route. Listing A-4 shows how to set it up.

Listing A-4. Serving static assets

```
if (config.useFileSystemAssets) {
  assets("/*", "src/main/resources/public")
} else {
  assets("/*", ClassPathAssetSource(this.classLoader, "public"))
}
```

When your web app runs locally, you'll serve assets directly from the file system. Otherwise, Jooby will load the assets from the class path. Like in the Ktor setup, all assets in *src/main/resources/public* are available through the Jooby HTTP server.

Responding to Requests

You'll respond to request the same way in Jooby as you do when you use Ktor, except you'll have to use `joobyWebResponse` that maps to Jooby, instead of the old `webResponse` that maps to Ktor. Listing A-5 shows how to perform some basic response handling.

Listing A-5. Responding to requests inside the `coroutine` route wrapper in Jooby

```
get("/", joobyWebResponse {
  delay(200)
  TextWebResponse("Hello, World!")
})

post("/db_test", joobyWebResponseDb(dataSource) { dbSess ->
  val input = Gson().fromJson(
    ctx.body(String::class.java), Map::class.java
  )

  handleUserEmailSearch(dbSess, input["email"])
})
```

Make sure you put this code inside the existing `coroutine` block inside your Jooby `runApp`. If you put it directly under `runApp`, the call to `delay(200)` won't compile.

This demonstrates how your code is reusable. You wrote `handleUserEmailSearch` for Ktor, but because it takes a Kotliquery session and normal Kotlin data types as input and returns a `WebResponse`, you can easily invoke your existing business logic from a completely different routing library than the one you've used it from so far. The main difference is how you parse the request body as JSON. But `handleUserEmailSearch` has no knowledge of this.

Authenticating with Forms

Jooby has support for session cookies, so you can add support for HTML-based form login in a Jooby app. You can also adapt it to work for cookie-based single-page app authentication, just like in Ktor.

The first step is to set up the session cookie itself. Listing A-6 shows how to configure Jooby with a session cookie.

Listing A-6. Adding session cookie support to Jooby, inside the `runApp` block

```
sessionStore = SessionStore.signed(config.cookieSigningKey,
  Cookie("joobyCookie")
    .setMaxAge(Duration.parse("30d").inWholeSeconds)
    .setHttpOnly(true)
    .setPath("/")
    .setSecure(config.useSecureCookie)
    .setSameSite(SameSite.LAX))
```

Unlike Ktor, Jooby only signs the session cookie and does not encrypt it. In addition to the session data itself, the cookie also includes a signature. This means that third parties cannot forge values in the cookie, as they do not have access to the signing secret. But any value you store in the session will be accessible to anyone that has logged in, by inspecting the cookie contents.

The HTML for the login form is identical to the one in Ktor, but it's repeated here in Listing A-7, along with the code for handling the actual login request.

Listing A-7. Displaying a login form and handling the form submission request

```
get("/login", joobyWebResponse {
  HtmlWebResponse(AppLayout("Log in").apply {
    pageBody {
      form(method = FormMethod.post, action = "/login") {
        p {
          label { +"E-mail" }
          input(type = InputType.text, name = "username")
        }
```

```
      p {
        label { +"Password" }
        input(type = InputType.password, name = "password")
      }

      button(type = ButtonType.submit) { +"Log in" }
    }
  }
})
})

post("/login") {
  sessionOf(dataSource).use { dbSess ->
    val formData = ctx.form()
    val userId = authenticateUser(
      dbSess,
      formData["username"].value(),
      formData["password"].value()
    )
    if (userId == null) {
      ctx.sendRedirect("/login")
    } else {
      ctx.session().put("userId", userId)
      ctx.sendRedirect("/secret")
    }
  }
}
```

Jooby abstracts away the details of the storage and conveniently lets you write to a key/value-like API. This code stores the ID of the logged-in user in the session cookie, so that you can retrieve it later.

To protect routes that require login, you'll wrap them in a decorator. Listing A-8 demonstrates how to set that up.

Listing A-8. Securing routes with a login requirement

```
path("") {
  decorator {
    val userId = ctx.session().get("userId").valueOrNull()
    if (userId == null) {
      ctx.sendRedirect("/login")
    } else {
      ctx.attribute("userId", userId.toLong())
      next.apply(ctx)
    }
  }

  get("/secret", joobyWebResponseDb(dataSource) { dbSess ->
    val user = getUser(
      dbSess,
      ctx.attribute<Long>("userId")!!
    )!!
    TextWebResponse("Hello, ${user.email}!")
  })

  get("/logout") {
    ctx.session().destroy()
    ctx.sendRedirect("/")
  }
}
```

The decorator extracts the userId property from the session. Jooby automatically handles the underlying cookie and provides the same key/value-like API for retrieving values as for setting them. If the userId is null, you'll redirect back to the login page. If not, you'll call the special next value with the current context, which calls the actual response handler that Jooby has matched for the current path.

You can use path to wrap routes in a path prefix. In this case, you've used path to wrap a set of routes in a decorator. You could also set this up so that all the routes that require login get a */secure* prefix. To do that, replace path("") with path("/secure"). Then, the route that was available on */secret* will instead be available on */secure/secret*.

You can then use `ctx.attribute<Long>("userId")!!` to extract the actual value. You're using the non-null assertion operator (`!!`) here, as Jooby will never invoke the handlers you've wrapped in the decorator if the value is `null`.

Authenticating with JWTs

Jooby has support for JWTs, but not the same way Ktor has. There's a JWT session store module, documented at *https://jooby.io/modules/jwt-session-store/*.

This module stores the JWT in the session cookie and does not give you control of how to utilize the token. For example, in your Ktor handler, you return the full JWT in a JSON payload to callers that successfully authenticate against your API. There's no way to do that with the Jooby JWT plugin.

However, Jooby doesn't stop you from using a third-party library such as `jawa-jwt` by Auth0 (*https://github.com/auth0/java-jwt*) for generating JWTs and writing a few handfuls of lines of code to add support yourself. So you can still make it work if you need JWT support in your Jooby-powered web app.

APPENDIX B

Using Hoplite Instead of Typesafe Config

In this appendix, you'll learn how to use Hoplite instead of Typesafe Config. You'll end up with the exact same WebappConfig data class as before, so the only code you need to change is the config loading itself.

Hoplite (*https://github.com/sksamuel/hoplite*) is a Kotlin library for type-safe and boilerplate-free configuration loading. By following a small set of conventions, such as naming the config properties in your config files the same as the properties on your data class (which you're already doing), all you need to do is to point Hoplite at your config files and your WebappConfig data class, and you're good to go.

One of the reasons that I use Typesafe Config in most real-world projects is simply that it's a Java library. I use it in both Clojure and Kotlin projects, which I tend to work on frequently, and it's nice to be able to use the same familiar library everywhere. But if you're purely on a Kotlin project, and that kind of mental portability isn't important, Hoplite works almost the same as Typesafe Config and is a little bit more convenient to use in some ways. So choose based on your own preferences.

Loading Config Files

Before you can use Hoplite, you need to add it as a dependency in *build.gradle.kts*:

```
implementation("com.sksamuel.hoplite:hoplite-core:2.6.3")
implementation("com.sksamuel.hoplite:hoplite-hocon:2.6.3")
```

© August Lilleaas 2023
A. Lilleaas, *Pro Kotlin Web Apps from Scratch*, https://doi.org/10.1007/978-1-4842-9057-6

Hoplite has support for many different configuration file formats. You'll use the hocon plugin for Hoplite, so that you can reuse the exact same config files for Hoplite as the existing Typesafe Config–based files.

Next, tell Hoplite to load your config files. Listing B-1 shows how to do that.

Listing B-1. Loading your config files with Hoplite

```
val config = ConfigLoaderBuilder.default()
  .addResourceSource("/app.conf")
  .addResourceSource("/app-${env}.conf")
  .addPreprocessor(EnvOrSystemPropertyPreprocessor)
  .build()
  .loadConfigOrThrow<WebappConfig>()
```

The values in *app.conf* are the base, and any value in *app-<env>.conf* will override the default.

The EnvOrSystemPropertyPreprocessor enables inlining of environment variables in your config files, which you do in *app-production.conf*. Conveniently, the syntax in Hoplite is identical to that of Typesafe Config. So your existing config files will work out of the box.

Finally, loadConfigOrThrow takes a data class as a type parameter, and that's the data class that Hoplite will serialize your config properties to.

That's all there is to it. Run your app, and you have an instance of WebappConfig available, just like you had before when you used Typesafe Config.

Handling JVM Target Version Errors

Note that by default, IntelliJ generates Kotlin projects with a JVM target version of 1.8. You can change this default when you generate your projects, but at the time of writing, you'll end up with 1.8 if you don't change anything. Hoplite ships compiled class files that are compiled using a JVM target version of 11, so if your project still specifies 1.8, you'll get the following error message at loadConfigOrThrow:

```
Cannot inline bytecode built with JVM target 11 into bytecode that is being
built with JVM target 1.8. Please specify proper '-jvm-target' option
```

To fix this error, update the `jvmTarget` property in *build.gradle.kts*:

```
tasks.withType<KotlinCompile> {
  kotlinOptions.jvmTarget = "11"
}
```

When you set the JVM target output version to 11 or later, your code will compile.

Handling Unknown Environment Variables

When you run your web app in the *production* environment, you'll need to set all the environment variables that the config file refers to. If you don't, both Typesafe Config and Hoplite will crash.

In Typesafe Config, you'll get errors like this if an environment variable is missing:

```
Exception in thread "main" com.typesafe.config.ConfigException$Unresolved
Substitution: app-production.conf: Could not resolve substitution to a
value: ${KOTLINBOOK_HTTP_PORT}
```

Hoplite, however, has error messages that are a bit less informative:

```
Exception in thread "main" com.sksamuel.hoplite.ConfigException: Error
loading config because:

  Could not parse classpath:/app-production.conf
```

Be aware of this when you run your web app. The error message from Hoplite makes it look like nothing works and that it can't find the config file or something like that. But that's the error you'll get if you refer to a nonexisting environment variable in your config files.

Masking Secrets

Hoplite has built-in support for masking config values, such as database passwords. This makes it easy to print the value of your config when your web app starts up, where you want to make sure that you don't print the actual secret keys and password that your config provides.

To create a masked value, you'll update the `WebappConfig` data class and replace any `String` you want to mask with `com.sksamuel.hoplite.Masked`:

```
data class WebappConfig(
    val httpPort: Int,
    val dbUser: String?,
    val dbPassword: Masked?,
    val dbUrl: String,
)
```

Originally `dbPassword` was a `String?`, but now it's a `Masked?`.

Hoplite will automatically convert strings from your config files into instances of `Masked` and makes your config print `"****"` instead of the actual value.

Note that you also need to update your code. `config.dbPassword` will now return an instance of Masked, not a String. So update your code to extract the value with `config.dbPassword?.value` instead, which returns the underlying `String`.

You can also use your own code for printing the config file when you switch to Hoplite. Your own code prints all config values except those that contain "password," "key," or "secret" in their name. If they do, it masks out the secret, but includes the first character of the secret as well, which lets you check that you at least have something that resembles the correct secret if you get errors about missing properties when you run your web app. Hoplite and Typesafe Config generate the same `WebappConfig`-type class as output.

APPENDIX C

Using Spek Instead of jUnit 5

In this appendix, you'll learn how to use Spek instead of jUnit 5 and `kotlin.test`.

Spek and jUnit 5 are similar in many ways. One of the main benefits of Spek compared with jUnit 5 is that Spek is multi-platform. So, if you use Kotlin/JS or Kotlin Native, Spek works well.

Spek also supports a multitude of test definition formats, such as a DSL that maps to the Gherkin format (*https://cucumber.io/docs/gherkin/*).

The Spek Framework (*www.spekframework.org/*) is a Kotlin-native test framework. You write your tests in "specification style," which means you use words like "describe" and "it" to define your tests. This helps enforcing good and descriptive names for your test cases.

Note that Kotest (*https://kotest.io/*) is a popular library for testing in Kotlin. It also has support for specification-style tests and assertions and has even wider support for property-based testing and more. If I were to start a new Kotlin project today, I would research using Kotest instead of Spek. But I've never actually used Kotest in real-world projects, only `kotlin.test` and Spek. So that's what I'll use in this chapter.

Additionally, the main point of this chapter is to teach how to use a different testing library than the one in Chapter 7, and it's not intended to be a full-featured tutorial on Spek.

Writing Spek Tests

To start using Spek, you first need to add it as a dependency to your *build.gradle.kts*:

```
testImplementation("org.spekframework.spek2:spek-dsl-jvm:2.0.19")
testImplementation("org.spekframework.spek2:spek-runner-junit5:2.0.19")
testImplementation(kotlin("test"))
```

You probably already have `testImplementation(kotlin("test"))` in your dependencies block. Even though you're not going to be using jUnit 5 directly, Spek still uses jUnit 5 under the hood as the actual test runner. You'll also need the assertions that come with `kotlin.test`.

To test that everything is working, you should first write a failing test. Listing C-1 shows how to do that with Spek.

Listing C-1. A basic failing test, in **src/test/kotlin/kotlinbook/UserSpec.kt**

```kotlin
package kotlinbook

import org.spekframework.spek2.Spek
import org.spekframework.spek2.style.specification.describe
import kotlin.test.*

object UserSpec : Spek({
  describe("Users") {
    it("should run tests") {
      assertEquals(1, 2)
    }
  }
})
```

Run the Gradle task named "test," either with `./gradlew test` or by running it from the Gradle sidebar in IntelliJ, at _kotlinbook_ ➤ _Tasks_ ➤ _verification_ ➤ _test_. When everything is set up correctly, you'll get the following error:

```
> Task :test FAILED

expected: <1> but was: <2>
Expected :1
Actual   :2

org.opentest4j.AssertionFailedError: expected: <1> but was: <2>
```

That's it! You now have a fully functional setup for writing automated tests using Spek instead of `kotlin.test` and jUnit 5.

Since you're using the same assertions library as before, you can copy/paste your existing `kotlin.test`-based tests into your new `UserSpec` specification. The only thing you must change is that you'll need to wrap them in `it("...")` blocks instead of functions annotated with `@Test`.

Structuring Spek Tests

With jUnit 5 and `kotlin.test,` all your test cases are top-level methods of a class. With Spek, you can nest your tests and group them in logical units.

For example, in `kotlin.test`, you might have a set of tests that look like this:

```
@Test
fun usersVerifiedShouldBeAbleToLogIn() {
  // ...
}

@Test
fun usersVerifiedShouldBeAbleToChangePassword() {
  // ...
}

@Test
fun usersNotVerifiedShouldNotHaveAccess() {
  // ...
}
```

With Spek, you can define those tests this way:

```
describe("users") {
  describe("verified") {
    it("should be able to log in") {
      // ...
    }

    it("should be able to change password") {
      // ...
    }
  }
```

```
describe("not verified") {
  it("should not have access") {
    // ...
  }
}
}
```

This lets you group your tests in natural groupings where you have multiple tests that test the same thing from multiple angles, so that you don't have to repeat the group name multiple times.

Skipping Tests

If you're in the middle of a rewrite or need to temporarily flag a test so it's skipped, you can do that with Spek.

Anywhere in your tests where you use describe and it, you can instead write xdescribe and xit. That marks the test as skipped, and it won't run the next time you try to run your tests.

You could just comment out your tests. But the benefit of marking them as skipped is that the test runner lists all the tests that it detected, but that you've flagged for skipping. That way, you don't forget about them and accidentally leave them commented out.

Running Individual Tests

Spek does not support running individual tests with Gradle. Instead, you can install an IntelliJ plugin for Spek that adds green arrows next to all Spek specifications, so that you can run either individual tests or a whole file, but not your entire test suite.

The name of the plugin you'll install is "Spek Framework." There's another plugin available, called "Spek." That's an outdated community plugin, so don't use that one.

To install the plugin, open IntelliJ IDEA's Preferences, and select *Plugins* in the sidebar, as seen in Figure C-1. In the Plugins search box, type in Spek Framework, and install it.

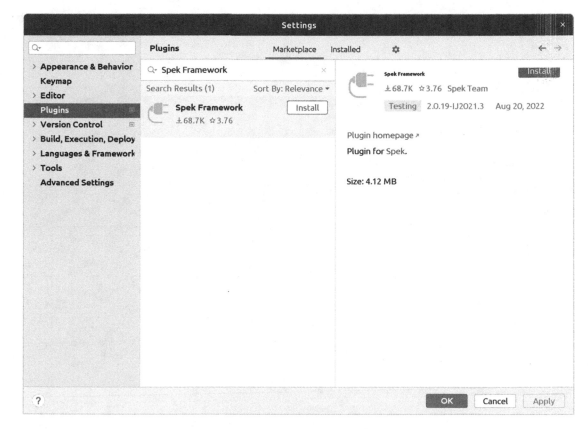

Figure C-1. *Installing the Spek Framework plugin*

When you've installed the plugin, each Spek test gets a little green arrow next to it to run just that test, exactly like the `kotlin.test-` and jUnit 5–based tests you've written earlier.

Index

A

M

N

O

P

Printed in the United States
by Baker & Taylor Publisher Services